*A Line of
Tiny Zeros
in the Fabric*

A Line of
Tiny Zeros
in the Fabric

*Essays on the Poetry of
Maurice Scully*

edited by

Kenneth Keating

Shearsman Books

First published in the United Kingdom in 2020 by
Shearsman Books Ltd
PO Box 4239
Swindon
SN3 9FN

Shearsman Books Ltd Registered Office
30–31 St. James Place, Mangotsfield, Bristol BS16 9JB
(this address not for correspondence)

ISBN 978-1-84861-729-2

Copyright © 2020 by the authors.

The right of the persons listed on page 5 and 6 to be identified as the authors of this work has been asserted by them in accordance with the Copyrights, Designs and Patents Act of 1988.
All rights reserved.

Acknowledgements

'A Line of Tiny Zeros in the Fabric' is from 'Song', in *Humming*, p. 93.

An earlier version of the essay by Kit Fryatt was published as '"AW.DAH.": an allegorical reading of Maurice Scully's *Things That Happen*' in *POST: A Review of Poetry Studies* 1 (2008). Many thanks to the editors of that journal for permitting the reproduction of the text here.

Note

Page numbers of poetic texts referenced parenthetically in the essays herein refer to editions of the texts as identified in the respective lists of Works Cited. On occasion however, the texts presented here may vary slightly from their earlier appearances. These revisions reflect minor changes made by Maurice Scully in the new complete edition of *Things That Happen*, which is published simultaneously with this collection of essays. The decision was made to reflect these corrections in the essays, but to retain the original citations and acknowledge the original publishers of the texts in question. One exception to the foregoing is the essay by Philip Coleman (pp.176–196), where no changes have been made to the original quoted texts.

CONTENTS

J.C.C. Mays
Preface / 7

Maurice Scully and Kenneth Keating
Introduction / 10

Aodán McCardle
We Have to Ask: 5 *Freedoms of Movement* / 21

David Lloyd
Intricate Walking: Scully's *Livelihood* / 36

Kit Fryatt
Meeting a Giant:
Allegory in Maurice Scully's *Things That Happen* / 68

Lucy Collins
The End of the Line: Maurice Scully's *Tig* / 102

Michael S. Begnal
"the fabric / through which":
Immanence and Ecopoetics in Maurice Scully's *Humming* / 118

Eric Falci
Scully's *Several Dances* and the Play of Genre / 132

Mairéad Byrne
The Shed of Poetry / 151

Philip Coleman
Between the "Canon" and "Oblivion":
Looking in the Books of Maurice Scully / 176

Bibliography / 197

Contributors / 210

Preface

J.C.C. Mays[1]

The paradigmatic Scully situation describes someone sitting in a tin shed, rain drumming on the roof, spiders lurking, a few books on shelves, erasers and Tipp-Ex on the table. Nothing peculiar: unless young readers haven't heard of Tipp-Ex. A poem emerges out of a situation that is about writing a poem and is, in effect, a celebration of ordinariness. The situation here usually has a prolegomena, a rallying of forces, and there's a lot of middle but no real end to what has begun: there's a wind-up but no dramatic turn, no transformative illumination; what transpires in the course of the poem isn't parcelled into wholeness, harmony and radiance, and thereby dispatched as a means to an end. The celebration of what happens is inflected in some way – it can be tentative, or robust, or hedged with anxiety; it can sometimes divert into complaint about pressures that kill the joy in simple things – but, whatever the distractions and hindrances, the poems repeatedly enact the urge to move out, to prevent the spirit of creativity getting overtaken by material creation. They describe no-one's and yet everyone's life while it is mobile, before it has settled into the mould: "Every-/place is Here and is Today."

There are threads of biography to be sure – places lived in (Lesotho and Italy), people in supportive roles (Mary and children), jobs acknowledged (language teaching and around the house) – but this isn't the point. The poet is not pushed forward as a surrogate hero, an ideal fictionalised presence in whose identity we lose ourselves: he is, always, just (just!) a person making. We are offered a poetry of witness, not of personality and career-accomplishment. We find ourselves watching what's happening, as it happens, with little concern for personal achievement. What can be constructed upon an event is not the point: the point is, very differently, what seeming non-events provide. Eventing, or getting and spending, we lay waste our powers, as another poet said. The poems don't promote a line of their own so much as transform the space around them. They communicate a level of attention to small particulars – caring, thoughtful, unadulterated –

---

[1] Words on the launch of *Doing the Same in English: A Sampler of Work 1987–2008* (Dedalus Press, 2008).

even if sometimes streaked with a few hard truths. This is what is special about this poetry. It finds a way to say this: a way of writing that comes together but remains open, and embodies the principle in the means.

Three-quarters of Maurice's new book – his "sampler" – reprints a selection from a multi-part sequence with the overall title, *Things That Happen*. The parts came out as separate books and chapbooks over twenty-five years (1981–2006) and they challenge the claim that poetry makes nothing happen. They instead suggest that poems can reach out like a handshake. Again and again in these poems you find a voice saying "How-do", prompting a reader to respond likewise ("And you"). The poems are not to do with history – "that which happened" (what happened in the life of a nation to bring us to the state we're in) – but rather with renewed encounters in the present. These encounters are easy and polite; no anxiety about identity, no gushing confidences; just even-handed, as if "The things never happened; they always are."

I can put this another way. Maurice is not a poet for whom experience is shrouded in words. He doesn't begin with complicated patterns of sound that disentangle into conventional forms, or a neat trope that encapsulates a truth that oft was thought but ne'er so well expressed. He begins outside the job, the task ahead of him and the Tipp-Ex on the table. The poem, as it writes itself before our eyes, is not a particularly desirable consumable; it is not a hoarded memory or a discovered analogy worked up into universal truth. Objects and events are left alone to retain their ordinariness. This is not high-octane performance; the poet is not a magus overwhelming us with rich metaphor and heavy consonants, tricksy rhymes and deft analogies. It's instead more like the work of a verbal mime artist: nothing permanent is involved except what's conjured up; making poems is work as play. While poems that seek to impress their skill can lose touch with that aim – be overtaken by ambition, rivalry or simply the need to put bread on the table with a new USP –, differently, here, the self-deprecating humour undercuts pretension. The formula is low-energy and sustainable, a manner of proceeding that doesn't exhaust the available means, that leaves its readers a decent breathing space.

I don't know of another poet in Ireland who writes poetry of this sort. Maurice has been linked with events and presses that connect with a so-called alternative tradition. As he says himself, it's a connection without much consequence:

> They take a poem of yours
> & put it in a book called *Other*.

I know he's more widely appreciated in the U.K. and U.S., where most of the books and chapbooks that make up *Things That Happen* were published. I could spend time talking about what his writing shares with this and that poet but it would again be an idle exercise. While the larger British and North American scene has space for many different kinds of poetry, Maurice is there pretty much out on his own. There are points of contact, but they are points only; they don't supply a key to how it all works. I only add that anyone who is hooked on this line of approach should consider painters as well as writers: Klee's juxtaposition of translucent colours, for instance. Maurice's way of being a poet (it seems to me) is consistently that of a visual artist who uses words, whose poems create a space whose deliberately ordinary contents are perceived afresh. Many of them perform an exercise, like a painter of still life. The inner life of art is manifested in its being made so, and for Maurice, I repeat, the means of the making are most trustworthy when most simple, for reasons of art and moral principle.

Introduction

Maurice Scully and Kenneth Keating

Love Poems & Others, published in 1981, is a debut volume of often intense lyric poetry, a mode you soon decided to abandon. Its titular reference to D. H. Lawrence's 1913 collection of the same name suggests a desire on your part to foreground a specific literary inheritance. If this is the case, why D. H. Lawrence? And what other writers informed the work of 29-year-old Maurice Scully?

OK this goes back a long way but I do remember being interested in the longer prosey lines of the later poetry of DHL. I see now I think I was trying to stretch out or make elastic the limits of the lyric my education had presented me with.

I did two Leaving Certificates. The second had a wholly new curriculum. The first, up to and including 1970, ran a little early Yeats along with people like Masefield, Padraig Colum, James Stephens, Walter de la Mare & J. C. Mangan. In 1971 suddenly: Eliot, Kinsella, Kavanagh, late Yeats, Emily Dickinson … Wow. This was the first shift in canon I experienced.

This was in Rathmines 'tech'. The year in Rathmines was terrific: the adult atmosphere, the good teachers – James McGowan in English, Mr Hoare, a practising sculptor, for Art, easefully communicating their love of their subjects.

The '70s were my apprenticeship years. I think a 10-year apprenticeship is pretty normal for an artist.

In the late '70s I met Eoghan Ó Tuairisc & his wife Rita Kelly & visited them at the Lock House in Maganey on the Barrow River. My partner, Mary, & I spent our first summer living together there when Eoghan & Rita had to leave for health reasons.

Ó Tuairisc produced both Irish-language & English-language texts across multiple genres, yet his legacy appears to rest on the 1964 long modernist poem *The Weekend of Dermot & Grace*. Did Ó Tuairisc's presence or example help inform your move away from the lyric?

I don't think Eoghan Ó Tuairisc's work pushed my younger self away from the lyric. Ó Tuairisc is a very lyrical poet. The *Weekend* was published simultaneously with *Aifreann na Marbh* whose title poem innovatively and lyrically merges urban Dublin of the 1950s with the horrors of the atomic bombing of Japan.

It was a delight and a surprise to meet *The Weekend* for the first time. My enthusiasm must have had a grain of pathos in it for the older poet.

What was the literary milieu like for you at this time (late '70s / early '80s)?

I was editing *The Beau* and of course had correspondences with various writers. It was around then I got *Colonies of Belief* in the post from Randolph Healy whom I'd known at the Grapevine Arts Centre, Raven Arts Press's HQ, which bowled me over. He visited us at the Lock House & got lost on his way to our isolated spot on the river. He had a tough time getting directions in those dark years – the 'Troubles' etc – when few were willing to open their doors in the dead of night to strangers. Anyway, he arrived on our doorstep in a dishevelled state, but greatly relieved! We had terrific fun the next day with the locks, experimenting with the tremendous forces of the water.

After the birth of our daughter, Leda, in the bitter winter of 1981 – we were snowed in for three weeks with our new baby in a friends' house in Dublin – we moved to rural Wexford for a year. I'd been awarded a Macaulay Fellowship on the strength of *Love Poems & Others* (I suppose) & of course continued writing there. I see now that that was a key period of unwriting the aesthetic of *Love Poems & Others*. In 1982 we returned to Dublin & happened to settle off Clanbrassil St., neighbours to both Michael & Irene Smith & Billy Mills. All by pure chance. Billy was working on *Genesis & Home*, an extraordinarily original début. I started work straightaway on *5 Freedoms of Movement*. There was a buzz of excitement about the place. Billy gave me the addresses of Halsey's Poetry Bookshop & Peter Riley's poetry book outlet. That was a treasure trove of new attitudes to writing.

I began to organize fortnightly *Beau Events* & publish Randolph's *25 Poems* under the *The Beau Press* banner. The 'events' consisted of talks, performances, presentations, readings by actors, architects, painters, musicians as well as poets. These took place at Kevin Connolly's Winding Stair Bookshop/Café overlooking the Ha'penny Bridge.

In 1981/2 you say you were 'unwriting' the aesthetic of *Love Poems & Others*. What was that aesthetic?

Well, 'naïve' is the first word that springs to mind! Take quotation for instance. In *Love Poems & Others* it is always literary, always poetry, and always poetry of the past at that, and famous of course (it needs to be recognized by the reader). A trick learnt from T.S. Eliot maybe in the 70s. To give prestige and resonance to the text.

In *5 Freedoms of Movement* quotations can be more raw, in the form of found texts, not poetry at all – scientific prose, and different 'discourses' – bureaucratic, psychiatric – everyday objects – letters – and everyday voices: family, friends, the street outside, not necessarily in English either.

There is an obvious difference between *Love Poems & Others* & *5 Freedoms of Movement*. Would you say there's a difference between the *Freedoms* book and subsequent books? And if so, what?

Yes, the difference is less striking (or more 'subtle' let's say) but there is, yes. Principally *5 Freedoms* is contrastive, subsequent work more filamental.[1]

And while you were working on making this shift, the 80s were a busy period for you…?

Oh yes, in life & in letters. In 1984 we went to live in Italy where I continued work on *5 Freedoms* & then back to Dublin for a bit, finishing *Freedoms* in '86. It was published by Pete Hodgkiss's (he of *Poetry Information*) Galloping Dog Press in January 1987.

Did you submit it to your first book's publisher, Raven Arts Press?

Yes, but they read it as a collection of poems. And who would blame them? That was the only model available to an Irish poet at the time, I think. *Freedoms* is constructed as an arrangement of checks & balances, not discrete 'poems', a bit like a Calder mobile. The book is the poem.

---

[1] For a detailed discussion of this topic, see Marthine Satris's interview in *Contemporary Literature* 53.1 (2012): 1–30.

Can you offer more detail about the dynamics of this period?

Michael Smith was generous with his books & chat. I had already read a good deal of NWP's output. The flow of books from small UK & US poetry presses through Halsey & Riley's outlets was a terrific stimulus.

It was also, in a curious way, a great advantage in my view *not* to be in situ – New York, London, Cambridge, wherever – and read the productions of these writers & presses at a distance and without the entanglement of their literary & academic politics on the ground.

In 1987 you organized the Coelacanth Press Reading Series. What was the motivation behind the press & also the reading series?

Coelacanth, after the fish thought to be extinct but very much alive (I'd been a little irked by attitudes such as 'Oh all that avant-garde stuff is so passé!' as if the new writing modes were merely fashions). The 'press' itself was a very simple thing. Two booklets nicely produced by Randolph Healy's Wild Honey Press for Coelacanth in small hand-stitched editions, *Arcs Through the Poetry of Randolph Healy, Billy Mills & Maurice Scully* (2002), by David Annwn, and *N11 A Musing* (2003), by J.C.C. Mays, then some items I made myself, photocopied, hand-decorated, of short extracts of my own work in process – *Paper Token, Tree, English/Greek Dialogues* etc – to circulate among the sympathetic.

The Reading Series was attempting to introduce (younger?) Irish poets to the poetic avant-garde. Venue: Winding Stair again (but the more extensive place post-Beau Events). Among the participants: Tom Raworth, Peter Riley, Alan Halsey, Wendy Mulford, Paige Mitchell, Allen Fisher, Lee Harwood, J.C.C. Mays.[2]

I think I failed spectacularly in stimulating a debate, but it was a success in an unforeseen direction: it suddenly became evident to the UK poets, and poets elsewhere, that contemporary Irish poetry was not necessarily all of one block.

---

[2] The Coelacanth Reading Series ran March through April 1987 and was funded by the Arts Council, the British Council & Irish Ferries. Venue: The Winding Stair Bookshop/Café. Line up: Friday March 20th: Geraldine Monk & Philip Casey; Sat March 21st: Lee Harwood, Brian Lynch; Fri April 3rd: Tom Raworth, Peter Riley; Sat April 4th: John Freeman, Alan Halsey; Fri April 10th: Wendy Mulford, Allen Fisher, Ken Edwards; Sat April 11th: Forum chaired by J.C.C. Mays, Panel: Wendy Mulford, Paige Mitchell, Allen Fisher, Ken Edwards, Alan Halsey.

Between 1981 when *Love Poems & Others* appeared from Raven Arts Press & 2004 when *Livelihood* appeared from Wild Honey Press you had no book publication on the island. What was happening in the interim?

Well after the Coelacanth Reading Series we went to Patmos with a view to settling in Greece for some years. I was offered a job on the mainland, but – we had 2 children by then – Louis had been born some months before – the accommodation was inadequate. We were in almost daily contact with the US poet Robert Lax who had lived on Patmos for many years and who had arranged our lodgings there with the local postman. I was writing a post-*Freedoms* book. That book didn't work, as a book.

What was the problem with the Patmos book?

I was trying to write a prose book that included poetry, a kind of internal/external diary in a way, of our stay on the island. And what we hoped was the beginning of a new life. Unsuccessful because the prose style got eroded by the poetry. I couldn't get the two to sit together. Of course I excised things from it: *The Pillar & the Vine* in *Prelude* is reworked from that and p 69 of *Tig* is from that Patmos book too. Maybe other bits & bobs but I don't remember. 'Failure' isn't always failure.

So, after *5 Freedoms* & the 'failure', as you say, of the Patmos book, what were you writing?

Not long after we came back to Dublin we went to Lesotho. There I was working on what was to become *The Basic Colours,* the opening volume of *Livelihood.*

Africa, was a huge & complex stimulus. We came back to Dublin in late 1990 where I assembled *Zulu Dynamite* & after a year, moved to Clare for a few years. It was there that the *Things That Happen* project (not yet called that) took off. At a distance now I see that I was digesting the experience of Africa in my writing in those years in books like *Priority* & *Steps.*

Following these peripatetic years, with no publisher on the island, and with a sense that you were writing into a tradition other than the dominant Irish one, was it difficult to settle into Irish cultural

life again and did any of this inform your decision to commence the *Things That Happen* project in a formal sense?

Yes and no. Soon after our arrival back I got a teaching job in 3rd level. I was dealing mainly with Japanese students, which was very new, & interesting, to me. Then we went to live in Clare & I commuted to work in Dublin. We settled in a house that hadn't been lived in for decades – broken windows, a dead tree outside, the local kids called it 'de divil's house'. We made it habitable and not long after this the twins were born, doubling the size of our family. I was writing *Priority* and *Steps* at this time, and interest in my work was growing in the UK. My parents were ageing and ill and died in this period too. Obviously with all this going on, and more, there wasn't time to organize readings, edit magazines and so on.

There was no decision to begin the *Things That Happen* project, it was more tidal than that. A willed project fails almost from the start somehow, for me. One must somehow sense a flow and be humble, and nuts, enough to go with it. Vague, huh?

In the mid-90s you participated in the *Assembling Alternatives* conference of avant-garde writing organized by Romana Huk in New Hampshire...[3]

Things began to take off somewhat in the mid-90s. Ric Caddel's Pig Press in Durham did *The Basic Colours* in '94 and Ken Edwards' Reality Street Editions did *Steps* in '98, Bob Cobbing's Writers' Forum did a tiny edition of *Priority* in London in ... was it '97?

It was in this period too that what became *Things That Happen* began to move under the general title then of *Livelihood, the set*. I'd always been a busy writer, never hanging around for 'inspiration', but kept the shredder busy too. This period was different. There was a new confidence. Through publication in the UK, I was invited to read at the Cambridge Conference of Contemporary Poetry. At Cambridge Rosmarie & Keith Waldrop (of Burning Deck Press) were in the audience & they invited me to read at Brown in Providence.

Hey-ho. Meanwhile Peter Riley did a beautiful production of a snippet from *Priority* in his Poetical Histories series.

---

[3] Assembling Alternatives: An International Poetry Conference / Festival, 29th August–2nd September 1996.

The *Assembling Alternatives* event was a bolt from the blue. So much so that Randolph and I wondered if it was perhaps a hoax! It was there that we met Trevor Joyce for the first time. Imagine. By 'we' I mean: Catherine Walsh, Billy Mills, Randolph Healy & Geoffrey Squires. Very stimulating.

The year after this conference saw the emergence of the first Cork Conference on New & Experimental Irish Poetry, and the formation of Randolph's Wild Honey Press and the publication of *Prelude, Interlude & Postlude*. Is it fair to say then that this marked a point of culmination of the momentum built up in the preceding years which then brought renewed energy to your writing, and to the writing of your peers?

Well, all of those things were great, *SoundEye*, as it later became known, meeting Trevor at last, Wild Honey, the vigorous continuation of Catherine & Billy's *hardPressed poetry*, meeting up at least annually (we'd moved to different cities & were busy raising kids & earning a living), meeting Jim Mays again, all of us making links together that help. And getting to know the Coracle Press people, Erica van Horn & Simon Cutts.

Renewed energy? I can't speak for the others, but I just tend to plod on regardless anyway. Of course, it is heartening to know that there is some kind of audience out there, and though small, a pretty well-informed one at that.

Did this encourage your return to some editorial work with *Súitéar na n-Aingeal / Angel Exhaust* and Coelacanth Press?

Súitéar came out of an invite from Andrew Duncan who'd heard me read in Cambridge and London and got interested in my work. Coelacanth arose out of the need to circulate some things to a small, but I hope interested, readership.

Sonata and *Tig*, both published in 2006, mark the completion of the 25-year *Things That Happen* project. After all this time, how did you know the work was finished? And did you achieve in this project what you had hoped/intended to?

Sonata had a circular motif to tie things up, the elegy for Ric Caddel at the centre, itself circular, the Tzuba language piece about how movements up & down can be dealt with in language, echoing the Swahili placement motif etc and while writing that I think I thought that would be that. And yet … there was a draw towards a coda too and that became *Tig* where I dissolved the dominance of 3 & 5 that had been rippling through all the books preceding.

Achievement? Well my Inner Critic seemed happy enough. Just about. Silent anyway. And that really was that.

Was it difficult to leave this expansive project behind and move on to a more self-contained book like *Humming*, or did you find the experience in some way liberating? Was there a transition period, and was there a shift in your writing process or practice?

Not difficult. Liberated? Not really. *Humming* was a very demanding book to write though. It is an elegy written in the form of a paean, to life, to the privilege of that adventure, in memory of my brother. Through the period of writing *Things That Happen* there were many deaths: my parents, my two siblings, and all the aunts and uncles I grew up with, and Mary's dad.

There was a bit of a shift in my writing practice, yes. I used my Secret Emergency-Procedure-in-a-Fix more than I had done with other books. This entails recording the work, then listening to it, super-attentively, in the dark, as a critical, somewhat sympathetic, *impossibly* knowing stranger. This must be used very sparingly and with great concentration or it loses effect. Then revise and sculpt and work to keep the evanescent growing shape in your mind as you go. You don't know quite where you're going of course. To know that would be death to the vitality of the work.

I don't remember a significant transition period as there was say between *Love Poems & Others* and *5 Freedoms of Movement*.

Did this emergency procedure take place in your writing shed? If so, is there any comment you would make on the importance of the shed or the writing space, the shed itself, its surroundings, its symbolic or practical importance etc? Or is it just a shed?

The writing 'shed' is referred to in the family as the *chalet*. A step up, don't you think? The chalet is *very* important to me. Unlike some writers,

I can't sit on the edge of a bed with my kids tumbling about me and concentrate on the work. The 'shed' itself has a history. It was made by my father-in-law & his sons in the '60s out of packing cases and left-over steel single glaze windows of the period for his eldest son then studying at 3rd level and later used by the teenage kids in the family. One of Mary's brothers tells me Neil Jordan, the film maker and writer, who also grew up in Clontarf, played his sax there. Simple and all as the structure is, it has been completely waterproof for decades until a branch fell on it recently. It's quite cold – next to no insulation – but I don't mind that too much. I used to wear a Mosotho shepherd boy's balaclava-like hat there in the winters to keep warm. Unfortunately the weight of my books and papers has caused it to tilt and sink in recent years so I've evacuated many of the books and put in a false floor. Good to be flush with the earth when dealing with such a volatile material as poetry!

It was used by my late father-in-law to store apples and his bee-keeping gear after his children grew up & left home. It had the tang of all that for years afterwards.

I've written a lot there, *Humming, Several Dances, Play Book* and bits of *Livelihood* too as I passed through Dublin.

Between the completion of the *Things That Happen* project and the publication of *Humming* you also published *Doing the Same in English* with Dedalus Press in 2008. What guided your selection of work for this publication, and what did it mean to publish this 'sampler' with a more established Irish press?

In very simple terms I looked to what might make sense to a local audience with the Dedalus book and a very different audience for the Veer book, *A Tour of the Lattice* two or three years later. With the *Lattice* I took all of *Things That Happen* and showed I hope that it could be shaped into different things, that it could be taken as a block of malleable material, definitely not The Selected Hits, The Best Of.

With the Dedalus book I simply went chronologically through the work starting with *Things That Happen* and then on to *Humming* and *Several Dances*. The pieces from *Work* at the end of that book had been published as part of a pamphlet of that name in the UK by Oystercatcher Press and *Work* itself, some of it, was subsumed into the finished *Several Dances*.

I would very much like to have readers in Ireland, my native country after all, so the Dedalus publication meant a lot to me & I'm grateful for it.

Can you tell me more about your current work?

My current project is *Play Book*. 'Play' in the senses of 'strategy', 'pretend', 'game', 'musical' & so on. Quotation is used differently here, comically, satirically, critically, dislodging the prestige of the originals and representing too I suppose the echo chamber of a lifetime's reading.

Play Book's epigraph, a quotation in Early Modern Irish, is a stanza from a C13th bardic poem by one Giolla Brighde Mhac Con Midhe, and in the age of Google I choose not to translate it. If a reader does look it up, they're in for a surprise. The sentiment in it is very modern & rather echoes my own, but is a vigorous distortion of the bardic poets' own sentiments in general in their own time (1200–1600).

Throughout the book there are quotations from C19th correspondence, a 1960s novel by Angela Carter, modern scientific texts on evolution, anthropology, archaeology, entomology, biology, laser mapping, engineering dynamics as well as literary and domestic quotations and the lived urban environment, where neon signs urge us to "Eat-Eat" or transport platforms tell the – mostly Anglophone – commuters to *fan taobh thiar den líne seo* (even my washing machine is quoted, muttering Irish on the Slow Rinse setting). Let's say the texture of the writing is porous.

The quotations function differently in different pieces as you might expect: contrast, implicit point underscored, the texture of a life in a time … In a piece entitled 'Pool' the opening stanzas quote Dorothy Parker, Marianne Moore, Wallace Stevens, Sylvia Plath, Toploader's *Dancing in the Moonlight*, Wordsworth, Shakespeare, Emily Dickinson and also reference Mallarmé by indirection – it's a kind of surround-sound which as the piece develops dies away into an insistent dog's barking. Make of that what you will!

What now for your own writing in the shorter and longer term?

In the shorter term I think I'm close to finishing (I hope) *Play Book*, so will try to let that sit for a bit before offering it to a publisher. In the longer term … some buddings of what might be the beginning of another work have begun to appear. Each book takes me about five years, so that would bring me to my early seventies. If that's to be my lot. It would be good too to make all of *Things That Happen* (8 books) available, say in two vols of about 300+ pp each. Or, say, take another tour through that *TTH* territory to make a more manageable new book. In 2018 I sorted a good deal of my papers into decades from the 1970s to the present (20 large boxes) and sorted the notebooks I had to hand chronologically too (a full bookcase). The notebooks may form a ground for future work ... who knows?

We Have to Ask: *5 Freedoms of Movement*

Aodán McCardle

> *If a man does not hope, he will not find the unhoped for, since there is no trail leading to it and no path.*
> —Heraclitus, Fragment 18

I would say that Maurice Scully's *5 Freedoms of Movement* offers a way into the unhoped for.

This quote from Heraclitus comes at the beginning of Thomas A Clark's *Ways Through Bracken*. It has been a lodestone for me in writing poetry, in making art and finally in responding critically to art, literature and perhaps responses to life in general. I don't think there is a formal area saved for poetry or art, a definitive method of dealing with it, it is made of and in the everyday. I think it's accepted that we find what we are looking for when we respond to art or literature, but I would also like to think that it's possible to find not only what is unlooked for but what might even be unwanted not just in the response but in the making. Not that this will happen often but it is an aspiration. An artwork, or in this case a poem, then is something we engage with and it and we are changed in the process. Lee Harwood said,

> Ideally, I want the poem to be like a beautiful object, a box that's all slotted together; and then I leave it on the table and leave the room, and you come in and handle it and pass it on… When [the poem] is read it becomes bigger and has more power. (qtd. in Sheppard 110)

Robert Sheppard says "Harwood sees a poem as a catalytic object that causes various changes within its readers, without itself changing" (110). While he does go into more detail about what this means and how it happens, I disagree with that idea that the poem remains unchanged. The words on the page may remain the same but the poem itself is never just the words on the page. The poem or work of art is an environment one enters into an engagement with, one where you are subject to influence and in turn upon which you exert an influence but the key is that you are subject to the actions of the poem, the gravities, rules and energies the poem brings to bear upon you. The poem or artwork exerts some autonomy even while it admits your experience as a catalyst or prism through which it is activated. It is this crucial point which allows an outcome that may even be unwanted but may equally be unhoped for, a country never visited before.

> That's the way we'll go
> past where the fact is
> Pouncing on its prey
> from cliff tops (Clark np)

Hope and the unhoped for are intangible but in Heraclitus they become an action, something you do or need to do in order to achieve the intangible. For Clark the "Fact" is a dangerous creature which will devour you if given a chance. There is no way that a fact will lead you to the unhoped for. Knowledge then, however useful, is not the key to the poem, the substance of this trail is of other things. Indeed in Scully's *5 Freedoms* the extracted moment of measurement where any ruler of knowledge might be wielded never occurs. There is no opportunity to measure in that way. Charles Olson roots this as a response to the thoughts of Herman Melville, especially citing a line from a letter to Hawthorne, "By visible truth we mean the apprehension of the absolute condition of present things" (47). He says "[n]othing was now inert fact", and continues that man is "folded in (…) a thing among things, which I shall call his physicality" (48). This physicality is the condition of knowing, not the discrete, separate, knowledge, but as a condition of duration, 'continuous'. Olson says:

> Taking it in towards writing, the discrete, for example, wasn't any longer a good enough base for discourse: classification was exposed as mere taxonomy; and logic (and the sentence as poised on it, a completed thought, instead of what it has become, an exchange of force) was as loose and inaccurate a system as the body and soul had been, divided from each other and rattling, sticks in a stiff box. (48)

I would consider this stance, exchange of force, hoping as an action that might attain the unhoped for to be a basis for moving forward into a consideration of what this poem of Scully's might do. Scully's poetry allows us to arrive at a thought or destination we had not met before nor knew even to look for, but I think it's a question of allowing this to happen, allowing the poem to work on us as much as making it happen. What does it mean then to be folded into the poem, as material constituents of the poem?

In both "A Sort of A Song" and *Paterson*, William Carlos Williams argued for "[n]o ideas but in things' (133, 231), and poetry and performance for me must achieve the status of thing. This is as opposed to being merely a description of a thing. Robin Blaser says about Jack Spicer:

> It is part of his notion that poetry is necessary to the composition or knowledge of the 'real' and this drew him into a combat for the context of poetry – that it was an act or event of the real, rather than a discourse true only of itself. (271)

Yes, poetry is an "act" or "event" of the "real". It is not a writing about, it is not an adjective, it is a doing, it is a being in and of the real. Olson's "folded in" demands this. Robert Creeley in the 1965 essay "Introduction to New Writing in the USA", referring to writers such as Allen Ginsberg, William Burroughs and Michael McClure among others, contends

> writing (distanced) from the usual habit of description – by which I mean that practice that wants to 'accompany' the real but which assumes itself as 'objectively' outside that content in some way (…) one is either there or not, and being there, cannot assume some 'not being' so as to 'talk about it'. (45–46)

5 Freedoms of Movement begins with a photograph of movement, except of course the photograph in capturing the movement halts it and leaves us with either a segment within a narrative of movement or an illusion of movement. But perhaps movement is not the object of the photograph or the action within the photograph, perhaps illusion is the key. It is a well-known image, Klein's *Leap Into The Void*. The image is of a man leaping off a high wall as if he's going to belly flop onto hard ground. However the photo had been doctored and in the real leap a group of the artist's friends were there to catch him. The concept of taking a leap into the void is similar to seeking the unhoped for. What is there or how to get there are neither clear nor tangible. Klein uses illusion to make that leap or create that leap in the eye of the viewer but another aspect of this photograph is that it brings two different sets of space and time and melds them. This is a less dramatic element of the photograph but is perhaps the more fundamentally seismic and I think is for me the part of this image that speaks more throughout Scully's poem, the idea that we never really inhabit a singular moment in time. Three of the other images used as the opening to sections of the poem also represent different aspects of the illusion of movement or movement captured within a moment of its action, and the other image is of a little boy holding a picture of himself upside down in front of his face, again a consideration of individual moments of time and space as illusion. In that sense also I don't read this book as five poems but as one long immersion that considers or transitions through different environments of language or consciousness or doing.

We could take the title and use its material parts, 'Five' or 'Movement' or 'Freedoms' as keys to examine the poetry, we could build a series of research questions based on the photographs used to begin each chapter or the graphic figures on the cover or opening and closing of the book, and I wouldn't ignore any of these, but this would be like taking what you know and using them as bricks to build a house. This publication however would present a differing layout every time you enter a room and a different scene every time you look out the window. Rather I would allow one of the lines in the book to be more of a guide, "to pick up the possible & go on with that from there" (65). By this I think it's a matter of bringing all these possibilities with you as you read but perhaps hold them lightly and allow them to insert themselves or assert themselves as and when their influence waxes and wanes, coheres to or repels within each ongoing moment of reading, within a line or stanza or page. Given the variation in language and image in this poem we have to ask, what are the ambitions for this poetry. What does it not give, or allow us to settle for?

On first reading, it is poetry that allows one to glide along shifting from image to sound to sensory gleam with asides into questions, overhearings, intimacies of the now or a now all without challenging you to stop, to dwell in any sense of profundity or share any sort of heartache or heartfeltness, a gliding through anything important as if one of you is a ghost but then once you dec(i/o)de to stop or re-visit it becomes apparent that this gliding, almost like listening to John Cage's

Roaratorio, where the background and foreground words and sounds, fiction and reality mingle, a theme tune to what else is going on, it is at once both its own ephemeral background and its most intimate endless moments of now, some of these sentences might hold you forever like a fairy ring once entered.

I would return to that idea of Lee Harwood's, on seeing the poem as a box that upon entering the room he puts on the table and leaves then for you to open it and what's inside comes to a large degree from you. So here I might seem to be the one dictating what is in these poems, this poem, a serial poem. But what part do those passages play that seem to step outside any traditional understanding of poetry: what seems like sections of a 'bank letter' on pages 9 and 12 which have no explanation or introduction, and the swift changes in atmosphere at the start of "Side A" where the subject of a line becomes a mystery such that it must be measured by its actions, the actions of its part within the construction of the sentence or the actions of its parts within the overall lexicon of our individual experience, or, if not measured, then teased out by or inferred by and implicated in? What are we to do with these in an overall context? They do not give us a traditional character or subject to ride along with, the image to sound to sensory gleam I roll off as analogies is exactly what can happen in this poem if you don't stop to tinker with it. If you don't question but still at the point of close reading how does that bank letter work in the overall poem, that change of direction or atmosphere at the start of Side A?

Nothing gets to be isolated in life completely. Our deep thoughts, whatever they are, must be accompanied by the mundane and the everyday, or at least by breathing, or a sore throat, or tiredness, or excess energy, or restlessness, or the sound of the bus, or lorry, or child shouting, or crying, or the letter from the bank, or the niggling problem at the back of the mind, the worry or fear or love that insists, and whatever we are dealing with the exact same doing will be changed completely by its accompaniment. If the narrative of the film 'The Glenn Miller Story' with James Stewart is to be believed, then the big break for his style of music came because the trumpet player hurt his lip and the clarinet played the trumpet part and that made all the difference. Scully is not presenting us with abstract images and sounds with which we can simply paint, instead he is demanding commitment and engagement and yes doubt, or at least speculation, and input, and willingness to go ahead without fully knowing, dragging all those accompanying unfinisheds with us into/onto the next page. Is introspection something you do, you seek to do or is it something that comes upon you, a state you enter or a state that enters you? Is it then an out of control state, an improvisational state?

Side A, a generational response will attach this to the idea of the album, a Side A and a Side B, a physical demand for change and/or a demand for a distinct order within reality. This is Side A so there must be a Side B, there is a difference between them, and between them and what surrounds them. Side A begins with a page which is a puzzle. It hints at something, seems to be pointing, but what it points at is a semi-abstract notion, it has the shape of something familiar but not quite defined enough to recognize. We are excluded from the first line, "locked into themselves with their own / geometries private…" (31). But as the line continues, there comes a condemnation, "& for sale" (31). To be private, to have one's own geometries, okay, but then "for sale" seems a betrayal of that, but a betrayal of what exactly? It continues, "as if all the time / there is an echo to significance" (31). Two words bounce off each other here "echo" and "significance", the latter demanding presence and the former presenting as more of a desire than a reality and this then percolates into the rest of the stanza; "as disappointing as / memorable speech or mot juste/out of true/…"(31). As if these things sell themselves too cheaply, "it will fit no doubt if a bit bumpy… / … fit as much as matters / if, if yr sights are quite low enough" (31). Other materials of the stanza being "quirk" and "convention", finishing with "when you are old & grey & full of shit" (31). The convention of wisdom, of conservative values? It is not a language that surrounds a given subject, person, place, or thing. This is a different atmosphere to the earlier stanzas. This is the beginning of Side A and we know we are somewhere else. There is a collage or montage of materials here, depending upon how your brain chooses to process what comes at it.

The next page moves further into abstraction with a consideration of "happiness" and "hope" and "despair" with lines premising the impossibility of containing those conditions in language, "equal to the same thing" and "equal to each other" (32). However the line "eyewash in the romance mating strategy" casts an acerbic, cynical, satiric pallor on romance, and perhaps on the abstract as the rest of the stanza returns to the physical, what is there, what can be touched, what can be done (32). The next line presents us with "step foot hand dance fog" (32). No punctuation, not so much a list again as a continuance of materials in a moment. But if step, foot, and hand lead to dance, we are still left with fog. We can choose to read this as a retreat into the abstract or the physical reaching towards the impossible, or carry both ideas with us. The following line reduces us to "bipedal hominids", to a generalization, the generalization repeated in "you know these days", but the stanza ends with "& focus   shadowy   fix & / swirl away" (32). That "swirl" is all dance and "away" is an uncontainable condition of both time, extending the swirl, and space, extending the physical into the romantic, a condition that eludes the acerbic or the cynical. We then move through stanzas of children's story; ""I say, look," said Peter in amazement, / "a castle on a cloud. Who lives there?"" (33). Then, through simplistic phrases from a foreign language manual; "Please let me have. How do I get to…?" (33). While we are dealing with the seemingly unconnected, with the disparate and the diverse, we still have to acknowledge the ongoing to ourselves, that something however elusive is happening, even if we cannot grasp or understand it, nevertheless we are changed by it.

This type of writing and this type of reading have an effect on us. When we come across the seemingly straightforward narrative of page 35, a description of a scene, a landscape, our attention has changed. We no longer accept that the words themselves will dissolve into the message they carry, the image of "heavy chestnut blossom by a shed wall by a river. / Mud & buried bicycles & reflections in the channel" (35). Indeed when the next line comes in "Fifty-seven seagulls on a parti-coloured roof" (35), it is hard not to hear that specificity of gulls like a nursery rhyme and the next line "Your move. Maytime" (35). This sounds like a challenge, a direct address and soon we are back into "Sorry. Check. Counter-check. Re-do. Excuse me. Thanks. Sex." (35). And all that punctuation suddenly, full stops everywhere connecting as much as disconnecting. But page 36 tips us into the intimate privacy of a writer's space, an introspective between awareness that considers the self and the surroundings

> Making almost no sound in here in this other room
> curious turning pages quietly & taking notes
> […]
> … & yet in the next
> room my baby daughter wakes as if meticulous she can
> sense or dream my presence into her sleep … (36)

This is the active state of writing, attentive and drifting, and therefore passive, at the same time. Doing and being done to.

This passage contains silence, awareness of each other, and silence. An unworldly communication, waiting for sound, aware of silence, but a silence that gets its presence from an expectation, a waiting for sound, "& each extension failing / to predict the silence like this now broader without / prelude sleep" (36). These atmospheres of language are uncontainable, we are cast adrift upon them. To try to tie a narrative or a context to them demands a violence of imposition that would separate the reader from the poem and whatever gratification is in that it would be a removal from the sense of "folded in" (Olsen, 48), an illusion of singularity that this poetry seems to deny us with every line. "Listening" is defined by Barthes as

> not the advent of a signified, object of a recognition or of a deciphering, but the very dispersion, the shimmering of signifiers, ceaselessly restored to a listening which ceaselessly produces new ones from them without ever arresting their meaning: this phenomenon is called signifying [significance], as distinct from signification. (259)

The ability to "not" arrest meaning is essential here. When is the present the present? Where is our attention while listening to something, what else is going on? If a memory encroaches then how present in the present are we? What is the difference between overhearing and being addressed? What is the difference between listening to or reading information or instructions compared to opinion or fiction? How do we move between these modes of processing, receiving?

Is "Side B" a declaration of change, a notification of difference, a conceit or formal game of clarification? "Side B" opens with materials, "To make a table / you need wood" and on "to make the wood / you need a tree" and onward "a seed" to "a flower" (40). Is this a refiguring of the common to understand its greater dimensions? Smacking of profundity, or simply a transition? As the pages go by we have more transitions: "childhood adolescence adulthood" (41); "addenda minutes instructions" (42); and "caterpillar", "larvae" and "parasitic grubs" (43). And between these moments we have "the colour black the colour the sheerness / the colour hostility. what these squabbling / natives lack" (41) and "the hinges of civilization opening / & closing   distinctly"

(42). What are we to do with these, where is the main thread, the dominant narrative? Is this about colonialism, or is it only this little bit, and is this a bit of these bits or an overhearing, how close to it are we, is it of us or an overhearing and do we have to deal with everything? Again and again the stanzas in this poem leave us with more questions than answers and we move on impelled by the lines' action left to right from the top of the page to the bottom and these images and ideas swarm with us.

By page 45 we have an almost setting, an almost subject, a context which teases us but never coalesces, a form of stasis and a continuing now.

> & lights change red & breezes turn
> the waves/you can feel them. sensible creature.
> you & I together have been sometimes
> hands held tight the sweat in the centre
> creases where those fingers that you've had for quite
> some time now & since then & where they begin (45)

Substance material and action seem endless, "breeze", "wave", "traffic lights", "begin", "repetition", "retrospect", all states without detail, coming from or going towards, a stasis of continual flow. Even the word "time" repeats itself at the end, as if time was ever other than eternal or ever stopped (45). The lyrical "songs about its periphery fill the gap" (46), a sonic emotional image that dissolves in an abstract edge, a non place this "gap", a space where things are not; "if accuracy is anything / singlemindedly aimed at / that single is wrong there" (48). The intention of accuracy, the "single" in the mind is questioned.

> reason shaped
> tapered
> blurred &
> bland too (48)

Reason shaped is qualified as tapered and blurred and finally bland. Bland as an action as much as a description, the action of reason is to bland. "Slot into anywhere / where/one usually can" (48). The "usually" is almost bored now as reason is pared down or pares down to fit anywhere, "but nothing gets finished. & nothing goes on. / deeper in debt & richer by half transferring / deference from one day to the next" (52). Life impelled towards a greater complexity but

> to recapture details
>
> before the decision
>
> just as they were   exactly so
> is not possible (53)

There's no way to measure here, no way to grasp and weigh, reason is only a convenient mould:

> that "now" can mean
>
> nothing
> as I say ... (54)

    Everything is something on the way to something else and we revisit images in page 47 "to make a table / you need wood" and the chapter/section ends with "flower   table   stem" (59). But even these are not quite what they were. So how do we keep from spinning out of control in this poetry, how do we play our part, engage and be engaged by, exert upon and suffer exertion? There is no clean now, no discrete moment in life, control is a refusal of possibilities. The beginning of the next section is a photo of a child holding up a photo as if it were a camera taking a photo. A confused leap of sequence and reason that disturbs and crystallizes the functions of the object, the portrait, the photo, the idea of camera, of being photographed, of an image stopped in time, a moment frozen, the madness of capturing light from the sun as it reflected off an object and holding it forever just there is beyond a reduction to any reasonable explanation. This poetry makes us aware and allows us to find alternative futures through awareness even of not knowing.

    We become aware of our expectations as we read. The "Two Caterpillars" section opens with a line that sets up our expectation of a fairytale, a parable, a joke or a story, not a novel or a poem, a story; "*There once were two young caterpillars*" (63). Something that at least mirrors or plays on the form of a children's story, a fable that might deliver a life lesson. Then we come on the lines "*One day a bankman came to the tree with his / money*". Now a slightly discordant note enters our expectations, the word "bankman" is out of kilter with the tone of "two young caterpillars". Is it a childish compounding, bank+man, or a problem of translation that this term, bankman, doesn't fit the technical nouns we associate with the profession of banker? It skews the semantics. Now our expectation is that the story will relate to money. The weight of that one word draws other concepts to it. However, in the context of this book the term bankman is no stranger than the two young caterpillars. Because of the variation in language, variation in forms of use, formal address of a business nature, instruction manual, poetic formatting in stanzas or disjointed lines and narratives, then we are more aware of being played with. We are aware that there are expectations on the part of the author as much on the part of us as reader. We are aware of the author's awareness. With this in mind we come across dream sequences, dreaming about dreaming. Awareness of lack of awareness. A dream in which one is aware of dreaming is an illusion of control and of the lack of need for control. So happiness in a dream is an illusion of happiness, but tangibly real in the dream within a dream, but then happiness as a realization of a present state is in itself both an illusion and a reality. The tangible reality of a given moment in the world may be felt by two people at the same time standing side by side but one of them may in that moment feel happiness while the other may not so the concept of happiness is both an illusion and yet perhaps a constituent part of the truth of any moment. Awareness of awareness is an atmosphere that surrounds us as we enter the rest of the poem.

> *Until one day an Autumn Leaf fell on the Fatter*
> *Caterpillar to the sinister snip of scissors*
> *and the day went black. Like that : ☞* ▮
> *How interesting. You can't do much under an Autumn*
> *Leaf though, so the Fatter Caterpillar, sensibly,*
> *fell asleep…* (64)

That finger pointing hand and the little black form it points at is from another universe than any fairytale or parable. It is almost another language except that it remains within the formatting of the line. A visual language that ties itself directly to the typewritten space and time format. The blackness a redacted language that enters the head as a sensation rather than the thought that a word has been withheld from us but just as happiness is both an externally unproduceable illusion and yet a concrete constituent of a moment of reality so this blackness has a corresponding resonance inside the head. Light is redacted, the white page is redacted, the access to words as language is redacted but these symbols point directly to the short circuit agreement we make with language as we learn it as children. Here that agreement is laid bare for us, the awareness of awareness is foregrounded, what is outside in the world, what is on the page, what is inside the head are no longer simply stages of transition but each parts of an ongoing reality in congruence. Charles Olson again touches on this necessity to carry seemingly contradictory modes of being or doing within us at the same time:

> Melville couldn't abuse object as symbol does by deprecating it in favour of subject. Or let image lose its relational force by transferring its occurrence as allegory does.... Melville wouldn't have known it to say it this way, but he was essentially incapable of either allegory or symbol for the best of congruent reason: mirror and model are each figures in Euclidean space, and they are *not* congruent. They require a discontinuous jump. (50–51)

In Scully the line is at once a part of a linear traditional narrative and congruently has its own gravity.

The next page presents us with an almost kaleidoscopic series of images, sounds, observations, thoughts with the last line "to pick up the possible & go on with that from there" (Scully, 65). So our ability to stand, to balance, to walk, demands that we take for granted gravity, joints and muscle and tendon, a brain and heart that never switches off and get on with walking, with that part we can make use of, indeed if we are to try to acknowledge all the moving parts needed for walking while walking we would not be able to walk.

Pages 70 and 71 provide a repetition of ideas, images, subject from earlier but the rhythms of page 70 in particular come to the fore. The "our" is repeated from 7 lines down as if revisiting an idea to qualify and clarify; "our what really is matter to be expressed our / our bright tininess our understandings reticulated" (70). This is repeated with "look"; "on fire they look / look at you look at them…", and "memory"; "where memory & / remembered memories diverge & play over the air / as the air itself is known to play diverging" (70). This repeated grasping at the direction or articulation of a phrase or word is like memory, it overlays and reworks, rewrites. A dream within a dream, awareness of awareness, but at the same time a lack of control. Page 70 begins with "diverge" and ends with "diverging". The repeated words as sonic, grammatical and conceptual reverberations begin to slip their moorings, become the song of a dream, impossible to hold onto, you bring with you into the present almost the scent of it but not the it itself. This amorphous presence of presentness, this dream within a dream, this everyday life we pretend to be in the present of in some logical reasoned sense is exposed as an illusion of reason. Reason is blurred as an instrument or tool in this poem.

From this we step into page 71 and "doing business. / getting your knife in deep & clean" (71). This first line seems to begin with the intention of refuting the blur, "doing business", a controlled factual employment of language, but then "getting your knife in deep & clean". An actual knife? A chef? Or a metaphor, the language used to justify business, to paint its practice in another light, "preferably into as many as it is possible / to line up simultaneously in a good / straight voluntary & vulnerable file" (71). And there the language begins to sway. There is intent, a driving intent in "doing business" and in the "knife" and in "preferably into as many as it is possible". There is a control in the "good straight" but with "voluntary" there is a clash from the intent of one to the influence upon the intent of others, that their intent be "voluntary" and from that we quickly enter the territory of the word "vulnerable" and the neutral atmosphere of unambiguous "business", business as usual, articulation of the "knife" with surety, an action already come to terms with, its consequences "deep & clean", trembles. The words "voluntary" and "vulnerable" attached by their alliterative umbilical to our awareness of awareness betrays our lack of control here. We travel between meanings looking for clues and connections but not in a linear sense, we need to return and revisit what we thought we knew, where we thought we were going, looking for directions.

Then the word "(memory)" appears in brackets, an instruction within a play, a direction or observation? We are propelled forward by the energy of the line itself as a form, "then suppressing that adrenal twitch / to simplify the mind / & steady the hand (memory)" (71). There is a sense that this makes sense and we should know or be familiar with it. Surrounded by "(memory)" this phrase resonates as if outside the dominant narrative of reading, a now overall instruction, a base operation upon which reading is fixed. An instruction on how to master an action, an intention, bracketed by bracketed "(memory)" as if this is the purpose or possibility of memory, that it offers control. Is control due to the memory of having done? The line impels us on "turn hard & true. through memory. / through life. a package deal one says. / to make a killing one says" (71). The language of business returns. The latter part of this stanza delivers us again into earlier imagery and ideas from the poem of larvae and host, of parasite, of unheeded behaviour or unheeded language, "a package deal" already prepared, "to make a killing", language that agrees to only accept or consider one aspect of its intent and meaning. A convenience, but with the words "one says" there is the implication that something is not as it says, some doubt is cast upon the ready meaning, an accusatory tone. "Through memory" and "through life". The word "through" as in a passage, into and out of, to get from one place to another, memory as a tunnel or a tool through life, a simplifying passage as in the "package deal" where decisions and possibilities are simplified rather like the tapered and blurred reason earlier in the poem, a justification of inattention to consequence. (memory)?

In page 72 we are again emptied into an account or accounting of the space of writing, this time via an inventory of the material physical detritus of a writer's writing place. Books, pens, pencils, typewriter, coffee, Odes, hymns, "Notes for Book in Process" (72), an implication of mental industry as thoughts move between object and idea, actions and concept. Then the mind wanders outside in the next page to "leaves" and "street" and back in to "glasses   plates   dishes   stray spoons" and "my daughter playing. quaint notion of permanence!" (73). Not a question, an exclamation, we arrive into a moment of discovery, a come-upon thought of the roving mind, the writer's outside and inside coming together upon a moment. And off again out and in "open yr head & gather it all in" he says and on the mind wanders:

>   ... trees
>   stains on a wall sunlight on
>   a wall sunlight through leaves &
>   branches sunlight on water moving & still
>   sunlight somebody combing her hair ... (73)

The wall moves from an actual wall through a sentimental state, identified initially in the environment of physically writing, being in the presence of sunlight on the wall, to the contemplation of sunlight "through leaves" "sunlight on water" to an association of "somebody combing her hair" and somebody "singing whistling watching herself shadows" and the play of the mind through associations to "I forget the most simple things elsewhere" and "wherever my mind elsewhere" and "as if" and "as if's" to "but I think I / think lost" (74). Lost is a condition, both I am lost and to think the condition lost into being, not to think of the condition of being lost, or to think of what lost means but to employ lost as a tool, lost as an awareness within doing, lost as an adverb, to think lost as a doing, just as hope is an action in Heraclitus, and we transition then back into fable where the "*river – which we forgot to mention – over-ran / its banks, and drowned*" (76). And the caterpillars dreaming are butterflies or the memories of butterflies over a drowned river. Sometimes reason needs to be blurred.

Works Cited

Barthes, Roland. "Listening." *The Responsibility of Forms*. Trans. Richard Howard. New York, NY: Hill & Wang, 1985.
Blaser, Robin. "The Practice of Outside." *The Collected Books of Jack Spicer*. Los Angeles, CA: Black Sparrow Press, 1975.
Clark, Thomas A. *Ways Through Bracken*. San Francisco, CA: The Jargon Society, 1980.
Creeley, Robert. "Introduction to New Writing in the USA." *A Sense of Measure*. London: Calder and Boyars, 1973.
Olson, Charles. "Equal, That Is, To The Real Itself." *Selected Writings*. Ed. Robert Creeley. New York, NY: New Directions Books, 1966.
Scully, Maurice. *5 Freedoms of Movement*. Buckfastleigh: etruscan books, 2001.
Sheppard, Robert. *The Poetry of Saying: British Poetry and its Discontents, 1950–2000*. Liverpool: Liverpool University Press, 2005.
Williams, William Carlos. *William Carlos Williams Selected Poems*. Edited by Charles Tomlinson. New York, NY & London: Penguin Books, 1976.

Intricate Walking: Scully's *Livelihood*

David Lloyd

> *The book
> is fat, contains code. The world,
> the water planet. The code contained in
> this thing in the world, the book, changes
> the things, the world.*
> —Livelihood, 228

Livelihood challenges reading. Like any important work of poetry, it poses immediately the question of "how to read". That question ultimately resonates for poetics in general, that is, for our habits and customary formulations about reading and about what a poem is as it lays itself open to, or troubles, or even forecloses our reading practices. More than any other volume of Scully's to date, *Livelihood* announces itself forcefully as a book: in its heft, its substantiality in the hand, in its imposing material presence, this is a very different object than the slim sheaf of carefully arranged poems that the prevalence of lyric forms has led the reader to expect will be the format in which poetry arrives. The materiality of the book as object is not irrelevant: it embodies and announces the gravity of the project *Things That Happen*, a twenty-five year long process of writing aimed at what Scully has famously described as constructing or assembling books rather than composing poems.[1] *Livelihood*, as a book constructed of five books, stands as the centrepiece of that project, transforming the previously published chapbooks or books that it assembles into parts of an imposing whole, making a "fat book" that communicates a certain monumentality.

Yet its monumentality and its gravity as an object in the world are counterpointed at once by its title, *Livelihood*. A livelihood is a means to life, but it is not a career, in the sense of a curriculum vitae that suggests a life that is a developing whole, an achieved and coherent vocation shaped by a singular plan or intention: say, "a 'career in/development', the 'management of the poor'" (186). A livelihood does not seem to

---

[1] Like many other critics of Scully's work, Harry Gilonis comments on this defining aspect of Scully's procedure in "The Spider, the Fly and Philosophy", 29. Scully recently described his work as "not making collections, but constructing books" at a reading in Cork, 21 June 2018. Author's recording.

lend itself to any idea of an opus, to a corpus of work bent on totality or monumentalising a "life work". It connotes, rather, a casual relation to gaining a living, an occasional relation to work and to the material necessity of some source of income in order that the work of writing might proceed. *Livelihood* reflects often enough and intimately on this conundrum of living and dwelling poetically:

> my wife & I worry about our debts & our spirited
> baby daughter. & the difficulty of getting out of
> this mess & learning the language & dodging main
> streets at rush-hour so as not to run into anybody
> we might owe money to. (97)

The scenarios of various modes of casual labour – "working as a/ teacher / porter / watchman / noteman / manman" (23) – and of the reproductive labour of raising children and making a home somewhere, somehow, counterpoint those of the poet at work, at, one is tempted to say, the real work:

> This is my desk. This is where I work.
> ....
> I work hard in my corner, any chance I get,
> really I do.
>
> ....
>
> And I've been busy. Busy eating, drinking, giving ear,
> listening to repetitive nonsense, setting out, getting
> a living, watching my children, teaching my children,
> making Lesson Plans, filling paper. ... (134)

In this counterpoint of labour and the work, where "getting and spending we lay waste our powers", chance governs the construction of the poem, the snatched moment of writing and the moments written of. However impressive the scale of the accumulated work, *Things That Happen* foregrounds happenstance, chance observation and encounter, the fleeting occasion, in defiance at once of necessity and of the Protestant ethic that responds to necessity with the injunction to steady labour. Scully's writing has, as Romana Huk has emphasized of another volume of Scully's, a lightness of touch that counterpoises gravity if it does not defy it altogether. (Huk 105)

Opening the volume more or less at random, the reader is faced with what appear to be some variety of lyric poems that often bear generic titles or subtitles that indicate one or other of the modes that form the repertoire of lyric poetry – sonnets, ballads, songs, rounds and even, for the Hibernophile, the aisling. Despite their highly various arrangements on the page, their allergy to the regularities of quatrain or tercet, they mostly share the visual form of lyric poems, sparse texts on the page descending through white space. At times, they even deploy moments of "vivid immediacy" and the invocation of the second person that, as Jonathan Culler has recently argued (Culler 887–91)[2], is the typical apostrophic stance of the lyric that floats ambiguously between self-reference (signifying "I") and address to the other:

> **sonnet**/a way peachtree branches arc
> loaded at the tip. I will please you
> with pattern & no one will read you
> no one will read you until you've been
> chopped & laundered. no one. if this
> worries you. someone will attempt
> taking the money if someone thinks
> they will read you. it's 4.02. dove-
> coo & a toilet tank filling & a cock
> crowing: nobody could not say it's not
> music, picking up the pattern by which
> to please the process receptors. ... (26)

This eighteen-line poem is scarcely a sonnet in any conventional sense, though closer to one in its appearance on the page than many so titled in the book. And yet, just as the rhyme scheme or the relation between octet and sestet in the sonnet establish patterns that, as formalists like Roman Jakobson have demonstrated to almost manic extent, operate across the whole sonic and semantic space of the sonnet, this poem establishes its own complex set of patterns, patterns that *please*. These patterns are indifferent to the tonal or social registers of the materials

---

[2] Kit Fryatt makes a similar comment about Scully, writing of the later volume *Humming* (2009): "Scully frequently employs, in place of the lyric 'I', a semi-imperative generalized 'you' ...." (Fryatt 101).

they orchestrate – "dove- / coo & a toilet tank filling & a cock / crowing" (with a buried pun on ball-cock and a deft allusion to the aubade) – and accommodate the most diverse materials without imposing hierarchies of taste or decorum. Indeed, characteristically the poems of *Livelihood* swerve and dip through multiple registers and levels, refusing both the high seriousness and the tonal consistency by which the lyric generally distinguishes itself and the alternative and equally consistent effects of comic bathos by which another vein of contemporary versifying stakes its claims on a democratic undoing of poetry's earnest moral pedagogy

But what differentiates this "sonnet" most of all from its archetype is its refusal of any closing *fabula* or *sententia*: the poem does not even conclude; at most, it may revert to its opening peachtree branches. It does not culminate in any rendering of epiphany or ironic reflection on the insights its transformation of experience into figure has yielded. Rather, it splits its sides:

> ... then I
> said. then a choir, I could hear it
> through doors, windows, fly-mesh,
> burglar bars, walls, tin roof,
> the page place — each filter in quiver — a
> choir, a magnificent hosanna, ooo ha-ha-ha
> a-appy day! blooming, spread. (26)

Much as a home may be penetrated by unearthly or disruptive musics from beyond that overwhelm its "filters" and defences, the poem ceases to be a self-contained artefact and opens itself to connections and relations infiltrating any closed structure that might even provisionally be thrown up. The apparently immediate image of the arching branches of the peach tree is not fulfilled in this poem but is picked up again in the following "sonnet":

> peaches whose fur   sweet fruit smell
>   curved groove   three senses
>   then taste one   (27)

Likewise, the tin roof is taken up again in a new conjunction across the page:

> tin roof + rain = tinroof rainmusic. (27)

In the subsequent "sonnet", the apparently imagistic tree opens once again, but now as matter for a school "nature walk" with all its pedagogical intonations:

> **sonnet/**(we went out to look at a tree.
>   we formed a circle around it.
>   this is the Bole, these the Branches, that the Canopy—
>   stand back. underneath you know
>   is where the Roots go
>   to live & hold the Ground together.
>   & look at its Top
>   how compliant it is to the weather. (28)

If I dwell on the recurrence and transformation of motifs among the poems – or verse units – from which the book is constructed on this local scale, it is to open the question which the book constantly poses, which is at what scale one is to think of pattern occurring, emerging or being woven. Repetitions across one or a handful of pages are relatively easily attuned to. When repetitions, echoes or variations chime across the distance of some hundred or even two hundred pages, how is one to think of poetic structuring?

Case in point: another sonnet placed early in the book captures a glimpse of a gull, that ubiquitous Dublin bird, perched on a roof:

> **sonnet/**There is a grey sky.
>   there is a white gull
>   on a black aerial
>   on a black roof
>   opening its yellow beak
>   wide & silently
>   calling calls. (21)

As if to arrest the reader's attention, a gull appears again at the opening of the following sonnet, where:

>   neon flecks join & pass
>   on black water
>   gull
>   teal
>   but ons in special in thyn arraye
>   I see well
>   it passes
>   clamp
>   two luminous blanks   rainbow splotch (22)

We are now all the more likely to recall this gull then, when some twenty pages later, it reappears in a further sonnet, but in language that slightly rearranges the initial version:

>   there is a grey sky.
>   there is a white gull
>   on a black aerial
>   on a black roof
>   opening its yellow
>   beak wide & silently
>   calling
>   calls. (45)

It takes a greater effort of attention for the reader to recall this when, on p. 205, the same scenario recurs, once again reconfigured and revised:

>   low sky
>   gull   aerial
>   head that way
>   this
>   beak wide
>   calls ("Fire", 205)

Likewise, the allusion to Thomas Wyatt's "They flee from me" (Wyatt 15) in the second of these poems recurs within that poem as a kind of parodic commentary on contemporary club-goers' fashion:

>   & close up
>   the Little Barrel's sexy sketches in thin array

>   gullwing
>   head flicking
>   claw in glove
>   though all curve & flow
>   stiletto clack   HEY   tap
>   seam of the knickers showing through
>   then not
>   engage the array of the discarded on the streets to live (22)

But allusion to Wyatt also detaches itself from this context and recurs over two hundred pages later as an echo indexed only by the little phrase "in speciall" (252), a reverberation so faint as to make one wonder whether in the complex array of the book's construction one has missed other iterations — as on p. 96, "where their dance in special", or the simple word "array" in "a life an array of related mistakes" (48). Missed patterning or mistaken patterning: in either case the "pattern-ache vanishing into life's pixels" (49) that the book both reflects on and induces in the reader is always in question. Pattern we inevitably, achingly seek, in the poem or book, in the world and in a life, ours or another's, haunted by the possibility that the patterns we decipher at any moment will the next dissolve into the pixellated textures of a world recalcitrant to processing by its very abundance and mobility.

This is therefore the most unmemorable of poetry, in the best sense. It resists easy appropriation and mental processing, proving almost impossible to commit to memory, "FORGETTING EVERYTHING" (303). It refuses the moralization of poetry as a mnemonic vehicle for crystallized *sententiae*. That is not to say that *Livelihood* abandons structure or the iterative patterning on which memory relies. Repetition is the condition of (having) experience: without repetition in memory or as a condition of learning itself ("repetitive nonsense" being the teacher's bane) there could be no experience, only a continuous influx of sensations and percepts; repetition is in the service of establishing relation and pattern, of making sense of and arresting what Beckett's Neary, stealing from William James, called "the big blooming buzzing confusion" (Beckett, *Murphy*, 6). Experience requires relation among its parts: "A mess of reminiscence is nothing" (Scully 130). Repetition is by the same token, in its various forms, the very condition of poetry, at times formally evident in devices like rhyme and metre, at others to be apprehended in the overall echoic structure of the work, what Scully calls variously the weave, the mesh, the net or the lattice, "this / impossibly repeating lattice" (43). Multiple "fibrous" connections proliferate across the poems that construct the book as a whole, producing a web of repetitions and resemblances that – for this reader at least – constantly multiply on each reading, overlooked on prior occasions and gradually generating an ever more complex tissue – or weave – of connection.

Scully has commented on this aspect of the structure of his work:

> Now, broadly speaking, for me, an entry into form in poetry would be to think of it as of two kinds, the architectural and the fibrous—two distinct ways of looking at it. Most of mine is fibrous—structure below ground. But *structured* for sure. The mycelium, the threaded web, connecting roots over long distances. Symbiotic not parasitic. My poetry has that sort of fibrous connectedness. It's all part of the way we experience the world, I think. (Satris 13–14)

Scully's preference for the fibrous structure reflects not only "part of the way we experience the world" but also an everywhere implicit aesthetic ethics of living. Anyone looking for a "politics" of Scully's writing might find it in that opposition of the symbiotic to the parasitic: the work refuses the relation of settling and colonization of the other, the exploitation of the host, in favour of a mutually supportive and constitutive relationality, in a "meshing" that can at moments become emphatic:

> when threads mesh as they cross
> over they sing to us.
>
> this is how to live. (219)

One is reminded that the sonnet (etymologically *sonitus*, little sound or song) was the form that inaugurated a Western poetics of interiority, adapted to ethical self-interrogation and the inner voice (Oppenheimer 183–5). Its cellular space of enclosure is the image of that interior space in which the project of self-possession unfolds. Scully's deconstructed sonnets – or song-nets — are lyrics that open out to let the world enter, analogues of the porosity of the subject to the world that may even open the body to cosmic as well as mundane forces, its threads pulled even as it pulls on threads of interconnection:

> ... From
> the outside of your life, a pattern threaded
> through, to the inside of your life, what at
> the back of your mind coming to the front,
> tautens. Look, I move my fingers. Oh. Feeling
> the pull of that nearby star the river twists
> and spins. Then I began to walk about with
> my body again. (199)

In one respect, the net or web furnishes a correlative to and attends an apprehension of living that is fundamentally generous, "giving back" in both a phenomenological and an ethical sense:

> Love plants peace. Not a catalogue of manipulative
> fairytales. Sky gives back. Gable-shape, tree-lines.
> The way the sunlight is, the way it comes down
> through leaves, and spider-silk gleams and
> doesn't suddenly, between lightly moving branches
> in the morning to be still. The order of the stones
> in the wall beside a yellow dust-track magnified,
> the insect ready, then away over and through a light
> dustfall in a sideways breeze gone but, very small,
> is noted. ... (163)

But the web or net, as Harry Gilonis has noted (30), is also a snare: both capture and entrap, as the multiple references in *Livelihood* to the spider's lethal webs and insect prey remind us. But the patterns and systems of patterning that web and net stand for are no less perceptual or cognitive traps. Gilonis acutely poses this issue as "the question of how to understand the world without clinging to, peering through, being jailed behind, some conceptual lattice". (39) For Scully, the question seems to arrive more as a problem of how to register the appearance of patterns, grasp them "precisely" (a term that echoes throughout the book), and yet not get trapped into mistaking the momentary or provisional pattern for a fixed and conclusive identity: how, in other words, to keep "moving in the weave" (Scully 128). Indeed, the untitled opening poem of the section "Prior" seems to map the relation between the "mis-taking" of the world and the "weave" that seems to make some momentary sense of it:

> Hopeful human mistakes. I think I see what I think
> (sometimes), but mostly I imagine where I am
> in the dark, feeling around, moment to moment,
> ready to respond to elastic surface, do you see what
> I hope I mean? A tap on a pipe, an insect clicks;
> deep in its pulp, a seed starts out. It's a long
> fantastic journey and nobody *really* believes the
> details. (129)

Mistaking is a function, on the one hand, of the slippage between names and phenomena, sense and signification:

> Yr name for the noise of what they were saying doesn't
> contain this or the web of the meaning of what they
> were saying and this together, shimmering, terrific,
> in the grass somewhere. (128)

On the other, whatever web of meaning is constructed, precisely as it offers the indubitable aesthetic pleasures of fit and harmony, confirms the distance of observer from world and carries the potential for complacency, another mode of mistaking the world – snug is a precise anagram of sung:

> When your pieces fit moving in the weave they make a
> noise together, snug in Disaster Depicted, not Disaster. (128)

The intrinsic distance of the poem from the world it orchestrates is at once its condition of possibility and its burden. The poet's stance at the window, catching glimpses of the world, or at the doorway, looking out at the rain-drenched or sunlit ground, is both a vantage and a threshold that hedges against "the strong tang / of the world impacting its *itself* on you, a / tide of smallest, simplest things" (208). The cascade of the real overwhelms and demands the response of a patterning that is, by the same token, defense and rage for order, conducing to limitation and the deadening of receptivity. "Habit", as Beckett's Vladimir said, "is a great deadener" (*Godot*, 91), product, in Beckett's own terms, of "a compromise between the individual and his environment" (*Proust*, 18). For Scully, the deadening effect is that of interpellation, the recruitment of the subject to the social order by the impact of instruction and media, for "If a system locks you to a screen / it directs your life" (186):

> learning to follow
> the way you hear the talk
>
> you will learn to follow
> the ways you see talk
> deployed
>
> & learn to initiate deployments
> in surprise
> measuring surprise
> crestfallen by the word *is*
>
> & this habit
> will facilitate & hinder
> yr ideas about the world
> skintight   to itself
>
> in the darkness
> (&) in the light. (189)

Scully's own relation to the interpellating effects of habit is not, however, to claim some ironically distantiated perspective that sees through the net of ideologies, but to recognize the constant possible oscillation between one's snug or smug satisfaction with the world as known and classified and the capacity of the world to derange or "dis-cord" that certainty, to slough the "skin" we stretch over its constantly shifting appearances:

> our problem
> was how the question was the
> more I thought I knew the more I
> "knew" I sank into those relative
> shadows that seem to cover the a-
> symmetrical skin that one begins
> to suspect anyway covers everything.
> full of. everything differently
> precisely in each different net.

> full of tiny bright word*ks* of
> discorded invention. our lives,
> glittering, reticulated. & from in
> here that edge where what you've
> been taught to imagine you know
> meets more ... (29)

Scully's initially stumbling and ambiguous syntax betrays here the awkward incoherence that attends any effort in *Livelihood* to "cover everything": nets are necessarily gapped. And the nets that are potential snares are countered by the "glittering, reticulated" nets that are *differential* in their function, establishing provisional constellations of the most disparate and disjunctive materials, assemblages whose momentary patterned stabilities are "discorded" at every moment by the insistence of the "more" that has necessarily been excluded from them.

Like constellations, then, Scully's weaves are the effect of a specific stance or angle of vision, an angle that shifts and changes with greater frequency than can that of any earthly observer of the heavens, but which are no less arbitrary than the arrays of stars that seem so persuasively to organize the night sky into constant and perduring figures. The poem as constellation, or as an assembly of constellations, speaks necessarily from what Paul Celan – one of the tutelary presences of *Livelihood* – called that "angle of reflection which is [the poet's] own existence, [the poet's] own physical nature" (49). Scully does not seek to "fly by those nets", in Stephen Dedalus's expression (Joyce, *A Portrait of the Artist as a Young Man*, 220), but rather captures himself as a constitutive presence in the nets that he weaves, no more nor less entrapped there than the reader or the friendly fly that each in their way find themselves landing "on a page" (Scully 7).

Dependent as they are on the particular "angle of reflection" of the poet, the patterns that form the local and extended constellations of *Livelihood* are nonetheless never understood to be the singular production of a peculiarly human capacity. On the contrary, the figures for the poems' and the book's structure are drawn from both organic and inorganic as well as artefactual phenomena: not only nets and weaving, but webs, crystals, honeycombs and birds' nests furnish the analogues for Scully's sense of structure throughout *Livelihood*. Additionally, the poems constantly stage the arrest of the subject's attention before the momentary, fleeting patterns that recur throughout, the net-like interference patterns of light reflecting on water or of the concentric ripple, also interfering wave patterns, caused by a pebble dropped in water, or the sunlight's dapple among leaves, or even the sudden, peripheral passage of a bird across the sky. Whether understood as architectonic forms constant in nature – like crystals or webs – or as fleeting effects of no less constant physical laws, pattern and structure seem to exist independent of the human observer. To Pound's triumphant "O splendor it all coheres!" and subsequent, repentant "I cannot make it cohere",[3] Scully responds with the architecture of the weaver bird in a passage of singular beauty:

    listeners there
        are &
    steady hey but

    cohere? go there
  look: hanker after
    people or a

    god or a blinding
        pattern
    one of the

    smallest birds in
the world its
    nest the size

    of half a
        walnut shell
    built to such

    deft such delicate
  these feathers
    leaves even telltale

---

[3] "What splendour, it all coheres!" are the words of the dying Herakles in Pound's 1956 translation of Sophocles' *Women of Trachis* (50), while the lines "I am not a demigod, / I cannot make it cohere" are from canto CXVI of the *Drafts and Fragments of Cantos CX-CXVII* (*The Cantos*, 796), that is, from the virtual conclusion of the work.

>   flower-petals moss
>   hair feet
>   bill spider-thread
>
>   weaving or the
> bird's own saliva
>   together or both
>
>   dancing in despite of even
>
>   out over
>   mimosa flicker past
>   the village to
>   the mountains
>
>   their eggs even
>   their eggs themselves
>   stuck down fast
>
>   against gales one
>   flat yes precision
>
>   stuck down
>   fast (Scully 272–3)

Pound's sublime ambitions here meet, perhaps in an echo of the *Pisan Cantos*' humble "lone ant" (*The Cantos* 458), with the miniature architect in nature whose delicate, deft operations find their equivalent in the minimal architecture of the poetic lines. Analogously, Gilonis cites Marx's famous remark that "a spider conducts operations which resemble those of a weaver, and a bee would put many a human architect to shame" (Gilonis 30).

Both the architectonic forms that appear in organic and inorganic nature and the beauty that the human eye may perceive in them raise more fundamental, and fundamentally aesthetic, issues than the humbling of human skills. Insofar as they are regarded not with respect to any function they may have, but simply as patterned objects, things like webs, crystals, honey-combs or nests correspond to what Immanuel Kant in the *Critique of Judgement* terms "free or self-subsisting beauties":

> Flowers are free beauties of nature. Hardly anyone but a botanist knows the true nature of a flower and even he, while recognizing in the flower the reproductive organ of the plant, pays no attention to this natural end when using his taste to judge of its beauty. Hence no perfection of any kind—no internal finality, as something to which this arrangement of the manifold is related—underlies this judgement. Many birds (the parrot, the humming-bird, the bird of paradise), and a number of crustacea, are self-subsisting beauties which are not appurtenant to any object defined with respect to its end, but please freely and of their own account. (I, 72)

Kant's point — which he extends to music and non-representational forms of decorative art and design — is that such "beauties" please independent of any concept we might have of what the object in question is *for* (its function or use) or of its adequacy to any moral idea (in particular with regard to human form). Nonetheless, they may still appear *as if* their form were "chosen as it were with an eye to our taste" (I 217). Later, he will add to these examples what he similarly calls "free formations of nature", all described with considerable knowledge of the physical laws involved, that include inorganic processes like mineral crystallization, the formation of ice in freezing water, or snow, "frequently of very artistic appearance and of extreme beauty" (I 219). Again the production of such formations in nature *appears* to suggest that nature has its own "aesthetic finality", that is, produces beautiful forms of its own volition. (I 219)

Still, according to Kant, to believe so would compromise not only the freedom of aesthetic judgement, but also the foundations of human freedom in general in the capacity for the free exercise of that power of judgement: "For nature to have fashioned its forms for our delight would inevitably imply an objective finality on the part of nature, instead of a subjective finality resting on the play of the imagination in its freedom, where it is we who receive nature with favour, and not nature that does us a favour" (I 220). Nature's apparent conformity to human aesthetic judgments that have universal if subjective validity "cannot belong to it as its end": "For otherwise the judgement that would be determined by reference to such an end would found upon heteronomy, instead of founding upon autonomy and being free, as befits a judgement of taste." (I 220)

Art for Kant is essentially a domain of freedom and as such a domain that must be divided by a carefully policed boundary from the operations of nature, however much these may appear to reveal the capacity of non-human animals to produce beautiful forms independent of any function they may have. Natural forms may be analogous to artworks (II 23), but only for the free reflective judgement of the human observer, not in themselves:

> By right it is only production through freedom, i.e. through an act of will that places reason at the basis of its action, that should be termed art. For, although we are pleased to call what bees produce (their regularly constructed cells) a work of art, we do so only on the strength of an analogy with art; that is to say, as soon as we call to mind that no rational deliberation forms the basis of their nature (or instinct), and it is only to their Creator that we ascribe it as art. (I 163)

As I have argued at greater length elsewhere, Kant's insistence on the realm of the aesthetic as that which grounds the very possibility of both human freedom and of the accord that guarantees the universality of the form of the Western human subject continues to shape a prevalent conjunction between aesthetic work and the ideal of human freedom and individuality. It cannot do so, however, without establishing differentiating thresholds between the free or autonomous subject and both natural phenomena and subordinate categories of humans, its racialised others. (Lloyd, *Under Representation*). Kant's *Critique of Judgement* thus inaugurates a tradition of aesthetic thought (which embraces poetics) that understands art to be the principal domain in which questions of human freedom and determination, subjectivity and universality are articulated. The artwork, in deliberate opposition to the products of nature, however beautiful they may be, is the archetype of human freedom from what Kant calls here "heteronomy".

In some respects, *Livelihood* might seem to extend that tradition: it is, as I have remarked, often scathing about the effects of a socially induced conformity, about subordination to the market (of labour and of poetry), and about the numbing impact of habits developed to survive in what the Frankfurt School named the "administered world".[4]

---

[4] For the notion of the "administered world", see in particular Max Horkheimer and Theodor W. Adorno, *Dialectic of Enlightenment*, passim.

> It impinges to such a degree that a minimum
> function required to remain the anonymous
> human agent in the world exerts a pressure
> disproportionate to the results required. *Chiaro?*
> Birdsong. I am that perfect citizen. Nothing is
> nothing. Yes-ing and no-ing and on-the-other-hand-
> ing my way through the mesh. I mean mess. Just
> pre-set the dial for Discipline: palm-frond in Harare,
> a bridge in Cambridge shiver a synapse. (Scully 201)

One of the volume's recurrent concerns is with the attainment of the means to a livelihood that might safeguard space and time for the writing to proceed in the face of the pressures of need and want. Writing continues to seem like a space that opposes heteronomy, that depends on the freedom from necessity that has always found its image in the free creativity of the artist, dismally as the concept of "creativity" has been appropriated in the lingo of Silicon Valley and sports good manufacturers and as the instances of transitory beauty – palm fronds and bridges – have been transformed into the routine metonyms of Discipline for the predisposed nervous system.

And yet *Livelihood* as a whole does not frame the issue with such finality. On the contrary, it establishes a constant oscillation between freedom and constraint, figured often as the relation between chance and choice. The sudden motion of perception or insight with which so many of the poems open or around which their movement turns alternates with the selection and patterning obliged by a world in which the poet "intent at desk" faces "the ten thousand / things that convene / shine escape / intermittent material" (279). In a world that is—to scale up—the product not of nature's subjective or objective finality, but of the accretion of dust particles through random collisions (168) or "colliding / high energy particles" (130), pattern and order are arbitrary or provisional, resembling the rules of a game that constitute the space and the instruments for a mesh (or mess) of chance outcomes:

> Giving back a black mesh, all the rules together, connected,
> or if all the rules together, dilated, make a path out then/
> Then our rules get up and shake hands. Game, set. No
>
> I mean yes ….

> If, stepping inside around and then
> outside and then again inside the circle of the rules of
> the game is the game, what then? Got that? *Chak*. But that's
> a new game. Turn, dance. ... (192)

Not only the game – including the "language game" of poetry – but even the players themselves are constituted by the rules of the game for the duration of the game. But in *Livelihood*, the rules of the game keep changing, shifting, the diverse units of the book refusing to stabilize into a single set of procedures; "Game, set. No…" (192). Any reader of Scully's work may have been struck by the extent to which the "second person address" characteristic of the lyric warps into the imperative mood, as if each verse unit required the iteration of "the basic instructions" (127) in order for poet and reader to proceed: begin, listen, turn, leave, breathe, step, open the book, close the book (Fryatt 101). The instances proliferate so extensively across the book that citation would be redundant. What matters is the function of the imperative mood and its relation to the order of poem that *Livelihood* enjoins the reader to engage with.

Critics have noted often enough Scully's antipathy towards the "well-made poem" that has dominated the Irish poetry industry and for which there seems an ever-avid market (Satris 1)[5]: product of what he dismisses as "the Gem School" (18), it circulates "bottled poetry" (Scully 132) whose characteristics he satirizes more than once in *Livelihood*, at times in terms that recall Beckett's enumerative comic turns in *Watt*:

> A mess of reminiscence is nothing. I was living
> on a small half-empty island, cold and wet, and
> many poets making much of their mothers and fathers
> and grandfathers and grandmothers and fields
> and ploughs and pigs as deeply gouged lies—the
> surface of Jupiter's Ganymede as I remember it—
> in the same breath, phrase-packets, a very I must
> say very slowed poetry: this was not Africa.
> Procumbent. I left. A weave is something. (130)[6]

---

[5] For a critique of this by-now received idea of Scully's practice, see Huk 105.

[6] Compare this passage to Samuel Beckett's rather more extended routine of the Lynch family in *Watt*, 101–11.

This is telling satire, directed at a familiar enough mode of Irish poetry, structured around the usually displaced, educated poet's reminiscences of rural childhood transformed into metaphors of belonging and cultural continuity. But there is more at issue than the anecdotal matter of poems that perpetually reiterate the conditions of deracination that has affected an agricultural economy undergoing rapid modernization, only to reassure the reader of the snug fit between the modern subject and the rural past. Ultimately, it is more about the inadequacy of a reproducible and widely reproduced poetic mode to the economic and social conditions of the present:

> I mean: everything run through this tensely amalgamated
> shadow-corps so that so many young practitioners
> don't even know how much's been filtered out or that
> anything has been *erase/erase* in the first place.
> Contact. Toy-like parallel movements. So complete, so
> concerted has been the walling round. To call repetitive
> clones "innovators" & get away with it. To inculcate
> a pathologically low tolerance threshold for complexity,
> & be thought intelligent. ... (107)

Generic ossification induces a kind of sclerosis of the attention, a "toy-like" automatism in which the poetic conformism of the clonic "shadow-corps" produces a "walling round" that peculiarly emulates the forms of enclosure that destroyed Ireland's rural communities and imposed the conditions for the emergence of an Irish version of the possessive individual of modern capitalist society.[7]

Irish poetry may be the immediate object of Scully's critique, but the critique is framed in such a way that it extends far beyond the poetic automatisms specific to Ireland's poetic culture. It aims at the ethical and aesthetic assumptions that are embedded in the "well-made poem". Scully has expressed often enough his distaste for metaphors and similes "(I dislike / similes, Mary, you know me)" (235).[8]

---

[7] On this transformation of Irish culture in the nineteenth century, driven by political economists' commitment to the formation of Irish possessive individuals, see Lloyd, *Irish Culture*, Chapter 1.

[8] In the reading cited above, Scully also reiterated his hatred of metaphors, introducing a poem in which, he claimed, he wanted to see what he "could squeeze out of the damn thing".

Metaphorisation is a fundamental operation or action of language and *Livelihood* is by no means devoid of either metaphor or simile. The antipathy is rather to the overall function of metaphor/simile within the "well-made poem" and as a model of the autonomous subject whose formation such poetry continually reinscribes, long after the conditions for autonomy have been eroded both by the thorough saturation of the social with the "codes" of automated responses ("repetitive cloning") and by the pervasive heteronomy of late or neo-liberal capitalism. The rote reproduction of lyric forms is symptomatic of a situation of unfreedom that Scully's fellow poet Trevor Joyce, no less dismayed by the automatisms of Irish lyric, described as "the common experience of seeming to act freely and spontaneously while even a minimal self-awareness reveals that this freedom is to a great extent generated and governed by forces and concerns in which one has had no hand, act or part" (Joyce, "Phantom Quarry", 6). The typical language of the lyric, that of "description, expression, aspiration", as Joyce goes on, "is constantly being sucked down the sink of calculated, monetised use. Moreover, even our means to refresh it have been appropriated" (6).

Both Joyce and Scully point to a larger predicament of lyric form than that evidenced in the routinised subject matter and "shape on the page" of the exhausted Irish mode. The so-called well-made poem reproduces the preset pattern of formation of the subject that integrates individual autonomy with the appropriation of the world. Its typical pattern is framed around metaphor: a vividly felt and particular moment of experience is rendered or recalled, usually in an ongoing present tense, only to be transformed – mostly by way of metaphor – into a figure for a generalized moral sentiment. The genealogy of the contemporary lyric may be traceable back to its Romantic forebears but as an exhausted form finally fails to partake of the imaginative imperatives that it now clones: both the illumination and the free relation to the social whole that it promises have declined into predictable "phrase-packets". What the form retains, however, is a specific economy of appropriation that informs the idea of the individual as autonomous or independent entity and an implied relation of author to reader in which the reader repeats the insight of the former in the interest of cultivating in turn his or her own self-formation. The poem stands as an act of appropriation that is in its turn appropriated or internalized by the reader as a model and vehicle of subjectivity. It thus lends itself consummately to the institutionalized practice and ends of the pedagogy of New or Practical Criticism, in which the student reader is formed as the self-possessed and morally discriminating subject. Metaphor is the vehicle by which experience is possessed and accumulated — "owned" as the current expression has it. Experience appears as a kind of raw material from which the individual is constituted in repeated acts of possession and processing *as* the "possessive individual". The type, however, is standardized and the poem that time and again relays the process by which experience is laid hold of is likewise standardized, offering the little "shiver" of recognition that fires the synaptic chains of pleasure. What appear as individual and spontaneous acts of perception in fact represent pre-programmed responses played out according to a fixed and pre-set pattern.

The correlative of that pattern and its capacity to circulate a standardized model of selfhood is money, the universal equivalent that succeeds in transforming every particular thing into a commodity form: money is, so to speak, the ideal form of metaphor, transforming difference into identity for the sake of realizing the potential exchange value that can be extracted from any thing, as the lyric transforms the specific moment of perception into a general equivalent. The association is explicit:

> Years ago one winter evening travelling
> through Ireland on a bus I watched a
> moon like money in the sky. (I dislike
> similes, Mary, you know me.) The moon
> was like money. Like money. Pulsing in
> my breast-pocket, bright sterile dust-
> rock, just like money. Circular shine
> against black, a brilliant silver, crystals,
> poison. (235)

Against the toxicity of money, transforming everything into sterile identities, the poem here seems to pose particular things — "that tree, this lake" (235) – if at the risk of transforming them in turn into "likenesses", metaphors rather than instances of particularity. More consistently, and more profoundly, *Livelihood* – and Scully's poetics as a continuing project – counterpose to the "money form" of the contemporary lyric an ethics and aesthetics of dispossession, one of whose crucial tenets is the refusal of a metaphoric poetics that converts its percepts into likenesses or equivalents, the mis-taking or misappropriation of one thing for another. The latter process repeats poetically the labour of global capital's sweatshops where everything, including human effort, is commodified in the entrapping net or web of circulation in exchange.[9]

Gaining a livelihood obliges the writer to engage in this dark parody of the poetic weave:

> I look at a thread. I watch, I hope, doing the sweatshop
> rag (pick up the whisper-movement in the grass, those
> insane harmonies of money) and in my hand
> mistake everything for everything else: floodlit factories,
> fences, dogs, men, uniforms. (127)

In this dark weave, the hopefully watchful attention of the poetic gaze at the world is perilously matched by the surveillance that guards the productive forces and fences the world into its enclosures. The "watchman" occupies the thin strip that divides these counter-domains of production and watching the world: his shed is the convertible site of watching and writing that generates the antithetical space of a counter-poetics that radically opposes the value system of accumulation and exchange. One of the recurrent locations of the writing throughout *Livelihood* furnishes also one of its pervasive puns: the shed where the writer produces his work, the shed where his writing accumulates along with other "clutter" (195), simultaneously and antithetically offers the term for this aesthetic of continual dispossession, its ongoing "shedding" of the particulars that risk being appropriated into congealed patterns and enclosures:

> Two or three small things, small, smaller, enmeshed.
> *Shed! Shed it all!* sings that strange bird I know of
> in the banyan tree. Quietly, quietly... (151)

Shedding counters the potentially endless round of "making and saving" where the appearance of choice manipulates the consumer-worker's desire:

---

[9] Gilonis refers to the networks "of electronic communication carrying signals, moving money and information" (37). Given the important place in *Livelihood* of the net or web as an analogue of natural and human patterning, including poetry, it may seem surprising that Scully does not play more with the idea of the internet or world-wide web, whose forms were coming into being even as the book was being constructed, between 1992 and 2004.

> Does matter stop at its edges? In a forest of false
> options your picture of the world inside your head
> is manipulated from outside to sell you a kind of hell:
> step onto that Desire-Wheel and start making and saving,
> making and saving, losing and making and losing again
> over the checkerboard. (151)

Shedding is the refusal of a fixed pattern in which it might seem that "matter stops at its edges", congealed in images of desirable commodities. It makes space for the renewal of attention to an unpossessed and unpossessable world of moving phenomena, of listening, of watching without desire to fix or appropriate:

> nervure of a fly's wings
> to blur the lens, difficult,
> working through, watching,
>
> taking note, watching, puzzled,
> delighted, in a presence
> (never anything by rote)
>
> beyond sense, sentient.
> Black green
> blue (249–50)

The composition of the weave of *Livelihood* out of such moments of precise, close-in attention, "puzzled" by fleeting and ephemeral glimpses of the world, its counter-sublime refusal of grand narratives or dwelling on historically significant events or figures, might seem to belie the immediate appearance of this "fat" book's epic scale. That is not to say that *Livelihood* is anything other than "a poem including history", in Pound's sense (Pound, *ABC*, 46), but its inclusion of the historical is not a matter of the citation of events but of being "in history" (Scully 61): as a poem, as a whole, it registers at every node of its net the pressures and possibilities of its actual historical moment, from personal and social economic constraints to the universe of theoretical physics, but with an ear attentive to what passes and, at times, "lodges obdurately (in the net)" as history (61). Likewise, in its adherence to "writing at the edge" (130), always at the cusp of what is emerging into attention, it honours its debt to Charles Olson's notion of "projective verse", but without the shadow of imperial desire that always haunts Olson's formulations, the desire for the work to match up to nature in its scale, to achieve "projective size": that belies the "humilitas" Olson espouses. (Olson 281)

Not that Scully's work is devoted to any kind of false modesty or minimalist reserve. It is, rather, a different conception of the projective that is at work here, one that connects Olson's injunction, "one perception must must must MOVE, INSTANTER, ON ANOTHER!" (Olson 273), to Scully's own suspicion of metaphor as an index of reduction to equivalence. For him, indeed, "one thing leads to another", but by a more tentative, less declarative movement, hedged around by the possibility of mistaking simultaneity or sequence for identity:

what is the name of the sound of the rain?

(none   a bell)
or anything echoing
between
one thing & another

one thing
of course

one thing

cedes to another
& stored
in

as a matter of

certain

coarsely sometimes
strangely
of

(tap)

> course
>
> one thing leads to another
>
>   fine
> through certainty
> in a sort of constricting ring.
>
> I thought the other hammering
> was the echo of another(tell/told)
> until the first(which?)stopped (Scully 94–5)

Here, indeed, one perception moves, more or less instanter, but hesitantly, towards another, or, more precisely, "one thing *cedes* to another", giving way as perception moves; and not only forward, but through interruption and the sideways flitting of the attention, *across* the field of composition, "mind skittering, touching/jumping / across a water-surface" (321). Ceding is the antithesis of "holding", accumulatively, to what is, to the imposition of a progression or direction. Like yielding, its giving way is productive, even if, as Scully jests, what it produces, one thing after another, might be "a terminal spinney / of ampersands" (49). Its law is not that of subordination but of seriality, "One one one one one" (259) in irreducible contiguity, not by likeness or resemblance. One is not mistaken for an other one.

In this respect, Scully's compositional practice seems radically musical, though not necessarily in the manner of the round or ballad forms his titles occasionally invoke, forms that depend on closed patterns of repetition. On the contrary, just as he deconstructs the sonnet form to open out its interior enclosures, so his musicality approaches rather the procedure that Adorno attributes to Alban Berg, and with similar demands on the "attentive listener":

> Even pointing to the presence of repeats does not count for much where the repeated elements are themselves so dissolved and transformed that they are scarcely perceived as an identity, and where no appeal is made to a feeling of architectonic symmetry. The complexity of the motivic elaboration, as well as the overlapping of formal ideas, transform the work into a piece of free prose despite, and because of, the bound nature of

every note. The only listener to take it in properly will be the one who follows its flow from one bar to the next, following wherever it chooses to lead him. The attentive listener must expand and contract with the music, instead of listening attentively for correspondences. (Adorno 188)

Livelihood is, of course, threaded through with repetition, but Adorno's description of repeated elements "so dissolved and transformed that they are scarcely perceived as an identity" could not better characterize the way in which Scully repeats motivic elements in *Livelihood*, suggesting itself as a very precise description of the musical function of a section like the *Postlude,* composed almost entirely of elements repeated from earlier in the book. Indeed, Adorno's provocative expression, "free prose" might well characterize large parts of *Livelihood* where the patterning of the verse moves not through interwoven sound- or image-scapes, but in a series of self-interrupting visions and revisions.

Adorno's description of Berg's method is no less apt in its application to Scully's refusal of subordination of the elements that compose the field of the poem:

> Berg does not begin by defining figures graphically in terms of rhythm, and then using them as models to be subsequently modified. Instead, one aspect of a complex, no matter what, is singled out because it is felt to contain seminal force. It is then spun out and transformed into the next one, without reference to any fixed point. The whole thing develops in a quite unschematic way. This may serve as the technical formula for that rampant proliferating growth in Berg's work, for that sense of an impenetrable undergrowth which may have been the core of its nature. (189–90)

Certainly, the reader of *Livelihood* is constantly aware that its structure refuses any central organizing motifs, no matter how often recurrences of materials may be noted. What is repeated does not organize metaphorically the meaning or even the form of the whole. Brief comparison with a more or less contemporaneous long poem, Derek Walcott's *Omeros,* may help to make the point, not least because so many of the figures that Walcott deploys find correspondences in *Livelihood.* For Walcott such elements as the African swallow that flies between Africa and the Caribbean, or the fishing nets of the islanders, or the criss-cross patterns of the waves are metaphors that undergird the larger moral significance of an epic that aims at reconciliation with the violent colonial past of the West Indies. Scully's repeating elements scrupulously refuse recruitment into such an epic resolution. One is not continually directed to contemplate the weave of the poem as an expression of the final harmony of both its structure and its evolution towards a well-prescribed and redemptive conclusion. Indeed, however much one is drawn to admire the sheer "craftsmanship" and technical achievement of the poem, sustained over so large a scale, *Omeros* inevitably feels archaic, not because of its allusions to Homer or Dante, but because it is so resolutely, even obstinately, committed to resurrecting an exhausted form.

Adorno's remarks on modern compositional form remain relevant here also, additionally offering another way than Olson's to think of "composition by field" (Olson 272):

> Composers now work in terms of 'areas' (*Felder*), instead of themes and thematic complexes. A path leads from each area to the next, but none is the logical inference or result of its predecessor. They all have equal status and stand on the same plane. They serve as prototypes of what must become of the symphonic form once the sonata system, and even more importantly, the spirit of the sonata, has been exhausted. The units within the movements are segments. They are connected by motifs which are divided up and shared between them.
>
> (Adorno 190)

It would not be wrong to consider the sonata form as the musical counterpart of the "well-made poem", each with their dominant thematic material, development towards resolution and metaphors or motifs that organize the progression throughout. If both are "exhausted" forms, it is not only because the techniques have come to seem so familiar as to appear rote, but also because their "spirit", the historically informing logic that dictates the laws of individual development that each obeys, no longer seem adequate to the condition of heteronomy that prevails in late capitalism. Adorno's subsequent analysis of the formal difficulty presented by the exhaustion of developmental forms, the danger of their reduction to stasis, incidentally offers remarkably relevant terms for describing the overall construction of *Livelihood*: "Where music does not unfold entirely according to the laws of development, but is composed, as with certain derivatives of dance, of segments whose meaning is not altered all that much if their sequence in time is changed, then a static architecture is not only possible, but it also assists in the articulation of events" (191). Ultimately, in Berg as in Scully, "the organized chaos of overlapping lines and sounds" allows for the "energy stored up in the simultaneous" to become "that of succession" (193).

Adorno's remarks throw into relief the tension throughout *Livelihood* between its peculiar stasis and its constant, restless forward movement, the way in which the poet's attention seems always "on the edge", alert at every moment to shifting movements internally and externally and propelled forwards or sideways by each instant of perception or apperception: reading through the poem, for all its lively movement, does not subject even the most attentive reader to the ironic effects of cumulative revisions of mistaken conclusions. This is not a poem "with designs on the reader",[10] moral or pedagogical, but a labyrinthine lattice, a "web of ... meaning" (Scully 128) across which connections may be made in any direction. Touring its lattice, to borrow Scully's expression (17), one reads and thinks across and around the poem, not through it to its destination: any node in the net is the switch to another point and a sum is never the product of its parts. The reader steps in and out of the poem in the tracing of the dance that is one of Scully's privileged figures for the patterns discovered in the natural world and in the movement of perception:

> the dance of rain
> snow   discovery
> taking in   letting
> go   molecular pavanes
> in rings & chains
>   pistons   combustion
> reading   doubt
>   day/night chequerwork
> cloud-dance   tidal-
> dance   dance of the whale
>   ants & bees   dance
> of the binary
> systems   dance of

---

[10] This comment is cited by Alex Davis in *A Broken Line*, 167, from an essay by Scully, "As I Like It", that appeared in his journal *The Beau* 3 (1983/4), 10.

>   regenerating
>   lithosphere   things
>   in relation   rippling
>   wing-edges
>   dance of energy
>   dance of the
>   blood
>   the dance
>   of the
>   blood
>   slow sets
>   shimmering nets
>   mountains
>   moving.
>   So. (268)

The dance, however, does not propose to be a Platonic idea of the harmonious universe, whatever harmonies may on occasion be descried among its "free beauties", constellations, webs, crystals or ripples. The dance is not an Order, even if lining things up produces momentary orders. On the contrary, the mis-step and the missing figure are as much part of Scully's complex weave as are things in their places, while order appears only in the commitment to the writing and its often uncanny moments of recognition:

> adding (down) leaning to the law that
> each thing its number its place
> between the/*because* of these shadows
> interlocked and separated figures
> things missing or things wedged side-
> ways that remind us that all orders
> have their justification in the end in
> an order of orders only our faith as
> we work, addresses – oh! – (260)

The poem is not the imitation of the Idea of Order; rather, the poem orders and in ordering changes what it orders. Not according to the model of exchange, where one thing may become any thing according to the law of equivalence for which money is the ultimate idea, but according to the model of intervention, where every thing, including the poem, acts as a thing in the world, changing and changed by what it changes:

> when the dance changes the world
>   changes the dance
>
> changes the dance changes: broken
> bits make a mosaic, mosaic a
> picture, picture a blur falling
> into darkness, darkness folded on
> darkness, old places shot through
> multiple veins of new surfaces
> in old places: (292)

As the foot moves through the dance, it leaves its trace, a vestige, like the prints in the snow or sand that pace through the poem, like the breath that mists the pane and in which other traces are inscribed, momentarily. Or like the handprint on rock: as the mosaic that forms a picture blurs and falls away, it falls down into the cavernous darkness whose rock-faces bear the imprint of the oldest human traces – artworks, perhaps – like those whose figures furnished the frontispiece and backpiece of the first volume of *Things that Happen, 5 Freedoms of Movement*.

As Jean-Luc Nancy has argued, such traces or vestiges are not mimetic, not efforts to present an idea of the world in sensible form or incarnation, but "present nothing other than presentation itself, its open gesture, its displaying, its aperity, its patefaction—and its stupefaction" (72). As he continues, these prints of hands are the signs of passage, not of grasping the world: "the hand posed, pressed against the wall, grasps nothing. It is no longer a prehensile hand, but is offered like the form of an impossible or abandoned grasp. A grasp that could well let go. The grasp of a letting-go: the letting go of form" (72). In its "intricate walking" (Scully 257), *Livelihood*, we could say, is the vestige of the poet's passage through the world, a letting-go of what passes into the poem, not as an array of things appropriated, nor as a presentation of ethical or political designs, but as a movement that sheds as a hand scatters what it holds in passing. It is a work that withdraws from all those forms in which writing has participated in the domination of the world and of the reader, offering itself instead as "the most estranged simplicity of presence" (Nancy 72): of presence in the world of which it is part and to which it is always "next", "deep in the world, / open, touching" (Scully 284). It offers us an unprecedented poetics of displacement and of dispossession, a weave for readers to lose their way in. We might say that therein lies the Irishness of Scully's work, but that no such identity category survives its shedding.

Works Cited

Adorno, Theodor W. "Berg's Discoveries in Compositional Technique." *Quasi una Fantasia: Essays on Modern Music*. Trans. Rodney Livingstone. London: Verso, 1992. 179–200.
Beckett, Samuel. *Murphy*. London: Picador, 1973.
———. *Proust and Three Dialogues with Georges Duthuit*. London: John Calder, 1976.
———. *Waiting for Godot*. London: Faber and Faber, 1981.
———. *Watt*. New York, NY: Grove Press, 1953.
Celan, Paul. "The Meridian." *Collected Prose*. Trans. Rosemary Waldrop. Manchester: Carcanet, 2003. 37–55.
Culler, Jonathan. "Lyric, History and Genre." *New Literary History* 40.4 (2009): 879–99.
Davis, Alex. *A Broken Line: Denis Devlin and Irish Poetic Modernism*. Dublin: University College Dublin Press, 2000.
Fryatt, Kit. "The Poetics of Elegy in Maurice Scully's *Humming*." *Irish University Review* 46.1 (2016): 89–104.
Gilonis, Harry. "The Spider, the Fly and Philosophy: Following a Clew through Maurice Scully's *Livelihood*." in *The Fly on the Page: The Gig Documents #3* (2004), ed. Nate Dorward. 29–43.
Horkheimer, Max and Theodor W. Adorno. *Dialectic of Enlightenment*. Trans. John Cumming. New York, NY: Continuum, 1972.
Huk, Romana. "'Out past / Self-Dramatization': Maurice Scully's *Several Dances*." *Irish University Review* 46.1 (2016): 105–18.
Jakobson, Roman and L.G. Jones. "Shakespeare's Verbal Art in 'Th'Expence of Spirit". *Language in Literature* (Cambridge, MA: Harvard University Press, 1987). 284–303.
Joyce, James. *A Portrait of the Artist as a Young Man*. Ed. Seamus Deane. Harmondsworth: Penguin, 1992.
Joyce, Trevor. "The Phantom Quarry: Translating a Renaissance Poem into Modern Poetry." *Enclave Review* 8 (2013): 5–8.
Kant, Immanuel. *Critique of Judgement*. Trans. James Creed Meredith. Oxford: Clarendon Press, 1982.

Lloyd, David. *Irish Culture and Colonial Modernity, 1800–2000: The Transformation of Oral Space*. Cambridge: Cambridge University Press, 2011.
——. *Under Representation: The Racial Regime of Aesthetics*. New York, NY: Fordham University Press, 2019.
Nancy, Jean-Luc. "Painting in the Grotto." *The Muses*. Trans. Peggy Kamuf. Stanford, CA: Stanford University Press, 1996. 69–79.
Olson, Charles. "Projective Verse." *Modern Poets on Modern Poetry*. Ed. James Scully. London: Fontana, 1973. 270–282.
Oppenheimer, Paul. *The Birth of the Modern Mind: Self, Consciousness and the Birth of the Sonnet*. Oxford: Oxford University Press, 1989.
Pound, Ezra. *ABC of Reading*. London: Faber and Faber, 1973.
——. *The Cantos*. New York, NY: New Directions, 1972.
——. Trans. *Sophocles: Women of Trachis*. London: Faber and Faber, 1956.
Satris, Marthine. "An Interview with Maurice Scully." *Contemporary Literature* 53.1 (2012): 1–30.
Scully, Maurice. *Livelihood*. Bray, Co. Wicklow: Wild Honey Press, 2004.
Walcott, Derek. *Omeros*. New York, NY: Farrar Strauss Giroux, 1990.
Wyatt, Thomas. "They flee from me, that sometime did me seek." *Silver Poets of the Sixteenth Century*. Ed. Gerald Bullett. London: J.M. Dent, 1947. 14–15

Meeting a Giant: Allegory in Maurice Scully's *Things That Happen*

Kit Fryatt

In his esoteric study of the Baroque *Trauerspiel, On the Origin of German Tragic Drama,* Walter Benjamin contends that within the hieratic and emblematic forms of figuration called "allegory" lies a revolutionary potential absent from the more elegant and seemingly organic forms elevated by Romantic philosophy and criticism as "symbol". The rigid morbidity of allegory emphasises the absolute divergence of signs from their meanings, liberating us from delusions of signification: "Ultimately in the death-signs of the baroque the direction of the allegorical reflection is reversed; on the second part of its wide arc it returns, to redeem" (232). Benjamin's "rehabilitation" of allegory has proved immensely influential – both directly and indirectly – on modernist poetic practice. Always bearing in mind the resistance of Benjamin's ideas to application by literary critics – as Charles Rosen writes, "His interpretations do not give meaning to, but strip meaning from, the work, allowing the inessential to drop off and the work to appear in its own light" (171–172) – I wish to propose, in this chapter, an exploration of the place of a broadly post-Benjaminian understanding of allegory in reading Maurice Scully's eight-book project *Things That Happen*.[1]

Given that Scully's work has still not received the critical attention it deserves, a description of the structure and technique of *Things That Happen* may be useful. The title, a late addition – for many years, Scully's working title was *Livelihood: the set* – alludes distantly to Paul Celan's Bremen Prize acceptance speech. Celan spoke of the effects of the Holocaust upon language: "It passed through and gave back no words for that which happened; yet it passed through all this happening" (29). The imprecision of the allusion is calculated to avoid appropriation of Celan's suffering and that of European Jews, while it quietly draws attention to everyday enormity. Celan's phrase is "that which happened", unnameable and unique. Without claiming

---

[1] Scully's continuing interest in the potential of formality and artificiality to effect liberation can be seen in his manipulations of the pastoral elegy in *Humming* (2009). See: Fryatt, Kit. "The Poetics of Elegy in Maurice Scully's *Humming*". *Irish University Review* 46:1 (2016): 89–104.

equivalence with "that which happened", Scully's title maintains that "things" do "happen" and the poetry "carries a lot of grief in its back pocket" (Scully and Fryatt 141).

The first volume of *Things That Happen*, *5 Freedoms of Movement*, was published in 1987 by Galloping Dog Press. It was reissued, with some revisions and in a different format, by etruscan books in 2001. The Galloping Dog edition is A4 format and uses a typewriter font, while the etruscan is shorter and broader than a standard trade paperback, almost square. In both editions Scully uses photographs to introduce each of the five sections, and the cover, frontispiece and end-pages feature his own drawings of moving bodies, based on Libyan cave paintings. *5 Freedoms* also makes extensive use of found material. A number of poems are based on creditors' notices, phrasebooks and Linguaphone courses, Enid Blyton's children's novels, works of natural history, medical textbooks and operating instructions. Scully revised the poems between the two editions, publishing some of the results in European poetry magazines and in *etruscan reader IV* (1999), alongside the work of Bob Cobbing and Carlyle Reedy. He deletes a number of poems, and makes a few additions, though the order and structure of the work remains fundamentally unchanged. The poems excised from the etruscan edition tend to be either lyrics apparently addressed to a lover, such as "I close my eyes" (10), or satirical work which identifies the speaker quite precisely as an impecunious writer living in Dublin during a bleak period of economic depression, examples of which include "Tart balm this: withdrawal from the salt details" (*5 Freedoms* [1987] 11) and "That winter I could hardly think" (*5 Freedoms* [1987] 39). Scully's purpose in reworking *5 Freedoms* seems to be to minimise the contribution of a lyrical poet-persona whose feelings and circumstances make a claim on importance simply because they are rendered in verse. The working poet is still a presence in the revised work, but inclinations towards self-pity and self-aggrandisement are muted, in line with Scully's ambition "[n]ot to write an autobiography, not to sketch a hero and edit amazing events, but to interact with the world... Not to meditate on the world, but to be *in* it" (Scully and Fryatt 143). The account of *5 Freedoms* below takes the etruscan edition, the most recent and most easily available text, as definitive.

The first section, "Unauthorised Credits", begins with a reproduction of Yves Klein's "Leap into the Void" (1960), a photomontage of the painter diving from a ledge, apparently part of a wall surrounding a suburban park. The title of this first section is taken from a creditor's letter, which appears as a found piece later in the section:

> It is disappointing to note that you have not
> responded to a previous communication in connection
> with your account and that you are continuing to avail
> yourself of unauthorised credit. (9)

The pun on "unauthorised" alerts us to Scully's disinclination to adopt the stance of a god-like author, or as Harry Gilonis puts it, the role of an "all-encompassing Master of Ceremonies" ("The Spider", 32).

"Instances", the second section of *5 Freedoms*, is prefaced by a photograph of a tiny figure leaping across the gap between two huge rock formations. His position in mid-air makes it difficult to judge whether he will make it to the other side, but if he does, he will certainly have to make the jump again, because the formation to which he is jumping is isolated from the main spar of rock, like a huge pillar for a modern Stylites. Befitting this implication of a desire for asceticism and isolation, the poems in "Instances" have a meditative tone, detailing precise effects in nature and art.

"A Record of Emotion", the third and longest section of *5 Freedoms*, subdivided into "Side A" and "Side B", uses a photograph of a stage magician holding a luminous hoop and apparently making his female assistant levitate. The heads of his audience are visible in the foreground. Again, this photograph seems to refer to Scully's distrust of the manipulative author, as the ironic title does to his scepticism concerning transparent communication between the poetic self and the world of objects. Elsewhere, Scully links sub-Wordsworthian sentiments about poetry's origin in recollected emotion to commodified and half-forgotten versions of "history" (Scully, *Livelihood*, 59–61).

The fourth section of *5 Freedoms*, "Two Caterpillars", starts with a photograph of a toddler standing beside a brick wall. The child holds a photograph in front of his or her face. The image in this photograph is of the same child and brick wall. In this section, a pastiche of a children's story about "Fat Caterpillar" and "Fatter Caterpillar" frames a series of vignettes about sexuality, consumption and the artist at work: a childlike idiom brackets poems which confront the subtleties of adult life. The caterpillars' life of consumption is naturalised by the distinctly mediatory tone of a children's story, while the poet, observant and detached, details economic and interpersonal nuance that belong most definitely to culture rather than nature.

5 Freedoms closes with "One Wallflower". The photograph associated with its lyrics of minute movement is a Muybridge stop-motion study of a man performing a long jump. Some familiar motifs re-appear here – an Italian children's poem quoted in "A Record of Emotion" is remade to describe intellectual motion, though the logic of the thought quickly breaks down:

> for argument you need words
> in blocks fit to ideas with
> sticky ends to fit block for
> block together. (88)

This final section leaves us with the impression of a mind at work, Scully's characteristic pose of watching, thinking and recording. It's also an optimistic finale for a book that has been preoccupied with straitened circumstances:

> that quite particular colour
> dark but clear & the cool smell of rain on
> a changed breeze
> [...]
> a tight schedule
> allows relief   elsewhere
> more air in lungs & cooler
> a white line in a blue sky
> moving & the mind   laughing at itself (91)

Livelihood (2004) is a work in five books and three "interstices", which Scully refers to as "the Ludes" – "Prelude", "Interlude" and "Postlude". Most of the work in *Livelihood* has been previously published, whether as extracts in magazines, chapbooks or book-length publications. Some of *Livelihood*'s texts also appear on a CD, *Mouthpuller* (2000), read by Scully. The frontispiece and end-piece of *Livelihood* is a sketch by Scully of a Sumerian clay container, the shape of which gave rise to the logograph for "legal", "decision", "trial" and "peace". The front matter of the book also features a childhood drawing of birds by the poet's daughter Leda, which first appeared on the cover of the pamphlet *Over and Through* (1992).

Livelihood opens with "Prelude", first published as a chapbook in 1997 by Wild Honey Press. Like all the "Lude" chapbooks, "Prelude" has a reproduction of a yarn painting by a Huichol artist on the cover. The Huichol are an indigenous Mexican people, descended from the Aztecs, who preserve shamanic traditions in their art and belief system. This artwork is not used in *Livelihood*. The poems in "Prelude", mostly arranged in irregular tercets, describe the world around the speaker in sometimes disturbingly galvanic terms: "a penpoint purred" (9);

> *take us*
>
> *home* pleaded the dice
> inside tight on
> the floor
>
> & whingeing ... (10)

The tone of puzzled grief that pervades much of the book is already evident in "Stone", in which the speaker finds himself before a grave:

> ... I who
> could never
>
> read you of a sudden
> reading yr
> stone
>
> reading yr
> stone. (11)

The first book of *Livelihood*, "The Basic Colours", was published by Pig Press in 1994. The Pig Press edition uses a different version of the Sumerian logograph sketch, and also reproduces Leda Scully's drawing. In addition to these there is an unidentified title-page drawing of shapes representing a fish, a cup, and perhaps a leaf, and an abstract pen and ink drawing between the poems "**sonnet/**flying past this impossibly repeating lattice" and "A maker of cages. whispers too, quite acute". Three poems in the Pig Press edition, "There is this specific machine", "parquet" and "THE START" (Scully, *The Basic Colours*, 51–54), do not appear in *Livelihood*. Otherwise alterations are minor, mainly involving changes in lineation. The revisions are like those to *5 Freedoms*, however, in rejecting the personal lyric and in particular, the elegiac lyric. In its Pig Press version, "**sonnet/**Open, wondering" confronts a recent death: "I'd like to thank you for the loan of the house. / crisp vertical layers. it's late. &…you're dead" (31). This has been emended to "it's late. you're gone" in *Livelihood* (40), and a later iteration of ellipses followed by the phrase "you're dead" is omitted altogether (*The Basic Colours* 31, *Livelihood* 40–41). According to Scully's note, "The Basic Colours" takes its title from an English/Greek phrasebook, *English/Greek Dialogues*, "in which there are no dialogues" (*Livelihood* 331). Pedagogical concerns – Scully has worked as a teacher of English to language learners for much of his career – animate this book of *Livelihood*. In "**sonnet/**(we went out to look at a tree", one of Scully's personae, a "literate / old Yahoo", mock-pedantically anatomises the rhetorical questions of W.B. Yeats's "Among School Children":

> this is the Bole, these the Branches, that the Canopy –
> stand back. underneath you know
> is where the Roots go
> to live & hold the Ground together.
> & look at its Top
> how compliant it is to the weather. (28)

The pedagogue's symbolic mode deranges cause and effect: because the individual integrity of the parts he describes are unimportant to him even as he names and distinguishes them, roots can "hold the ground together", the top of a tree be "compliant […] to the weather". The last line, in particular, parodies a Yeatsian vocabulary of complaisance and gracefulness. The conclusion of "**sonnet/**…" introduces an uneasy human relation – that between a teacher and his students – to the inherent instability of Yeats's rhetorical questions:

> *I see* nodded each student in this dance
> intent, pretending, chipping at the fact
> to teach me something, something quite different
> *I see*   I think). (28)

Like Yeats's poem, this engages with urgent issues of discrimination. What is the difference between intentness and pretence or between seeing and thinking? What is the different thing the students wish to teach their teacher? How can the grammatical structure "I see" contain these possibilities?

The subtitle of "The Basic Colours", "a watchman's log", and the section headings "On Site: A" and "On Site: B", refer to the watchman's job that Scully held to supplement his income in the 1980s. Many of the poems can be read as the observations, thoughts and dreams (the persona wakes with a start in the penultimate poem) of a man doing a very boring job. The watchman persona is sustained in "Zulu Dynamite", the second book of *Livelihood*, which opens with an account of his routine:

> It was one of my duties as a night watchman on the site
> to check the site every hour on the hour & to enter in
> the site logbook, every hour on the hour, *Site normal.*
> *Nothing to report* then to phone HQ to report that there
> was, in truth, nothing to report. (75)

Shortly after this, it seems, the watchman loses his job for excessive interest in the plans left in the site office, an interest Scully shared: "I used to pore over the plans in the engineer's office. Years and years of detailed work. Quite like art really" (Scully and Fryatt 143). "Zulu Dynamite" is arranged in five subsections, named after the notebooks in which they were composed. One of these, "The Yellow Logbook", seems to have been liberated from the building site. The contents of "The Red Notebook" are read by Scully on the CD *Mouthpuller*. "The Dun Copy" was published in 1997 as a folded card by Longhouse Books. The Longhouse Books version includes some italicised lines later omitted. These, like most of the material Scully excises in revision, are of a personal and confessional nature: "*the pain of waking up / can be the pang of love / yr hand*" (Scully, *From Zulu Dynamite*, np).

The third book of *Livelihood*, "Priority", is in two parts, "Prior" and "Over and Through", with a single-poem "Coda". Some of the poems in "Over and Through" were published in 1992 by Poetical Histories as a pamphlet which also includes some work not collected in *Livelihood*. "Work Day", the "Coda" to "Priority", appears in a slightly different form in the Poetical Histories pamphlet. In 1995

Scully published *Priority* as a book with Writers Forum. The Writers Forum book had an extremely small print run and is vanishingly rare. It does not include "Interlude" – "I wrote the 'Ludes last", Scully notes.[2] Parts of the Writers Forum book, omitted from *Livelihood*, appear in *Tig*. The closing pages of section II of "Bread" (Scully, *Tig*, 73–74), for example, are derived from the 1995 version of *Priority*.

"Interlude", the second of *Livelihood*'s interstices, is placed between "Prior" and "Over and Through". It contains some of Scully's most explicit engagements with authority and its symbolic forms, particularly in "The Sirens – a ballad", where we encounter Cuchulain, "the giant / spinning in his / skin", as a personification of Order (*Livelihood*, 140). The slender tercets of "The Sirens" also recall "Prelude", reminding the reader of formal links across the five books of *Livelihood*.

"Over and Through" differs substantially from the Poetical Histories pamphlet. Scully has added twelve poems, retitled two, and expanded two. The poem that appears as "Rain [A folder falls open]" in *Livelihood* has been both expanded and retitled. In a number of other poems he has changed lineation and syntax. The additions and revisions develop our sense of Scully as a political and social satirist. The precursor of "Rain", "Sound", ends on a note of multisensory observation: "Tensed rosettes of brilliance / patterns, chance, the seam glistens… / the hammer taps" (Scully, *Over and Through*, np). "Rain" replaces this with "Legislation is the rules of the fight, a rondo in / plot-pages, not a comfort, honey, or didn't you know? / Opulently produced by. Irk and then manipulate. Beware" (*Livelihood*, 156). The new poems in "Over and Through" also touch on literary politics: in "Fire", "a Language Poet grins & / flickers in the ghost of svarabhakti in the west of Ireland / risk misting the screen" (164). "Svarabhakti", a Sanskrit word meaning "loyal vowel", is used by some grammarians to denote the "helping vowel" sound interposed between consonants to aid pronunciation. Synonymous with the Greek "epenthesis", the effect is common in Irish, occurring for example in *gorm* ("blue") and *ainm* ("name"). It may also refer to the interruptive equals sign (=) sometimes placed between each letter of "Language" when referring to that poetic movement. Svarabhakti is disruptive of morphology but phonologically helpful; Scully, undogmatically but distinctly concerned with sound, relishes the idea of simultaneous interruption and facilitation. The

---

[2] Maurice Scully, "Re: Priority", email to Kit Fryatt, 29th July 2006.

juxtaposition of a Sanskrit word with "the west of Ireland" reminds the reader of connections between Irish and Indian nationalism, and the interest taken by Yeats and his circle in both Indian philosophy and the folklore of the Irish west. Svarabhakti might stand as a metaphor for Yeats's enabling and inhibitory effects upon his successors. Scully notes both Yeats's flexibility and his forbidding grandeur: "What I like about Yeats is his will to change. Right up to the end. The rhetoric can be just too hard to swallow, for someone of my generation anyway, sometimes" (Scully and Fryatt 139). "Language" poets typically oppose nationalistic literary culture of the type that Yeats seemed to promote, but their late modernist anti-identitarianism could not exist without the example of high modernist masks and personae. Scully's ghostly, flickering Language poet is an implicit acknowledgement of the spuriousness of a poetics which opposes the "creative" to the "communal".

Steps, first published as a self-contained book by Reality Street in 1998 and scarcely revised for the 2004 publication, has a simpler structure than *Priority*, which looks forward to the less intricate third and fourth volumes of *Things that Happen*. It is divided into three numbered sections and a coda. A number of the poem-titles used in *Priority* recur here. As Scully remarks, "[t]itles of 'poems' are a bit slippery in *Livelihood*. They can be 'serious', tongue-in-cheek, oblique, picking up a motif from elsewhere or pointedly omitting it and … sometimes a few of those things at the same time" (Scully and Fryatt 139). As an example, Scully compares the first piece entitled "Responsibility" in *Steps* ("the fid, stirps") and a later one with the same title ("Washing her clothes"). The first poem combines a carpenter's specialist vocabulary ("fid", "kerfed", "rabbets") and classification ("stirps") with an ironic attack on the centrality of religious institutions to Irish public life in the twentieth century. The Yeatsian metaphors of bole and blossom, used to satirical effect in "**sonnet/**(we went out to look at a tree", are revisited in the poem's coda (*Livelihood*, 204). The second poem is also concerned with specialism and knowledge, featuring "The Oxford English Dictionary of / Spraints, Pretoria Encyclopaedia / of Mortgages, Concise Cambridge / Political" (215) but this informationism is set against the optimistic figure of a young woman insouciantly washing her clothes in a rusty wheelbarrow:

> her bright brown eyes
> and mouth connect in a smile whose

> radiance and playfulness the fine
> skin black (215)

"Adherence", the fifth book of *Livelihood*, has a similar tripartite structure, with a coda. The parts are entitled "ABC", "Cohering" and "DEF". "Adherence" celebrates a stoical, though still minutely observant mode of life that looks back to "In Praise of Painting Doors" in "Steps" and forward to the elegy "A Song (& A Dance)" in *Sonata*. This book also contains poems with an explicitly scientific theme – "The Geometry of Soap Bubbles", for example – and some sorties in metacritical footnotes (290–291).

Of the final interstice, *Postlude*, Scully notes "guest appearances include: Paul Celan, George Herbert, Emily Dickinson, Miyazawa Kenji, Anatol Stern, the Great Vowel Shift, Lao Tsu and Mary E. Carroll [...] all a welcome set of hectics at the party" (331). Scully's allusions and quotations usually go unacknowledged in the texts themselves; many are not even mentioned in the concluding note. "Guest appearances" complicate Scully's attitude of "humility in the face of the material" (Scully and Fryatt 139). He imagines *Livelihood* as a kind of carnival, but unacknowledged quotation is nonetheless requisition of a kind. He misquotes, as in the title *Things That Happen*, in order to evade appropriation of other writers' substance, but that strategy itself acknowledges the risk of such appropriation.

Sonata, the third volume of *Things That Happen*, has a much simpler structure than its predecessor. Longer than any individual book in *Livelihood*, it is arranged rather like "Steps" and "Adherence", in three numbered sections followed by a coda. This arrangement establishes Scully's partiality to tripartite structuring, and echoes the construction of *Things That Happen* as a whole. Of *Sonata*, the poet notes, "[t]he binding motif is the circle, so there are lots of repetitions, doublings, turnings, arcs, zeros, returns" (Scully and Fryatt 143). Unlike his precursors Thomas Kinsella and Eugene Watters, however, Scully seems consciously to resist cosmic understandings of circularity. Where *5 Freedoms* and the first books of *Livelihood* were edited to exclude personal content, *Sonata* follows "Steps" and "Adherence" in admitting elegiac and more explicitly autobiographical poetry. "A Song (& A Dance)", written in memory of the poet and publisher Richard Caddel, stands out among Scully's elegies. The poem's variable rhythms evoke Caddel's own work, "a poetry rich enough to mirror the actual world, compositionally complex enough not to need an external music" (Gilonis, "Richard Caddel: Obituary", np). Caddel, an asthmatic, was particularly interested in the relation of breath and speech. He was also a distinguished elegist: his book *For the Fallen* (1997) commemorates his son Tom with a hundred versions from the old Welsh *Gododdin*.

Tig, the coda to *Things That Happen*, appeared in print in 2006, published as a trade paperback by Shearsman. Like *Sonata*, published in the same year, its frontispiece and endpaper feature a simple circle motif. "Tig" is an Irish word for "house"; Scully notes "English sense also intended" – presumably that of the playground game also known as "tag" or "it". The title is also reminiscent of Irish "tuig", "to understand", which gave rise to the informal English usage "to twig". *Tig* has two parts, "Stepping" and "Bread", each of which are subdivided into five sections: three numbered, followed by a coda and a "coda coda". These sub-codas, wryly acknowledging that the project's shape was not entirely planned in advance, "it just 'grewed'" (Scully and Fryatt 138), gesture towards the unfinishable nature of a poetic sequence.

Things That Happen is large in many senses: formal, chronological, geographical. The history of its composition demonstrates Scully's interest in mutability over ordered, preordained structuring. The "trilogy" is a psychological anatomy, in which different locations symbolise aspects of the speaker-poet, though he also tries to resist this kind of alignment of the outside world with the self. It is a *psychomachia*, in which the poet confronts psychic obstacles, grief and injustice. Because of its size and chronological spread, it is inevitably ambivalent and self-contradictory. It tries to evade coercive aggression towards its raw materials, but the speaker is often forced to acknowledge his ordering impulse in moments of irony. The growth of the project demonstrates an aptitude for infinite extension: although Scully has now finished *Things That Happen*, he acknowledges its actual, physical presence in his new work. For example, "The Pillar & the Vine" (*Livelihood*, 5–11) and certain parts of *Tig*, "I feel I should feel better now" and "fat stem. / tiny branches. / enormous yellow flowers" (Scully, *Tig*, 69, 29), were originally part of a "diary-book" entitled *The Pillar & the Vine* which Scully "disassembled" before 1990, but continued to use in composition: "That 'fat stem etc' even occurs in [the] present book I've been working on for some years now. This book is not part of *Things That Happen*".[3]

---

[3] Maurice Scully, "Re: anti-talent", email to Kit Fryatt, 9th August 2006.

Scully's account of the diary-book's disassembly powerfully suggests the apparent autonomy of the work, its independence from the poet's control and its almost non-human quality. In response to a question about when he decided to unpack *The Pillar & the Vine*, he notes:

> re: "decide to disassemble": much more organic than that: the mass of contiguous writing developed such a force that it burst apart anything in its way not strong enough to resist. P[illar]/V[ine] was in the way & had an unfinished feel to it. This would have happened perhaps (not sure exactly) late 80s, perhaps 1990.[4]

These qualities – largeness of scope, attention to the symbolic relation between the self and its surroundings, unfinishedness, mutability and autonomy – prompt a consideration of *Things That Happen* as an allegory. It is a self-reflexive one in that it takes seriously the ethics of allegory's fictive transfer of properties, as something that might have implications for real human bodies in the real world. If allegory is, as Joel Fineman puts it, inescapably the "hierarchizing mode" (32), then in *Things That Happen* we have an allegory by a poet concerned to resist hierarchy, yet drawn to a mode which offers the opportunity of making on a large spatial and temporal scale.

Dream vision and parable emerge as prominent modes in *Things That Happen*. "Two Caterpillars", from the first book, *5 Freedoms of Movement*, is styled as a parody dream vision. Its framing story adopts the deliberate tone of a story for young children: "*There once were two young caterpillars, Fat / Caterpillar and Fatter Caterpillar, that lived / on a windowsill under a tree*" (63). *5 Freedoms* contains a number of found poems based on children's books: Enid Blyton is a particularly useful source. Scully juxtaposes the limited vocabulary and simple syntax of such texts with the pedantic idiom of material for language students:

> "I say, look," said Peter in amazement,
> "a castle on a cloud. Who lives there?"
> "I don't know," said Chinky, "I do hope
> it's someone nice. I don't want to meet
> a Giant this morning."
> *

---

[4] Maurice Scully, "Re: pillar/vine", email to Kit Fryatt, 9th August 2006.

> Yes. No. Please. Thank you. I like it.
> I don't like it. That is too expensive.
> Please let me have. How do I get to…?
> What time is it, please? I need.
> I would like. I don't speak. I don't understand you. These
>
> are important expressions. (33)

Children and language learners are in similar positions of powerlessness, which is apparently emphasised here by the intrusion of racist vocabulary. (In the Blyton novel from which this is an extract, *The Adventures of the Wishing Chair* (1937), the character so named is a pixie, and no explicitly racist connotation pertains). They are patronised by teachers and adults, who are their authors as well as their authorities. The children's novelist writes ingenuous dialogue for her protagonists, the language teacher offers basics of communication, "important expressions" as pre-packaged units independent of grammatical understanding. Fictional child characters and language students, in that they are given words to say, have meaning imposed upon them, just as personification involves the imposition of meaning upon a human form. Meeting a Giant – that staple of allegory as well as fairy-tale – resonates, in this context, for both.

The Caterpillars of "Two Caterpillars" are Scully's own invention, influenced perhaps by Eric Carle's ubiquitous children's story *The Very Hungry Caterpillar* (1969). They present a more complex dynamic than the juxtaposition of Blyton with "important expressions". The Caterpillars are defined by their natural impulses to eat and sleep, which they do persistently and paratactically, "*they ate and ate and slept and slept / quite happily on the white windowsill under / the tree*" (*5 Freedoms*, 63). The windowsill, apparently not connected to a window let alone a dwelling, alerts us to the odd interplay between nature and the man-made in the following poems.

In the next stanza "a bankman" sits under the tree "balancing a book". At the end of "Two Caterpillars" we discover that "bankman" as well as his book-balancing is a pun, as he is swept away by a river in flood, but for the moment he serves to introduce the dream-vision motif:

> *in his dream he saw a bankman falling asleep*
> *under a tree with his money and a book and*

> *beginning to dream of a man dreaming he was*
> *making money out of a book (in which* he *featured*
> *quite prominently) under a tree beside a window-*
> *sill upon which were two young caterpillars,*
> […]
>   *that dreamed they lived*
> *on a windowsill under a tree.* (63)

It is not uncommon for the protagonist of a dream-vision to fall asleep within his dream, nor for him to enter a further allegorical vision upon doing so. Such a manoeuvre occurs in William Langland's *Piers Plowman*, for example. Riverbank settings are also an established feature, the 14th-century *Perle* being exemplary. Scully's parody of such dreams-within-dreams also evokes the sort of philosophical puzzlers – how do we know we are not simply figments of someone else's dream? – popular with children just a little older, perhaps, than those who enjoy reading about Hungry and Fat Caterpillars. The bankman is also related to the financiers who have pursued the poet throughout *5 Freedoms*, demanding the repayment of "unauthorised credit" (9).

The bankman's presence in the narrative allegorises it: because he and his only action of book-balancing are puns, the reader is alerted to the metaphorical implications of the caterpillars' consumption. As we might expect in a book about money and movement, "Fat Caterpillar" and "Fatter Caterpillar" are also capitalists or fat cats. In this newly allegorised world, nothing happens naturally. The coercive allegorist is always present: "*one day an Autumn Leaf fell on the Fatter / Caterpillar to the sinister snip of scissors*" (64). This action by an invisible human turns the caterpillar itself into a visionary, who begins to dream a human life, articulated in a series of ten brief poems.

Casting a caterpillar as the dreamer inverts allegorical hierarchy, whereby active human agents dream the world around them into significance. The poems which make up the caterpillar's dream vision in turn resist the imposition of allegorical meaning upon the world. The difficulty of such resistance is suggested by the structure of the poems, which often begin in a patient, observant mode and inch almost imperceptibly towards allegory or allegoresis, before stopping short in a moment of irony. The first poem of this dream vision sequence performs the manoeuvre twice before breaking off. It begins: "between paper & trees where the sun / gets through between the branches to the grass / under a leaf on a curving stem", but before the landscape can be moralised, it is dismissed as a "pseudo-fairytale" which abets a possessive "lyric" view of the world (65). The poet presents another scene, at first as if for someone's approval, from which he again draws away:

> how's this? a girl goes by from elsewhere
> to set street music its cryptic rhythm against another
> how you can live to a different beat an old radio
> in a hut on a deserted building site paid little to
> live & as to writing/well! but between stations
> to pick up the possible & go on with that from there (65)

The poet resists an impulse to find meaning in the girl or the temptingly "cryptic" street-sounds or 'music' and retreats to his night-watchman's hut (about which the reader discovers a great deal more in *Livelihood*), reflecting on his poverty. His ambition seems to be to exist in the white noise between definite and clear transmission of meaning: "between stations". In "pick up [...] & go on with that from there", however, there is wry acknowledgement that these "stations" might also be stages in a secular Passion: a shared mythology continues as a ghostly, ironic possibility.

The second poem in the series extends the theme of "street music": its first stanza imagines a troubled, restless woman suffering from "love-grief" (66). Her actions are self-conscious and distrait: she "pretends to try to read" and hears "the / wind in the street playacting along with   music" (66). In interview, Scully explains his attitude to what the interviewer terms "ambient noise":

> Ambient noise…oh, something wrong there, for me. [...] it's neither ambient nor noise, but the penetrating signature of… everywhere I've lived. All the many houses I've lived in, rooms worked in, they've all had their own highly distinctive song, sound. Composed certainly of quite mundane things [...] but in combination, extraordinarily distinctive. Not to privilege human language and stuff it with ego but listen, the poet a contributor not an imperious editor. (Scully and Fryatt 142)

For all its humility, this remark bears traces of an "editorial" attitude: unconnected noise is still gathered and processed into "the penetrating signature of … everywhere I've lived". Similarly, the woman performing her "love-grief" to herself attributes similar "playacting" to the wind outside. Allegorical manoeuvres – the pathetic fallacy being one such – are surprisingly difficult to avoid, as the second stanza of this poem notes. The speaker imagines a chilly, empty outdoor scene in contrast to the "clammy, tropical" enclosure of the previous stanza, and the main agent seems now to be a man, moving through a deserted urban space of "gantries" and "alleyways", turning his collar against the cold, sensing "wads growing with each / breath in yr breast pocket" (66). Money, which often behaves in a peculiar, galvanised fashion in Scully's poetry, seems to impede breath, stopper or "wad" normal human function. Such representations of polis and oikos, conditioned by economic concerns and conventional gender roles, the speaker concludes rather glumly, are "very popular very human" (66). The third poem in the series, like the last, records a moment of communication and the speaker's attempts to avoid analysing it. The exchange is a sexualised one, "tight cloth in motion / over the pelvic rhythm", followed by an "eye-kiss", "returned", with grave mock-formality, "with thanks   & best wishes" (67).

Scully then returns, with the fourth poem, to the question of sound and "music". The verse is more open here than in previous poems – Scully leaves large spaces between words to represent "pauses developing in places", and conversely, suggests rapid "bustle" by using an oblique slash instead of a space between words (68). The music begins to intersect with the poet's artistic practice, as he "wonder[s] how it works" and the music "leans / forward into its own   *danger*" (p.68). The dangers that the poet faces, in inadvertently endorsing egotistical, "editorial" ways of thinking about his surroundings, encourage him to develop a listening, contributory mode of being:

> tenacious details of daily getting by
> fog interspersing   as   no   some mist   emphasis
> counter simultaneous emphases/bustle in enclaves underground/
> & a ghost from another station (68)

Sibilance indicates the space "between stations", while the broken syntax suggests the poet's reluctance to invest the world around him with allegorical meaning.

This breakthrough is followed by another poem using the authoritative tone of a language primer. Simple sentences in French are undercut by reflections from a more involved and difficult life:

> *Marie est debout*
> *près de la fenêtre.*
> my wife the sun the rent
> *Je suis assis dans un fauteuil.*
> is due my headache is due
> to your headache
> *Pierre est a genoux sur le plancher*
> *il joue avec son train.*
> Pierre is screwing
> that tart from Kimmage.
> *Bonjour mon ami.*
> *Écoutez s'il vous plait.* (69)

Funny as this is, it represents a regression from the insights of the previous poem, in both its easily playful line-breaks: "the rent [...] / is due my headache is due / to your headache" and its facetious rejection of the bland simplicities of elementary language learning. The request "[*é*]*coutez s'il vous plait*", is, however, typical, and marks a mid-point in the dream vision. The following poems explore allegorical structures in more forensic detail.

The dense sonnet-shaped poem beginning "diverge these gaps" describes some of the structures that we employ in order to make the world meaningful: "our what really is matter to be expressed our / our bright tininess our understandings reticulated" (70). "What really is" becomes "matter to be expressed"; the allegorical protagonist understands himself to be "reticulated", tied into a network of meaning which pulls in and encloses everything it encounters. This speaker sees himself and other agents as microcosmic – "our bright tininess" – but nonetheless in competition with others for control and mastery of their surroundings: "we meet they-you-I & retreat / parry & plunge" (70). The poem ends with figures of mutability and flux, but it is far from certain that the speaker has been able to escape or resist allegorical hierarchy. Scully's choice of a sonnet shape for this poem is interesting, particularly in view of the many poems in *Livelihood* entitled "Sonnet", none of which take a fourteen-line pentameter form. (Not all the lines in the "Two Caterpillars" poem can be scanned as pentameters either, though a number can.) The sonnet shape conveys an enclosed economy which resonates with the poem's interests in reticulation and microcosmic ordering. That the last word of the poem is a participle form of the first emphasises this closure, while it allows for limited change and mutation. In *Livelihood*, Scully's understanding of networks which tie and bind, like the form of his "sonnets", becomes more flexible.

The seventh poem in the series takes further the brief evocations of allegorical violence in the sixth, and reminds readers of both the fiscal framework of this dream-vision and the monetary preoccupations of *5 Freedoms* as a whole. "doing business", in terms reminiscent of Kinsella's *A Technical Supplement*, sees the capitalist economy as a slaughterhouse:

> getting your knife in deep & clean
> preferably into as many as it is possible
> to line up simultaneously in a good
> straight voluntary & vulnerable file
> (memory) then suppressing that adrenal twitch
> to simplify the mind
> & steady the hand (memory)
> turn hard & true. (71)

The allegorical personality becomes almost psychopathic in its disregard for the bodies which it turns into meaningful objects: an analogy might be drawn between allegorical production of significance and capitalistic production of profit. "Memory" brackets an act of coolly considered violence – this is affective, coercive, instrumental memory, the kind which tears past events from their context in order that they may make an impact on the future. Of instrumental memory, Mary Carruthers writes, "the accuracy or authenticity of these memories – their simulation of an actual past – is of far less importance [...] than their use to motivate the present and to affect the future" (69). It "simplifies the mind" and makes violent action easier.

Scully then moves from the metaphor of the abattoir to a characterisation of a more profound allegorical violence:

> confidence in ignorance to be eaten
> hatch in the victim's alimentary canal
> laid in places frequented by any suitable
> victim species hatch into minute active larvae

> later stages Collide There are things we meet
> They have nothing to do with/Flash/Don't let it end
> (Scully, *5 Freedoms*, 71)

Scully is fascinated by parasitoids (that is, parasitical organisms which kill their hosts), and descriptions of their life-cycles recur throughout *Things That Happen*. Allegorical meaning can be understood as a literary parasitoid, inhabiting bodies and objects to obliterate and replace their integrity. Gordon Teskey, in *Allegory and Violence*, locates allegory's eradicatory impulse in a philosophical poser little more sophisticated than the childish solipsism implied by the dreams-within-dreams of the caterpillar story. We perceive that our consciousness is a product of nature, and yet we also perceive nature as something other than ourselves. This dilemma of consciousness is resolved by casting others as coterminous with ourselves: we assert that because the self is in the world, the world must be in the self. The microcosm-macrocosm analogy produced by the identification of self and world is one of allegory's most cherished features, cherished, argues Teskey, because it expresses the desire in which allegory originates. This is "the desire of the organism to master its environment by placing that environment inside itself" (Teskey 7), a desire which is expressed in the allegorical vision of the universe as a giant. Northrop Frye identifies this vision as characteristic of his "anagogic" phase of symbolism:

> when we pass into anagogy, nature becomes not the container but the thing contained and the archetypal universal symbols [...] are no longer the desirable forms that man constructs inside nature, but are themselves the forms of nature. Nature is now inside the mind of an infinite man [...] This is not reality but the conceivable or imaginative limit of desire, which is infinite, eternal and hence apocalyptic. (119)

Immediately, however, we perceive that any subject who desires to contain nature in this way is in competition with all other bodies, which all have the same desire. These other bodies must be eliminated in the most complete way possible: by devouring them. The structure underlying allegory is one of mutual devouring – Teskey calls it "allelophagy" (8).

Scully figures the later development of the parasitoid as a collision between it and its host: "Collide There are things we meet" (Scully, *5 Freedoms*, 71), which echoes, in a much more sinister fashion, the sexual exchange of the third poem in the series, and looks forward to the baffled chance meeting of the last poem. The last line appears to be a disingenuous denial of the violence underlying systems of representation, a reading that can be confirmed by reference to the 1987 version of *5 Freedoms*, published by Galloping Dog, in which it reads "They have nothing to do with life" (70). The parasitoids of this poem remind us that the series is the dream-vision of a larval creature, and while they contrast starkly with the anthropomorphised Fat and Fatter Caterpillars, they are also linked by their shared relevance to money and capital.

Emphasising this financial theme, the eighth poem in the series begins "Credit all this lumber!" (72). It lists the contents of the poet's study – a "shaky", "riddled", "overcrowded" environment in which there is little of purely economic value. The poet's poverty means that he cannot even consume: "gas fire – turned off: economy in the cold" (72). He reflects that he has some superficial resemblance to the insects (which, we recall, are dreaming him and his study) but their "madness of aggregation" has a "logic", which his collection of "lumber" lacks. The poem concludes with an ironic demand for the poet to be written into a system of meaning, made the subject of "a new entomology" (72). It inverts accepted allegorical procedure, whereby humans both give meaning to the non-human and encompass it through macrocosmic figuration, but it also endorses the aggregative potential in allegory.

The penultimate poem in the dream-vision series proposes a saner, less grasping attitude to the world. The poet returns to his observant, reserved persona, concluding:

> sometimes   sudden self-anger
> sometimes   blank falling
> I forget the most simple things elsewhere
> wherever my mind elsewhere taking a walk as if
> among very many as if's very
> demanding labyrinthine but I think I
> think lost (74)

The reticulated allegorical view of the world is exposed as a kind of madness "mind […] lost". The final poem in the sequence, meanwhile, suggests an awareness of otherness which undermines allelophagic competitiveness. The solipsistic poet, meeting others in the street, finds them grown older and unreadable: "a new solid film over their features / [...] masked" (75). Instinctively hermeneutic, he reflects that "I read too much into it or / [...] / they're half thinking the same thing / too *him!*" (75). Basic allegorical procedures – aggressive interpretation and violent conflict with other agents – are summarised here.

The dream vision ends with this articulation of fundamental structures, and the story of the caterpillars and the bankman is resumed. The bankman, who, it appears, must have been sleeping on the bank of a river, is drowned when it floods, and Fat and Fatter Caterpillar undergo their metamorphosis into butterflies, pausing "*as a mark of respect*" on the flowers on the bankman's coffin. "*Before / moving on.*" The bankman's death is a deliberately absurd *deus ex machina*, evoking not so much stories for children as stories by them (dream vision narratives, are of course, a staple of both). In parabolic terms, the bankman seems to be too obvious a representative of capitalism and the pain it has inflicted on the impecunious poet to be allowed to live. (The fish in the river catch his money.) Instead, the "fat cat" caterpillars are transformed into kinetic signifiers and diffused into the world, rather as ideologies penetrate consciousness by presenting themselves as natural objects.

The dream vision also appears in *Livelihood*, especially in the first half of the volume, in which the protagonist is a night-watchman, working on the building site from which he must report every hour "that there / was, in truth, nothing to report" (*Livelihood*, 75). The night-watchman dozes occasionally, and wakes up with a start, a motif that is continued, with variations, throughout *Sonata* and *Tig*.[5]

Another motif in *Things that Happen* takes parabolic form. Like the dream-vision discussed above, it begins as a found work drawn from children's literature. Gianni Rodari's poem "Ci vuole un fiore" is translated by Scully as:

> To make a table
> you need wood
> to make the wood
> you need a tree
> to make the tree

---

[5] For examples, see Scully, Maurice. *Sonata*. Hastings: Reality Street, 2006. 59 and 92. See also *Tig*, pages 44, 83, and 84.

> you need a seed
> to make the seed
> you need fruit
> to make the fruit
> you need a flower
> to make a table
> you need a flower. (*5 Freedoms*, 40)

Scully changes the poem's grammar: the passive voice of the Italian "ci vuole un fiore"[6] – "it takes a flower" – becomes an active construction which can be read as a direct address to the reader, a memorandum to the self, or an informal use of "you" to mean "people in general". This ambiguous use of the second person is very common in Scully's work, and relates to his impatience with the lyric self: "As a 'prentice poet in the '70s the 'I' was very big in Ireland. It still is? Me, my, I. I love you. You love me" (Scully and Fryatt 141).

Rodari's poem is a charming, if slightly saccharine, illustration of human dependence upon nature and the necessity of even that which we may regard as purely decorative. Scully's use of the motif in *Things That Happen* explores the allegorical structures which underlie even such an apparently innocent caprice. Rodari depends for most of his effect on a childish bit of illogic: the notion that "trees" and "flowers" belong to separate categories of being. It is not a very remarkable thing to state that to make a (wooden) table you need wood, which comes from trees, and from that point on the poem deals with different parts of a single organism: a tree, its fruit, seeds and flowers. So in essence, the poem states that to make a table you need a tree, which is not a delightful or charming thing to say at all. A further iteration – actually, simply a truncation – of the poem in *5 Freedoms* effectively makes this point:

> to make a table
> you need wood
> to make the wood
> you need a tree
> to make the tree (47)

"You need a tree / to make the tree" is true in a biological sense: it

---

[6] The poem was popularised as a song by Sergio Endrigo.

simply omits the intermediary stages which give Rodari's poem its piquancy. It emphasises the circularity of argument which makes this motif particularly useful to Scully in *Sonata*.

Scully's English distinguishes between definite and indefinite articles in a way that the Italian does not: "ci vuole il legno / per fare il legno ci vuole l'albero / per fare l'albero", but "to make the wood / you need a tree / to make the tree". "You need a tree / to make the tree" also expresses with remarkable concision a central dynamic of allegory: an ideal representation ("*the* tree") must find its substance in the world of individual trees. In becoming *the* tree, *a* tree suffers a loss of individuality which is smoothed over by Scully's idiomatic English translation. We might not mind it happening to trees, but the point is that allegory treats everything in this way, even human beings.

Scully demonstrates his concern with the violence involved in making objects and persons allegorically meaningful in his subsequent uses of the motif in *5 Freedoms* and *Sonata*. He criticises the weakness of Rodari's reasoning towards the end of "One Wallflower":

> for argument you need words
> in blocks fit to ideas with
> sticky ends to fit block for
> block together. (88)

Rodari's sentimental category mistake is implicitly compared to a child's toy – alphabet blocks, perhaps, or Sticklebricks – and his seemingly basic argument is actually constructed of 'blocks' of unexamined assumptions. The surprise of Rodari's poem depends on children *not* recognizing that tree, fruit and flower are part of the same organism, which resonates with Scully's allusive discussion of Yeats's "Among School Children" in *Livelihood* (28). In that poem, discussed above, the pedantic speaker shows a disregard for individual parts of a tree – bole, branches, canopy – which predisposes him towards a Yeatsian vocabulary of compliance with and acquiescence in authority. His mistake is the opposite of Rodari's, but it turns out to have similar results. Rodari places a tree and its own flower in artificially separate categories in order to make meaning, while the speaker of "**sonnet/**" implies a signifying unity which overrides the individual integrity of the tree's constituent parts.

Rodari's poem evokes natural cycles, and its flawed argument depends on logical non-progression, so it is appropriate that it is often quoted and parodied in *Sonata*, the governing figure of which is a circle. These parodies expose the violence that underlies allegorical signification: "to make a table / you need a gun / filled with rhetoric" (*Sonata* 55), perhaps also has Yeatsian rhetorical questions as its target, while other examples interrogate the hierarchical abstraction of the allegorical mode: "to make a table / you need power / pierced by childhood" (57), "to make a table / you need theory-in-excelsis / pierced by groundswell" (63). These examples also demonstrate the ambivalence of allegory, its propensity to incorporate (without necessarily modifying) even resistance to its own structures: power is shot through by powerless "childhood"; celestial theory punctured by reality on the ground. Can such ambivalence be liberating, or is allegory simply, voraciously encompassing everything which it encounters, even resistance to itself? In *Sonata*, the "to make a table" motif is always followed by an elliptical query or challenge to a writer or thinker:

> so you're another – what?
> storyteller twiddling dice
> in a game called Risk? two parts
>
>   confection, one part grit. (55)
> [...]
> so you're another lyricist?
> my mother
>   remembers
> yr brother. (57)
> [...]
>
> so you're another
>   novelist?
> tell me yr novelty. (63)

These are queries about making. The first offers a recipe for narrative in which toothsome make-believe is moderated by "grit", though the result is "a game called Risk" not risk itself. That the board game so named advertises itself as "the game of world conquest" might return us to the anagogic man. The second seems to challenge the familiar and familial context of much lyric poetry, with which, as noted above, Scully is often exasperated, while the third skewers the opposite vice, a preoccupation with alleged novelty. All three remarks implicitly question how the work of making meaning helps us live in the world, a concern which is made clear in the final iteration of this motif:

>   to
> make a table
> you need a
> leg to
>
> stand on.
> so you're
> another
> pragmatist? (82–3)

It is in *Livelihood*, however, that Scully's critique of allegory and authority is at its most angry and overt. "Pattern", Harry Gilonis notes, "is, for Scully, a net, a snare" ("The Spider", 30), and *Livelihood* draws close parallels between reticulation – the web of meaning – and consumption, as of a fly by a spider. Both of these allegorical processes are in turn connected to authority, order and power:

> /the Police are perfect.
> God is perfect.
> God is the Police/
>
> > and in a cabin on a building site
> > watching. hatching near spring
> > to net that one pet fly.
> >
> > thrums the web to lull her
> > then motions as to bind her
> > (blue whale's residual pelvis)
> > and rarely gets away.
>
> /the Rule is No.
> the Rule is Good.
> take take take take take/
> > > the pieces (*Livelihood*, 63)

Gilonis quotes the second stanza and remarks:

> ... there is positivity [...] in this passage. Even here in the natural world, our great cultural "other", not everything is red in tooth and claw. (The next stanza refers to mating and the birth of young.) Also, a spider – like a poet – is a pattern-making animal and activity in both cases is predicated on observation, on attentiveness. ("The Spider", 30)

While this is indeed a passage about the confrontation of the self with the "other" as represented by nature, it is perhaps more ambivalent about the desirability of pattern-making than Gilonis suggests. The stanzas about feeding and mating spiders are framed by an authoritarian syllogism and a sharply reductive account of the dynamics of inequality: a "Rule" which equates prohibition with "Good" while rapaciously and indiscriminately taking. The "pieces" are perhaps the disintegrating body of the male spider, who dies after mating, or perhaps his sloughed-off cuticle, which implies maturing and ageing, if not decease. These "pieces" appear alongside evidence of new life – "eggpouches" – as "little luminous pieces of the love story" (*Livelihood*, 63). In the end, the poet finds it difficult to refrain from being a "pattern-making animal", co-opting death and birth into a cyclical narrative, which may also enable and endorse authoritarianism. Gilonis is right to comment that Scully does not metaphorise spiders in the usual ways: they are neither loathsome "others" nor emblems of "industry and perseverance *qua* Robert the Bruce", but nor can they be, as Gilonis puts it, "simply [...] item[s] in the inventory of the world" ("The Spider", 32). Or, rather, they *can*, but being an item in the inventory of the world is not a simple matter. The idea of "an inventory of the world" immediately revives allegorical, hierarchising modes of thought, and returns us to the realm of the figural. Scully's spiders, because they are both predators and pattern-makers, often signal reflections on the nature of figuralism itself.

"The Sirens" revisits these concerns about authority. The title suggests that the alarm and action implied by a klaxon in the street is a form of seduction by power. The sirens offer wisdom, but the consequence of giving in to their temptations is a passive, lingering death; the only way to listen to them safely is in a state of enforced stillness. The poem's subtitle, "a ballad", indicates a narrative, though a vernacular one rather than formal epic, making it again "of the street". Other "ballads" in

Livelihood show humans working within and aligned with nature: "marram builds   directed   builds / my children too [learn, learn, learn & do]" (216), or demand a withdrawal from interference in the world. The first word of "Ballad" from the book "Adherence" is "Stop" (249). Echoing the importance of the form for Romantic poets, Scully's ballads confront and complicate distinctions between nature and culture.

"The Sirens" begins with a flat statement of the disparity between precision and function: "Everything *correct*. And no / use" (137). The italicisation of "*correct*" suggests that the speaker doesn't share this opinion of the rectitude of his surroundings; but given Scully's distrust of instrumental meaning, it might also be an expression of approval – such ambivalence is characteristic of allegory, given its purposeful muddling of nature and consciousness. The scenes that the poet observes might be *paysages moralisés*: "Broken glass blood- / stains / spiked fences desklamps dream- / homes" or "Lithified beach / densed starscrap" (137), but the speaker refuses any hermeneutic activity: "I mean as far as I can see / that's as far as I / can see" (137). The rebuttal is immediately undercut by *Livelihood*'s characteristic figures for consumption and pattern-making: "A spider eating jagged/ shadows under a / leaf" (137).

The syntax and lineation of "The Sirens" enacts the reader's search for allegorical significance, the singular goal that draws us into the realm of reticulated meaning:

> In a shimmer of
> hollow surfaces
> at so many
>
> removes from
> so-called
> reality
>
> in the unworld
> where *Unity*
> is
>
> and True/False
> tremble
> in

> the ring – darkness/
> coyote
> scat. (138)

The passage embodies allegorical distaste for "reality" and the search for unified meaning in an "unworld", but the search concludes with an animal howl, "coyote / scat". "Scat", by association with "scatological", suggests waste as well as the free-form vocalisations of jazz singers. "Scat" in both senses is free of semantic content: the allegorical pursuit of meaning is temporarily halted. The ballad continues with another reticulation, which this time involves human bodies:

> Let a skeleton set off
> then down
> a
>
> laneway through a gate and
> be gone. Gorgeous Art!
> Joints
>
> click. Blank. (138)

The skeleton, itself an intricate system, is dispatched on a quest "out of silence / and back into it / and out again" (138). The figure of labyrinthine pursuit which follows is emphasised by choppy line-breaks and discontinuous syntax:

> Of the many links in the set
> of all things
> plural
>
> that make up
> the twisted
> chain
>
> *i ngile an tráthnóna*
> *i mainistir na*
> *feola*

> sirens thread the streets
> ferry the
> dead – (139)

"Set" refers both to the totality of the poet's daily experience and the poetic work at hand. The title *Things That Happen* is a late addition: during the work's composition Scully called it *Livelihood: the set*. The "set" of books that eventually became *Livelihood* – "set" is a term Scully prefers to "sequence", because it is "more radial" (Duncan, np) – is visualised here as a "plural [...] twisted chain" (Scully, *Livelihood*, 139). It's a figure which fuses the hierarchical – the chain as *scala naturae* – with exploratory plurality. Similarly, "sirens thread the streets / ferry the / dead" suggests an eclectic myth, conflating the figures of Odysseus, Theseus and Charon with the mundane, though instrumental, urban sound of an ambulance on the street. As readers, we're tempted to install the mythic meaning above the everyday one, to consider it more important because it requires (only slightly) more recondite knowledge – this is one of the functions of allegorical hierarchy – but Scully insists on bodily reality:

> dying – injured – past where
> you live (repeat)
> (clack)
>
> to the table in
> the corridor
> or
>
> slab
> in the
> dark –
>
> splash of
> vomit on
> the path – (139)

In order to reject mythological significance, the poet must conjure pain: "dying – injured" and violent expectoration: "splash of / vomit". The violence of instrumental meaning intrudes even where it is consciously resisted.

Peace, "the sound of no-one there", disturbs the speaker no less (140). It admits possessiveness (here filtered through the poet's cat) and self-regard:

> cat vanishing from a
> sunlit ingle
>
> to brush your ankle
> as you pass: *mine:*
> *keep out.*
>
> *See!* said the Mirror
> *we are civilized –*
> subtle urbane
>
> tolerant witty – (140)

This self-caressing mood is immediately productive of an allegorical figure:

> Whereupon there
> rose up a thing
> called
>
> Order – the giant
> spinning in his
> skin –
>
> AW. DAH. (140–141)

"Order" both embodies allegorical hierarchy and is subject to it: he *is* the allegorical system (he is Frye's anagogic man), but in that he is a personification, is also contained by it, which impossible self-reflexivity produces the warp-spasm oscillation. Cúchulain's position within Irish culture is analogous: the ancient hero has meaning imposed upon him by modern nationalism, but as that nationalist icon he himself forces bodies into meaningfulness, impelling real violence and suffering. Allegory's uncanny interventions in our world have never been more precisely conjured than by Yeats in "The Statues": "When Pearse summoned

Cuchulain to his side / What stalked through the Post Office?" (Yeats 384). Scully can manage nothing like this, in which magnificence resides in absurdity, but "The Sirens" nonetheless registers allegory's persistent interference in the real world. The appearance of Cúchulain as the personification of Order further suggests a satirical swipe at Kinsella, the best-known translator of the *Táin*, whose portentous preoccupation with psychic ordering is the reverse of Scully's non-interventionist aesthetic (which is not to say that preciousness is entirely foreign to such an aesthetic). Scully's description of Cúchulain's warp-spasm – "awe-inspiring and a bit ridiculous" (Scully and Fryatt 138) – might also apply to his older contemporary. "The Sirens" concludes that "the point is":

> just to breathe
> and live
>
> sing/passing a little
> fruitshop on a corner
> by the lights/
>
> the sirens.
> Yr move. (*Livelihood*, 141–142)

Aspiring to a non-hermeneutic contentment, the poet turns over responsibility and agency to the reader. It is a weak conclusion to an attack on authoritarian ordering of experience, but withdrawal may be Scully's only possible response to allegorical voracity.

Allegory is powerful. Not only does it intervene forcibly to impose meaning upon things and persons, it takes up resistance to itself and rewrites it into its signifying system. *Things That Happen* opposes "AW. DAH.", but the pleasure that it offers is that of "tracing a clew", as Gilonis puts it, of spotting pattern and lighting on recurrence. Scully's strategies of evasion often result in poetic unsuccess, poems that equivocate their way to a muted whimper. "Backyard", one of two poems thus titled in *Tig*, attacks capitalistic avarice in terms which startlingly recall the notion of allegory's origin in "allelophagy". The poet, engaged on a quest through "chequerwork / barbed dazzle" of a rather Coleridgean "Difficulty- / in-Life", spies first a "gap in the defences" (*Tig*, 28), and then encounters an obstacle which is instantly personified: "boulder in yr / path: / Calculated Greed" (29). This obstruction prompts polemic:

> ... an accelerating bubble on a swollen
> tide – machines of war memory perception –
> whose meanings can't any more be pre-
> figured or absorbed cultures inverted
>
> to prey on not "cradle" "civilizations"
> lulling or eliminating peoples for the
> use of a few invisible manipulators of
> no country or allegiance – theft –
>
> parasitic on a scale never before thought
> possible to succeed – eating up humanity.
> eating it up. meanwhile old-world lyrics
> get prizes in small quaint corners. &
>
> good luck to them. (29)

This gets to the heart of what allegory does – "eating up humanity", both in that it is driven by devouring desire and it annihilates humane attitudes – but its devices are crudely imitative: the line break "pre- / figured" (worse, in the preceding stanza there is a "frag / mented"); the inverted commas cradling not just " 'civilizations' " but " 'cradle' " itself; the poetic sectary's attack on "lyric" as innately reactionary, immediately and ambivalently retracted.

On the other hand, some of Scully's most successful critiques of inequality in "our Overdeveloped Pig World" (Scully and Fryatt 139) are perilously near to "old world lyrics" both in their form and their deployment of symbolic material. "Liking the Big Wheelbarrow" advocates a characteristically attentive stance in a kinetic world:

> Wait. The instruction was to wait. Be still.
>
> Dust particles collide and bounce away, collide
> again elsewhere and stick until a thicker
> filamentary delicate medium sinks to the central
> plane of a disc which breaks into rings (*Livelihood*, 168)

Scully's resources here are aural and syntactic rather than spatial and typographic, and the result is a far more achieved poem than "Backyard".

"Liking the Big Wheelbarrow" concludes with that most "mainstream" of devices, an epiphanic anecdote which revises the foregoing lines:

> A four-year-old child who said to a pilot
> on their way to the plane on the air ferry tarmac
> "I like your big wheelbarrow." (168)

Allegory intrudes instantly, capturing the child's utterance, simultaneously making it significant of innocence and stripping it of innocence. Significance is inimical to such simplicity: to perceive it at all the reader must be self-conscious, not simple.

The success of "Liking the Big Wheelbarrow" and the achievement of *Things That Happen* as a whole suggest the difficulties inherent in moralising a poetic stance. Scully is painstakingly thoughtful about the implications of poetic form, and the ethics of organising experience into artefact. That he is perhaps at his best when he forgets his own strictures and dares to write a lyric which might win the approval of "small quaint corners" does not render invalid his reservations about instrumental meaning. And though some distrust of allegory's system, order and hierarchy is wholesome, we should not allow ourselves to become melodramatic or self-castigating about the violence done to raw material or experience in the creation of a poetic artefact. *Things That Happen* is large enough to admit some diffuseness, some allegorical ambivalence. Immediately after his attack on prize-winning lyric in *Tig*, the poet finds himself on the margins of the "Forgotten Gaelic Tradition", mediating the equivocal voice of the "Blackbird of / Anywhere-At-All quite likely to be in two / minds on one branch"(*Tig*, 29–30). The irony is heavy enough – at the beginning of the twenty-first century, the various poetic blackbirds of "Gaelic Tradition" are probably the least "Forgotten" thing about it (not to mention the boost they have received from Wallace Stevens). The line break "two / minds", meanwhile, is as deliberately unsubtle as they come. But the sentiment is large-hearted, and it alerts us to Scully's other deployments of Irish tradition in *Tig*: the allegorical-mnemonic kennings or *briatharogham*, which like *Things that Happen* itself, are "oblique, obscure and undependable. And extraordinary" (101).

Works Cited

Benjamin, Walter. *The Origin of German Tragic Drama*. Trans. John Osborne. New York, NY: Verso, 1998.

Carruthers, Mary. *The Craft of Thought: Meditation, Rhetoric and the Making of Images 400–1200*. Cambridge: Cambridge University Press, 1998.

Celan, Paul. "The Meridian". Trans. Jerry Glenn and Beatrice Cameron. *Chicago Review* 29.3 (1978): 29–40.

Duncan, Andrew. "Poems 14". *pinko.org*. n.d. <http://www.pinko.org/91.html>. Accessed 27th March 2018.

Fineman, Joel. "The Structure of Allegorical Desire." *Allegory and Representation*. Ed. Stephen J. Greenblatt. Baltimore, MD & London: Johns Hopkins University Press, 1981. 1–38.

Frye, Northrop. *Anatomy of Criticism: Four Essays*. Princeton, NJ: Princeton University Press, 1957, repr. 1971.

Gilonis, Harry. "The Spider, the Fly and Philosophy: Tracing a Clew through Maurice Scully's *Livelihood*". *The Gig Documents* #3 (2005): 29–43.

———. "Richard Caddel: Obituary". *The Independent*, 11th April 2003. Reprinted in *Jacket* 22 (2003): np. <http://jacketmagazine.com/22/caddel.html> Accessed 9th August 2006.

Rodari, Gianni. *Ci vuole un fiore*. Rome: Gallucci, 2003.

Rosen, Charles. "The Ruins of Walter Benjamin". *On Walter Benjamin: Critical Essays and Reflections*. Ed. Gary Smith. Cambridge, MA: MIT Press, 1988. 129–175.

Scully, Maurice. *5 Freedoms of Movement*. Newcastle-upon-Tyne: Galloping Dog Press, 1987.

———. *Over and Through*. Cambridge: Poetical Histories, 1992.

———. *The Basic Colours*. Durham: Pig Press, 1994.

———. *From Zulu Dynamite*. Guilford, VT: Longhouse Books, 1997.

———. *5 Freedoms of Movement*. Buckfastleigh: etruscan books, 2001.

———. *Livelihood*. Bray, Co. Wicklow: Wild Honey Press, 2004.

———. *Tig*. Exeter: Shearsman Books, 2006.

Scully, Maurice and Fryatt, Kit. "Interview". *Metre* 17 (2005): 134–143.

Teskey, Gordon. *Allegory and Violence*. Ithaca, NY, New York & London: Cornell University Press, 1996.

Yeats, W.B. "The Statues". *The Poems*. Ed. Daniel Albright. London: J.M. Dent, 1990. 384.

The End of the Line: Maurice Scully's *Tig*

Lucy Collins

Tig's position as the concluding part of *Things That Happen* has a scope that is at once contained and vast, achieving its own unitary focus as the single work of art, but also gesturing towards the encompassing vision – spatially and temporally – of the larger project. *Things That Happen*, described by Marthine Satris as a project "of movement and process, and also one of cross-weavings" (Satris, "Selection as Rewriting", 195), draws attention to the relationship between lines that move the reader forward, and those that make close and subtle connections of inference between elements. The idea of 'verse' is held in the Latin *versus*, the act of turning that approximates the tilling of a field. The transformation of this rhythm into a flexible and varied measure marks the need to represent a more complex relationship between humans and their world, and to trouble the referential power of language. In this essay I want to examine the idea of the line – both the poetic line, and the line as a means of tracing a journey or a line of thought, a line as movement and containment – as a way of exploring the temporal and spatial co-ordinates of the volume. An implicit part of this examination is the relationship between the part and the whole, and the role of such a relationship not only in the construction of the work of art, but in the individual human's understanding of the world. In the words of William James: the vastness that sensation renders must "be measured and subdivided by consciousness, and added together, before they can form by their synthesis what we know as the real Space of the objective world" (James 145). The larger world can only be rendered by the fragmentation and reassembly of these forms of apprehension, and in this respect *Things That Happen* suggests a world broken apart and reunited in varied forms. The dynamics of fragmentation and reconstruction speak of the larger concern with death and dissolution with which the volume is preoccupied. This tension is what sustains language and observation, the bodily sensations and thought processes that move and change as the book progresses. In this respect, *Tig* at once expresses the energies of the project as a whole and breaks from them in order to represent an advance or a closing statement to that project, as well as a transition to new modes of work.

A poem, as Heather Yeung observes, both represents and constitutes a particular understanding of space and time. The ambitious scope of *Things That Happen* emphasises the role of art not as an immediate response to particular experiences and conditions, but as a way of engaging with larger questions of human connection and understanding. By extending and varying his practice of publication, Scully enters the act of reading into the realm of provisional meanings and deferred closure. Though *Tig* is the culmination of this project, it is not a resolution – the dynamics of expansion and refinement remain the hallmarks of the work, and these continue to present new challenges to Scully's readers. We encounter *Tig* with an awareness of its important transitional status, and a fuller appreciation of the impact of Scully's cumulative creative strategies on our larger acts of reading.

Our engagement with this work unites a specific experience of reading with a sustained reflection on being in the world. This combination is intensified by the organic development of *Things That Happen*, which records the continuous interaction of sensory and creative processes. Tim Ingold explores similar dynamics in his examination of the relationship between humans and their environment. Invoking Kant's statement that the surface of the earth is "the ground on which our knowledge is acquired and applied" (qtd in Ingold 46), he elaborates on the expert's encounter with landscape in ways that inform our approach to Scully's textual spaces:

> What distinguishes the expert from the novice, then, is not that the mind of the former is more richly furnished with content – as though with every increment of learning yet more representations were packed inside the head – but a greater sensitivity to cues in the environment and a greater capacity to respond to these cues with judgement and precision. (Ingold 47)

In this way the experience of reading, while it may mark an accumulation of knowledge, is in fact a way to transform our relationship with the world. Unlike our encounters with Scully's interim volumes, this act of reading is at once complete and incomplete; it follows lines of thought and composition yet registers the fact that these no longer explicitly reach forward to the text yet to come.

In spite, or perhaps because, of this apparent closure, the book enacts a play of form that reinforces the importance of larger networks of understanding and their representation in poetic form. Scully distinguishes between forms that are architectural and fibrous, identifying most strongly with the latter: "the mycelium, the threaded web, connecting roots over long distances. Symbiotic, not parasitic. My poetry has that sort of fibrous connectedness. It's part of the way we all experience the world" (Satris, "Interview", 14). Importantly, this structure accommodates growth and change, and understands the human mind – and the language of its expression – to be in a continuous state of interaction with the world. Sharon Lattig draws explicit conclusions about poetry's capacity to mirror the represented world in its own aesthetic practices, and expresses this in dynamic terms: "The poem is a kind of cognitive hinge referring in both directions, outwardly to an apprehended cognitive environment and inwardly to the cognitive process by which it apprehends" (Lattig 454). Though her focus is the lyric poem, Lattig's perception of the mobile connection of text and world illuminates Scully's own practice, and in particular the concept of the lattice, trellis or net as both a method of arrangement and a means to express the larger human relationship to language and materiality. Eric Falci has explicitly linked the poem as net as a new way of thinking about form:

> Imagining a poem as a net provides a new way to conceive of it as both a closed and open form. A net holds things and lets things go, and what "belongs" in a net is partly a function of what happens to have made it into its openings. As a way to describe individual poems and longer aggregations, it suggests both arrangements and porosity and indicates both structure and structure's hollows. (Falci 149)

This attention both to the structure, and the space between, is central to a reading of *Tig*, a book in which the lines of movement, both as tropes and linguistic structures, must always be seen in relation to the terrain that is traversed, and to the gaps in time and perception that trouble semantic unity. The reader simultaneously follows the unfolding elements of language, and recognises that the transference of meaning through repetition and association is more than a linguistic game, but is instead a form of entanglement that represents the complex relationship between humans and their world. Ingold's concept of "meshwork" perhaps comes closest to this expression of these implicated forms of existence: "Nothing can hold on unless it puts out a line, and unless that line can tangle with others …. To describe the meshwork is to start from the premise that every living being is a line, or better, a bundle of lines" (Ingold 3).

The idea of the line brings the dynamics of movement and stasis to the forefront of human acts of representation, not only confronting the transience of individual animate existence but the question of how certain ideas and modes of representation can become fixed. At first glance *Tig* appears to have a comparatively stable form, comprising two sequences, "Stepping" and "Bread", each with three parts and two further codas. This apparent symmetricality is an illusion, though, and Scully's conviction concerning the generative power of three ("three is the beginning of plurality in the Irish language, not two") and the pleasurable asymmetry of five (Satris, "Interview", 23), alerts us to the productive instability of the volume. The tensions between renewal and loss are mapped in the poem's terrain of sensory experience and memory that is inseparable from its processes of thought and understanding. In Ingold's construction, cognition is itself spatial, because inseparable from the observable world:

> Far from being confined within the skull… the mind extends along the pathways or lines of growth of human becoming, just as do earthly roots and aerial foliage. Thus the ground of knowing – or, if we must use the term, of cognition – is not an internal neural substrate that resembles the ground outside but *is itself* the very ground we walk, where earth and sky are tempered in the ongoing production of life. (Ingold 48)

Tig thus bears witness to the mobility of mind and body, and to the close connections between observed reality and the experiences held in memory. This understanding is not so much "represented" in experimental form but constructed through attention to the relationship between language and the external world.

I

The question of duration is an important dimension of the act of reading from *Tig*'s opening page. We are already coming to the end of this poetic journey and the image of the migrating butterfly suggests both the larger patterns of human and non-human migration, and the particularity of the experience for the single organism. It also returns us to an earlier reading episode, the sound of butterfly wings from "In the Music", which were "made quite / clearly quite a way off" (Scully, *Livelihood*, 162). In *Tig* the lifecycle of the butterfly is first given in detail (birth in the Great Lakes of America, then the journey towards the Mexican border), but there are sensory details too – the "immense blizzard of wings" (*Tig*, 11), and its tiny counterpart, the "*flash!* fold *flash!*" of the minutely observed creature (12), its wingbeats concealing and disclosing its identity. This transition from the scientific to the sensory is closely linked to other acts of apprehension, and to the ways in which these are processed by the mind. The shadow of the passing train, with its hints of relentless modernisation, does not at first disturb the concentration on the migrating insects but it opens the scene to human experience paving the way for scientific explanation to be overtaken by joy in the moment of witness. Does this shift in perspective permit a memory of joy to emerge? Or is joy at the centre of this passage, its dispassionate language an essential precursor to the registration of delight, designed to capture how we apprehend difference – light absorbed and refracted, nature in motion and stillness?

This opening section initiates the attentiveness to physical mobility and emotional response that goes on to shape the volume as a whole. It alerts us to the inherent instability of the act of reading, which may reverse or reframe a process of thought or memory, rather than presenting it as it emerged in the mind of the poet. Thus these early pages offer the reader routes through space and time that emphasise the tensions between continuous existence and fragmented memory, as well as asserting the capacity of language (remembered and invented) to alter both past and present experience. The infrastructure of the text, which comprises both its structural boundaries (between sections and segments) and its shifts of language and mode, speaks to its engagement with movement through time and space. The migrating butterfly expresses the resilience and fragility of the living world as a whole, and invites reflection on the relationship between larger patterns of repetition and change, and specific moments of witness. Multiple yet exact, like the pattern of the raindrops on glass, these creatures reveal the design of nature, in which difference and similarity are always in play. In a typographically condensed page from the book's final coda, the butterflies "erupt & disappear over a hedge" (86). Yet later they feature in a list of key images and phrases at the close of the book. This strategy reveals the double existence of the butterflies, and indeed of all the key images in the poem: they are first material and then linguistic, presenting a representation that is at once dynamic and containing, offering a self-reflexive conclusion but no promise of closure.

The image of the train is a recurring element in the poem, unifying its disparate parts and reinforcing the impression of simultaneity created by the folds of the text. Here is an image of multiplicity and sameness, endlessly repeatable yet distinct. The empty rectangle with which the opening section closes allows us to contemplate the train from within, understanding the motion of language as that of the journey, and the blank space as the gap in perception that incomplete memory supplies. In this way the train becomes both an image of movement and a space of memory – first its shadow is seen (11), then its sound overheard (19); soon it prompts a return to the past, offering a vantage point on the "sunny external world" apprehended by the speaker's companion and – in the form of a reflected image – by the speaker himself. He is transported in memory, and in reality:

> listen I saw what
>
> I meant you saw
> & the sunny external
>
> world slid past over
> yr shaded spectacles
>
> & for the sake of
> the rhythm I suppose
>
> of the train on its
> track you smiled.
>
> it all takes you back. (35)

Yet it is perhaps the rhythm of the train that most clearly imposes itself on the reading of the poem – its shadow "flickering / over the fields" (37) before the childlike "*baaah!* goes the train on the line" (43). Its constant motion offers a pathway across time and, together with the "great liquid spine" of the river (34), transports the speaker through time ("older... older" (34)) and from land to sea. Alongside these structures, including the "pouring canal" with which the poem ends (99), are the journeys – borrowed and remembered – that criss-cross the landscape of the book. "(*then // crossing the / mountains we / got stranded / one night*)" (28) introduces a letter from D. H. Lawrence's 1912 trip to Austria, and with it the account of his relationship with the still-married Frieda. This interweaving of emotional reflection, complex family relationships, the business of writing and the liberations of travel offer a microcosm of *Tig*'s varied concerns.

The second half of the book radically alters the smooth process of movement set up here. In "Bread" the bringing together of flour and water creates, not life-giving sustenance, but a near-comic collision of slipping pedestrian, toppling cyclist and crashing van, breaking the lines of continuous movement. Here the scene combines death (the hearse) and life (the joke, the rising loaf). Everything on the street stills, but the goods train trundles overhead, its black and orange livery glimpsed through the bridge. There are Joycean echoes of the destructive goods train in "A Painful Case", but here it seems to pass in another dimension, though more vividly present than before.

II

The transition between spaces is an important means by which the materiality of memory is handled by Scully in this volume, and the structures of this movement are subtly linked to the flux of nature, to its dispersal and growth. The migrating butterfly finds a visual analogue in the poem's vegetative landscape, its dispersing seeds and falling leaves, implicitly connecting the cycles of generation and death mirrored in human representation. The leaves that land on the grass are like the butterflies alighting on the trees and gesture to the connections between processes of growth and decline. Experiences, as well as organisms are distinct, yet there are networks of recognition that exist in the most diverse circumstances. These cycles are made more complex by the acknowledgment of evolution: "the need for flattened ... wings" (13), so that repetition and change are allied in the larger contemplation of life's meaning. From the singular "little seed / in the big black earth" (47) to the "*multiple as seeds / in tight array*" (73), we are driven to attend to the precise manifestations of the natural world as central to our own constructions of meaning:

>   let yr eye travel
>   slowly
>   up the stem
>   green
>   up along it
>   in a pocket of light
>   leaves
>   light cilia
>   to the shaped
>   silver in the air
>   then
>   to flowers
>   moving &
>   leaves
>   & the light in them
>   up
>   inhale it
>   pass
>   green
>   blue
>   red (86)

This minute scrutiny of the single growing thing also follows a line of observation and attention, mirrored in its compressed representation on the page, the font opening out into the white space in organic development.

The vegetative texture of the book is linked also to its treatment of space, as the singular fibrous structures relate to larger constructs of form. The two variants of "[A Place to Stay] / [A Place. To Stay]" (43, 95) invoke the provisional nature of the spaces of belonging. The phrase is used multiple times across the volume, and illuminates the experience of houses and the built environment in *Things That Happen* as a whole, where the organic and the constructed are brought into complex alignment. Just as MacNeice's "Snow" uses the windowpane at once to separate and draw together diverse sensory experience, in *Tig* too doors and windows both facilitate the movement between distinct states and gesture towards their disparity: "different (or) touching a windowpane where / drops gather ( ) difference ( ) & / or different" (17). Rooms and houses offer spaces for contemplation, that signal separation as well as connection. The "dark & haunting house // off the South Circular" (36) is a hall of mirrors that reflects and enlarges the images of a previous life and, by extension, their sounds. Bachelard notes the comfort associated with the "old home" that is never available in more transitory spaces (Bachelard 43) and this space, despite its "dark and haunting" quality is not construed negatively. It is significant, though, that this house is associated with the road that runs to the west of the city, but is set apart from its connotations of movement and change. By contrast, the "white house outside the village by the sea" (*Tig*, 39) is in a liminal coastal space, and is further linked to the natural world by proximity to the found nest, another image of simplicity and return (Bachelard 99), which here expresses the notion of shared human and animal life directly. In both cases, though, these houses are set apart, and distinct from the enmeshed lives of the city streets depicted elsewhere in the book. Other built spaces, notably the shop and the hospital, juxtapose the sensory experience of observing and touching the fruit, and noting their arrangement and smell, with the emptiness that is the hospital's blank transitory space. Here the relationship between the familiar and the strange is key: If "a place is made local because of its familiarity to the body" (Davidson 4), then it is only spaces through which we move that may be construed in this way.

These spaces are understood to be part of larger movements of experience and perception. Two early sections titled "[Backyard]", and linked by the narrow, oscillating "[Waterway]", intensify the use of space as a means to deepen engagement with memory and experience. The falling leaf – reprised in another section from the book, and depicted on its cover – draws attention to the particularity of the material world, even of its most transient natural elements:

> fall detached from
> their place at
>
> each point (exact) landing in even
> circles anding at different
> times ... (*Tig*, 17)

When the backyard is re-imagined, it has become a watery environment, its reflective surface and tidal bubbles emphasising mutability and the necessity for self-scrutiny. Despite its domestic connotation, the backyard is a space of risk and predation where cat and spider await their opportunities to catch and kill. The human subject is implicated in these anxieties, weathering the "elongated crisis" of life but aware of the faceless destruction of the modern world:

> machines of war memory perception –
> whose meanings can't any more be pre-
> figured or absorbed cultures inverted
>
> to prey on not "cradle" "civilizations"
> lulling or eliminating peoples for the
> use of a few invisible manipulators of
> no country or allegiance ... (29)

This new understanding of space as opening to the violence of the contemporary political world is supported by the porous nature of Scully's poetic form. This particular representation, however, has been reached by means of the elegiac "[Waterway]", which juxtaposes the fixity of the burial place with the onward flow of life. Here the name, the presence, runs away through the weave of single word lines, not moving downstream but into a zone of uncertainty that blurs the lines between elements – stone, water, air. Here we recognise that the flow of water, and of language, at once removes and carries the past, which can now be apprehended only by the closest attention. The form of this section, with its narrow weave of language, captures first the flow of time and meaning, and then the slowing, dwindling human movement towards death:

> step & then
>   a step
>   (gone)
> reading out
>   *reading out*
> the signs
>   for you
> in the park

>   *loud*
> step
>   & then a
> step (21)

The concept of the lattice, which creates a network of spaces and connections, is key to the relationship here between fixed space and the process of movement, and also between the perpetuation and cessation of existence. Drugs may prolong life, but give rise to changing perceptions on the part of the patient and his loved ones:

> the
>   drugs
> (step)
>   given you
> oh to
>   help you
> to help
>   you yes
> the packet
>   says
> Lethe
>   or
> Lever
>   or
> Leave It
>   can you
> hear it? (21–22)

The necessary repetition suggests failing attention on the part of the listener but also records the speaker's own need to process this experience. Lethe, the river of forgetfulness, is linked through sound to the pharmaceutical company – the way to oblivion is natural and manufactured, imagined and material. The spatial construction of this section, with its strange combination of forward momentum yet halting expression, heightens its sense of loss. Both cerebral and sensory awareness informs the process of grieving, which begins in the presence of life and continues into the future.

The mutability of this world is most strikingly understood in the struggle that attends human endurance. In the first "[Backyard]" the memory of the father is invoked, when the pattern on the sunlit wall is turned to reflect crisis: "stunned/back from hospital / on the way back too / back to the wall // my old dead / father in / shadow" (18). Recurring illness and frailty shadows the book from the start, carried like sediment in the river of its language. The suppleness of the form renders this dissolution with painful immediacy but offers an energy of perception that is sustaining for the reader. Throughout *Tig* texts and their means of creation – paper, pen, books, a desk – are a central part of everyday life: "amid gambits   crypto-babble /   paper clips   staples / books   papers" (52). These echo the crowded workspace of "Two Caterpillars" (1987) – "Pages. Five hundred books / at least. Shelving (shaky). A desk (ditto). Typewriter. / Erasers. Tipp-Ex, blade, pens, pencils, markers, chalk" (*5 Freedoms*, 72) – the earlier text more compact in form and expressive of a layered life as reader, writer and teacher. The business of writing is threaded through *Tig* too, and everywhere the limits of language are tested. Memories of teaching emerge again in "[Picking Persimmon]" where the "intense cone of light" marks a labour without aesthetic ends – the passable grasp of *béarlagair* describing the struggles of his students as well as his own bilingual heritage. Though his parents were not themselves fluent in Irish, Scully was sent to an Irish-speaking school as a boy, and would find himself "thinking in that language and translating as I spoke, dreaming in that language, or a jumble of both," his early attraction to words marked by the interwoven processes of meaning (Satris, "Interview", 11). His awareness of English and Irish as distinct yet interwoven in his own mind informs his attention to the slippage of language, its movement across space and time, and its inexhaustible formal potential. The emergence of transcribed text in *Tig* is part of this process of accretion. "Splendid & unforgettable are the shrines of the gods …" (*Tig*, 53), a passage from "The Tsurezure Gusa of Yoshida Kenkō", is first quoted from, and then incorporated into, Scully's text. Its intention – to be found in the preface to Kenkō's work – expresses the need to capture thought directly: "To while away the idle hours, seated the livelong day before the ink-slab, by jotting down without order or purpose whatever trifling thoughts pass through my mind" (Kenkō 3). Acts of reading are another line that can be traced through this work, emerging in such quotations, but also in references – both direct and indirect – to specific authors such as James Joyce, and Séamus Dall Mac Cuarta, a seventeenth-century Irish language poet, whose reputed blindness did not limit his vivid appreciation for the natural world. Mac Cuarta's life and work introduces the bardic tradition with its own sense of movement and its historical specificity.

Scully remains conscious of the fate of the poet at times of radical change and recognizes the distance between his ambitious experimental project and the "old-world lyrics/[that] get prizes in small quaint corners" (*Tig*, 29), going on to make fun of Seamus Heaney's "Digging" in an (almost) pen-shaped page of text:

>   dug
>   every body
>   said
>   yep-yep
>   petty
>   gun-squat
>   yup that
>   sit
>   dug
> what a pin is (56)

His renunciation of "Creativity // Free Expression, Genius & all that" in favour of direct communication suggests the extent to which we need to open our minds to the unpredictable forces of language (57). The need to move beyond established forms has shaped Scully's accretive process, which sees him re-interpreting, rather than discarding, inherited techniques. For him the mastery of form is "mechanical, even childish… I think my work is very formal, in that it keeps the old forms in mind and searches for different ones at the same time. And drops the whole caboodle if it feels like it, goes underground" (Satris, "Interview", 22).

The function of the sonnet form in *Tig* is a case in point: it appears three times in the sequence, once as a "Sonnet Ode" and twice as two sections simply titled "Sonnet". The second of these is a ten-line poem, positioned at the end of the first part of "Bread", and reads as the answer to a puzzle concerning the identities and locations of four women: Alice, Betty, Charlotte and Doris (*Tig*, 66). The alphabetical denotation, and the introduction of Pythagoras, seems to confirm this as a mathematical problem, but Pythagoras is most closely associated with *metempsychosis*

– the transmigration of souls – familiar from Joyce's *Ulysses*, where Leopold Bloom unsuccessfully attempts to explain the phenomenon to Molly: "O, rocks! she said. Tell us in plain words" (Joyce 77). This juxtaposition of ancient and modern, poetry and puzzle, confronts us with incomplete knowledge and a parody of deductive reasoning that seems remote from the deeper currents of thought that have emerged in *Tig* so far. It seems to reinforce the limitations of closure, especially when it is not derived from a deeper, and more enduring, process of thought. The earlier sonnet reflects on poetic form in quite different ways. Presented as a poem in fourteen brief sections, each separated by a printed line, it considers the interface between human and natural worlds – and more specifically the role of nature in the shaping of language – in a series of discrete yet interlinked glimpses:

the word for *quick*
in this language

a dog at a door
barricade

blackback tilts & turns
robin under privet (*Tig*, 46)

There is both repetition and newness in this poem, as befits a reinterpretation of this most familiar of all poetic forms. "She left a leaf on my desk" returns to the image of the falling leaves, but transforms them here into gift and inspiration. The sonnet ode also links art and the feminine. Here nature offers itself as art – "moving over hills / in silent ripples / wild brushwork /   colour-intricacies" – linked by association with the abandoned canvas "her sister had left behind" (51). This emphasis on the making of art is linked here with the books and papers that mark the writing of poetry, emphasising the body in time as productive of painting and text.

Here the lines on which Scully's poetic project is built have become brushstrokes, expressive of the unique nature of each movement. The image of the incomplete circle with which the book closes conveys this co-existence of cessation and continuation, its fading brushstroke marking the subtle changes within the cyclical process. The shape of the circle or spiral is significant in this transference of momentum, as Ingold notes by likening this to the movement of the line from singer to singer in a choral round (Ingold 55). In *Tig*, the return of images and phrases enacts this kind of transference, so that the picking up of these elements is also their transformation.

Tig explores, in moving ways, the relationship between human and non-human worlds and the persistence of human meaning that is linked both to suffering and to art. These are age-old preoccupations but in this work their impact on thought and feeling is recorded in new ways. The single mind holds fragments of time, which can be formed and reformed in language. This language defines our humanity and places us in meaningful relation to all that is around and beyond us, both in the present and the past. The world of the text – like the wider world it meditates on – is constructed from the smallest particles: the sand on the beach, the weeds and wildflowers. Even in the presence of suffering, the poet is attentive to these elements, because they are central to the web of life. This web connects us in ways that make meaning possible. "What happens when people or things cling to one another?" asks Tim Ingold. "Nothing can hold on unless it puts out a line, and unless that line can tangle with others" (Ingold 5). *Tig* enacts just that process of putting out a line, and illuminating our response to the idea of ending itself. Even this has continuing momentum, though, "for, wherever you are, there is somewhere further you can go" (Ingold 5).

Works Cited

Bachelard, Gaston. *The Poetics of Space*. Trans. Maria Jolas. Boston, MA: Beacon Press, 1964.
Davidson, Ian. *Radical Spaces of Poetry*. London: Palgrave, 2010.
Falci, Eric. "Joinery: Trevor Joyce's Lattice Poems." *Essays on the Poetry of Trevor Joyce*. Ed. Niamh O'Mahony. Bristol: Shearsman Books, 2015.
Ingold, Tim. *The Life of Lines*. London: Routledge, 2015.
James, William. "The Perception of Space." *The Principles of Psychology*. Vol. 2 1890. New York, NY: Dover, 1950. 134–270.
Joyce, James. *Ulysses*. London & New York, NY: Penguin, 1992.

Kenkō, Yoshida, *Essays in Idleness*. Trans. Sir George Bailey Sansom. New York, NY: Cosimo 2009 [c.1332].

Lattig, Sharon. "'A Music Numerous as Space': Cognitive Environment and the House That Lyric Builds." *The Oxford Handbook of Ecocriticism*. Ed. Greg Garrard. Oxford: Oxford University Press, 2014. 440–58.

Satris, Marthine. "An Interview with Maurice Scully." *Contemporary Literature* 53.1 (2012): 1–30.

——. "Selection as Rewriting: Maurice Scully's Re-Envisioning of *Things That Happen*", *Golden Handcuffs Review* 1.16 (2013): 195–200.

Scully, Maurice. *5 Freedoms of Movement*. Buckfastleigh: etruscan books, 2001.

——. *Livelihood*. Bray, Co. Wicklow: Wild Honey Press, 2004.

——. *Tig*. Exeter: Shearsman Books, 2006.

Yeung, Heather H. *Spatial Engagement with Poetry*. London: Palgrave, 2015.

"the fabric / through which": Immanence and Ecopoetics in Maurice Scully's *Humming*

Michael S. Begnal

At the end of a 2012 interview with Marthine Satris, Maurice Scully discusses his book-length poem *Humming* (2009) and avers that "The title could be taken to be anything from the background radiation of the universe to the babble of languages irradiating our planet, to the buzz of bees pollinating plants across the earth" ("An Interview", 30). Scully's first new book after his epic-scale *Things That Happen* series, *Humming* is – connective threads to other works notwithstanding – a stand-alone text. Firstly an elegy for the poet's late brother, in its unfolding it becomes something more than a means of mourning. Scully's interview comments suggest variously the Big Bang, the role of language in our perception or understanding of the world, and the fructifying interchanges between beings in nature. The elegy, then, prompts questions not only on the nature of death or grief, but on the nature of life in the world and the best way(s) of being in it. For Scully, the response is often a kind of ebullience in living and in exploring the workings of language and poetry, seeking a form capable of connecting oneself to the environment rather than merely depicting it, in other words a form of ecopoetics that, as the poet Evelyn Reilly describes, "coheres with evolution, with our destiny as animals among other plants and animals. A search for a poetry that is firmly attached to earthly being and that is thus *dis-enchanted*, in the sense of being free of the mesmerizing spell of the transcendent" (257; italics in original). Here, the confrontation with and contemplation of death leads not to the transcendent or the spiritual, but instead illuminates an immanent, "humming" life-force inhabiting the cosmos, our senses, our language, even as these latter are stretched to their limits in articulating both the material world itself and the ineffable that lies beyond our ability to perceive it.

As an elegy, *Humming* fulfils certain conventions of the form and radically departs from others. In her article "The Poetics of Elegy in Maurice Scully's *Humming*", Kit Fryatt observes, "It is in many ways a traditional one, working within and commenting upon the constraints of the genre, but especially compared with other modern Irish examples, it may strike the reader as unusual" (90). It is "unusual" for a number of reasons, including the lack of detail about the deceased subject, the muted or often even absent expression of grief, the sometimes self-mocking tone of the speaker persona, and the employment of bathos. Fryatt has percipiently analysed these and other aspects of *Humming* as elegy, so the present essay will not recapitulate them in detail. Instead, while keeping the elegiac aspects of the poem in view, I hope to shed light on some of the wider ontological and epistemological issues that spring out of Scully's death-vigil and the ways in which he goes about elaborating them. Specifically, looking at this text through an ecopoetic lens emphasises Scully's desire for an unalienated relationship to the material universe and how this plays out in his poetry. Reilly conceives of "ecopoetics as a search for a language congruent with a world that is not filled with objects or subjects, that is not 'the context,' nor 'the setting' for subjects or objects, but that is a permanent state of flux…" (257). In other words, ecopoetics posits a conception of the self as constructed and possibly illusory and explores ways to create art that, as Scully wrote as far back as 1984 in a statement of his poetics in the journal *the Beau*, concomitantly "moves with the shape of the world" ("As I" 10), rather than with the shape of the poet. The exigency of death, of course, brings the issue of the loss of personal identity to the fore.

Although Scully has said that in *Humming* "There's only one piece that focuses on the actual death" ("An Interview", 30), I would argue that there are actually two. The first occurrence comes in the poem "Ballad (Argument)". This piece begins, "My brother is dead. I found him at the end of his bed. / His brain weighs 1565g, his heart 465 / the document says" – and ends, "My brother is dead. His wristwatch laid face up beside his bed" (35). Then, in the closing "Coda" section of the book, the scene leading up to the death is briefly restaged: "Take yr wristwatch off and lay it on the bed – / good – its three hands – *haa, ha-ha* & *ha-ha-ha* / circling circumstance under heaven" (93; italics in original). Both of these moments provide useful jumping-off points by which major themes in the poem can be discussed. The response to his brother's death in the first instance exemplifies Scully's thinking regarding the "humming" connections in the natural world and the art of poetry, while in the second instance it crystallizes his arguments about the limited nature of human perception as well as further highlighting the cosmic "fabric / through which twists *this* to *this*" (93–94). All of this further suggests the idea of immanence as put forward by Gilles Deleuze and Félix Guattari in their *A Thousand Plateaus* (1980), where the breakdown of categories such as self and other (or subject and object, which, as we have seen Reilly note, is an aim of ecopoetics) opens up a "plane of immanence":

> In any case, there is a pure plane of immanence, univocality, composition, upon which everything is given, upon which unformed elements and materials dance that are distinguished from one another only by their speed and that enter into this or that individuated assemblage depending on their connections, their relations of movement. A fixed plane of life upon which everything stirs, slows down or accelerates. (255)

While it might be sufficient to understand Scully's radiant "hum" as immanent in the basic sense of "dwelling within" the material world, it is advantageous to understand it as defined in Deleuze and Guattari, where the dismantling of hierarchical self/other distinctions implies "not the unity of substance but the infinity of the modifications that are part of one another on this unique plane of life" (254). This, it seems to me, is one of Scully's overarching concerns, both in *Humming* and throughout his work.

Since death reminds us that personal identity is subject to inevitable dissolution in the ineffable void, it is no surprise that the death of a loved one would prompt questions about one's self and one's place in the world. Scully's first iteration of the "death scene" in *Humming*, in "Ballad (Argument)" – "My brother is dead. I found him at the end of his bed" (35) – is quickly followed by the speaker's harsh assessment of his own life and career as a poet. In stanza two, he writes, "I am 52. How old are you? I'm old enough to take a knife / to any letter from the Arts Council for instance regretting et cetera", and then in stanza three he further characterises the Irish poetry world as one of ruthless opportunism: "You will discover starfish ingesting molluscs & ugly / dishonesties between people. You will have been a poet. Why?" (35). The initial mood of the speaker is sadness not only about his brother's death, but for himself; "I know the facts are rough" (35), he adds. Fryatt describes the situation as an "infernal complex of brutality, mortality, and money [where] elegy turns inevitably and swiftly to self-elegy" (95). How, then, to proceed?

The first section of "Ballad," the initial "Argument," is followed by a "Response" in which the mordant tone disappears and the form changes from the long lines of the previous section to clipped, mostly single-word lines. The effect is to radically quicken the pace and create a sudden sense of ebullience, as Scully turns to the natural world in a reaffirmation of life. Specifically, trees, interacting with the wind, now seem to speak:

>   trees
> hiss
>   trees
> bend
>   &
> sway
>   &
> grow
>   that
> way
>   &
> this
>   the
> trees
>   whis-
> per (36)

The message that the trees whisper is one of swaying and bending with the wind, or again as Scully had put it in 1983, "mov[ing] with the shape of the world." The trees also urge him

> to
>   never
> be
>   still
> ...
> in
>   all
> this
>   space
> ever
>   open (37)

This is both a credo for living and a kind of *ars poetica*. In other words, Scully's response to death is to redouble his efforts to create the kind of art that is in tune with what he sees as the actual nature of the cosmos, open, in flux, moving like the trees. In imparting to the trees the ability to "whisper," Scully seemingly makes use of the pathetic fallacy, which as Pádraig A. Breatnach points out is a particular feature of the Irish bardic and other European elegy traditions,[1] where "natural phenomena are depicted as sharing the sorrow of the bereaved" (52). Here, the trees do not necessarily share in the sorrow, but it is to their consolations that the poem's speaker turns. They act as the catalyst that propels him back into his work after the despair over the gnashing Irish poetry business (and his brother's death), exhorting him to simply "listen / in / the / dark" (38).

The natural world figures prominently throughout Scully's oeuvre, for example as the subverted or deconstructed pastoral encountered in his book *Livelihood*.[2] As Fryatt notes, "*Humming*'s arrangement ... reflects the intricate patterning created by apparently random action in the natural world. The appeal to nature's cycles and systems, whether as a source of consolation or of horror, has been fundamental to the European elegiac tradition since Bion and Theocritus" (90). Such strands of elegy unfold into wider considerations of the ways in which nature functions as a structuring model, both formally and philosophically. Throughout *Humming* there are numerous references especially to flowers, bees, and pollination, which, as observed earlier, Scully states in his interview with Satris are central tropes in the book. They serve as unifying metaphors, connecting the recurring descriptions of the Neanderthal grave (the funeral flowers of which are known by their pollen deposits), honey, and the grains or "dots" of pollen and seeds that all recur throughout the text, bringing together great swathes of physical space and time. Meredith Quartermain further "connects the dots," as it were, between pollen and ink, thus emphasising the writing act in all of this, describing "another

---

[1] Scully acknowledges the influence of Irish bardic poetry on his work in his interview with Satris ("An Interview", 24).

[2] See especially Scully's poem "Four Corners" (*Livelihood*, 227–28), which complicates and ironises the bucolic aspects of traditional nature poetry. In his ecocritical survey of Irish poetry, James McElroy writes that "Maurice Scully ... envisions the natural world as a universe of close coordinates in 'Four Corners' where he initiates an instructive exchange about the neo-negatives of [the] pastoral" (61).

rhyme of ideas around the word *dot* (the materiality of ink on the page), the grains of pollen picked up from bees humming in flowers and the pollen from flowers used at a Neanderthal burial site in Iraq – the pollen being the only ink from which we get a record of the first known use of flowers in a burial ceremony 60,000 years ago" (236). Pollination in this poem is both fructifying and communicative, opening up connections between humans, animals, and the environment, across landscapes and history, showing individual death to be only part of the larger fabric of life.

Scully's use of the fabric metaphor occurs numerous times throughout the book in various forms and finds expression in terms (or variations of terms) such as "fabric" itself, "thread," "tapestry," "stitching," "fibre," "weaving," and "lattice," some of which are common to his oeuvre.[3] In a 2013 essay on Scully's *Things That Happen*, Satris states, "Coming across the words *weave* or *lattice* in the project, I saw these moments as connections between the poet and myself, moments in which he acknowledged the scaffolding on which I could develop an understanding of his concerns" (195). In this way, the fabric metaphor tells us much about how he approaches his work on the formal level, revealing it as a recursive process and in a sense teaching us to read it. As Scully urges in one of the pieces in *Humming* titled "Sonnet," "know the connect-points" (27). In linking up these repeating themes and phrases, new layers of meaning accrue, and what can initially seem overwhelming or chaotic in its parataxis begins to cohere. Reilly identifies this as an ecopoetic strategy, writing that "Ecopoetics points to a poetry that attempts to trace the kinetics of whole systems, and to enact connections rather than to mark distinctions. As such, ecopoetics might be called democratic in the most aspirational meaning of the word" (258). Registering the "connect-points" is one way to engage in an active reading of Scully's work, to participate in it, in a sense, rather than passively consume it.

Scully has further described his conception of the poetic structure of his work as "fibrous." In his 2012 interview with Satris, he states, "My poetry has that sort of fibrous connectedness. It's part of the way we all experience the world, I think. And a different way of looking at structure" (14). It is a poetry in which the firm line between form and

---

[3] To mention one example, the poem titled "Song" that begins "Two palace guards" includes the phrase "I was touring the lattice" (Scully, *Humming* 73), which readers will recall as the title (*A Tour of the Lattice*) of a volume which remixes parts of Scully's *Things That Happen* that Veer Books published in 2011. Variations of the "lattice" motif occur throughout *Humming* as well.

content has dissolved – and certainly in *Humming* there is the sense that the text is constructed so as to function in consonance with this particular philosophical view of the natural world. The term "fibrous" calls to mind Deleuze and Guattari, who also use the term to posit connections among entities in nature: "A fiber stretches from a human to an animal, from a human or an animal to molecules, from molecules to particles, and so on to the imperceptible. Every fiber is a Universe fiber" (249). Quite possibly, this passage is even one of the sources for Scully's interpretation of the fibrous structure of both his poetry and the human experience of the world. At the same time, Deleuze and Guattari warn against seeing a hierarchical relationship along this string, asserting instead that "Each multiplicity is symbiotic; its becoming ties together animals, plants, microorganisms, mad particles, a whole galaxy. Nor is there a preformed logical order to these heterogeneities..." (250). The emphasis on symbiosis and "becoming" suggests a universe in which the individual self is fluid rather than fixed, forever in process, changing in accord with the environment and in response to ongoing communication with others.

Concomitantly, in one of the "Ballad" sections of *Humming*, Scully limns a world where boundaries between self and other, and human and nature, collapse:

> ... at night then after
> the bees' forage in the foxglove and return
> in the dance to the hive – who? – *I* am that
> constant upstairs star you spy across the fields
> by the river, O – (31; italics in original)

Here, the bees, after continuing their pollinating work in the plant world, engage in an orgiastic dance where their individuality is deferred to the collective hive. There is an "I" speaker voice in this extract, which is even emphasised, but it is not the traditional poet entity asserting himself or the emotions that nature may elicit. The human has instead been diffused to the universe, transformed into the molecules that make up the stars.[4] While the star is described as "constant," which implies a

---

[4] For Deleuze and Guattari, the "becoming-molecular" is a key node on the continuum of transformation; "all becomings are molecular," they write in *A Thousand Plateaus* (275).

certain priority, Deleuze and Guattari argue that "A constant or invariant is defined less by its permanence and duration than by its function as a center, if only relative" (95).⁵ Thus, there is a speaker persona of sorts in *Humming*, but one that is relational, a temporary "center" only out of exigence – be it as a star the reader ("you") spies in a pastoral-esque vista, as a listener to the whispers of trees, or as someone grappling with the death of his brother and the slings and arrows of a hostile Irish poetry industry. John Goodby observes that "the self in Scully is wholly constructed, or improvised, created *from* language ... beset and at the same time validated by its involvement in the contingent" (622; italics in original). What Scully images then is a poetic self always in the process of Deleuze-and-Guattarian becoming, eco-conscious of itself as a part of a broader continuum of nature.

One's perception of oneself and of the material world is for Scully always inherently limited, and so as we have seen he constructs his poetic speaking voice accordingly. The second of the two poems in *Humming* in which the "death scene" occurs emphasises the related theme of the limitations of the senses. As earlier noted, the scene is recapitulated in the closing "Coda" section (in one of several pieces titled "Song") that begins, "Take yr wristwatch off and lay it on the bed – / good – its three hands – *haa, ha-ha* & *ha-ha-ha* / circling circumstance under heaven" (93; italics in original). In this version, the perspective has shifted to the imperative mode, instead of the earlier first person ("I found him at the end of his bed"), and is now addressed to Scully's brother. Breatnach notes that such a direct address to the deceased is a feature of the Irish bardic elegy, employed "with a view to giving dramatic effect to the expression of personal loss" (52–53). However, as we have seen earlier, Scully in this poem largely avoids overly dramatized gestures, leaving personal expression understated. Here, the shift in perspective provides a sort of alternate take on the events leading up to the death, a new and further dimension, implying that there is always some other way of seeing that we may or may not be aware of or even capable of grasping. It becomes an opportunity for exploring the nature of consciousness, which reveals that not only may the distinction between self/nature (or, between subject/object) be arbitrary and artificial, but ultimately so too the binary of life/death.

---

⁵ Reilly similarly argues that "ecopoetics requires the abandonment of the idea of center for a position in an infinitely extensive net of relations" (257).

This theme of the limited capacity of the senses to know the world is articulated overtly at the end of the first stanza of "Coda"/"Song," where Scully writes of "Distorted places between / yr eye & the lens, yr eye & the surface, & yr eye /   & yr mindbits & the world" (*Humming*, 93). The idea that the mediation of the senses creates "distortion" between the world and the mind's perception of it is not new, and need not be seen as something esoteric or mystical. For Deleuze and Guattari, "perception is molecular" (282), and thus its workings are ultimately grounded in materiality even if it is highly subjective in practice. Similarly, in his ecocritical essay "Sustainable Poetry," Billy Mills advocates for a poetry that "accepts the sceptical view that full knowledge of the world cannot be attained through the medium of the senses. However, it sees this as a failure of the senses, not as an argument for the idealist position, and works towards the clearest possible approximation"(np). This is Scully's view as well, and, in an interesting moment of trans-species empathy, he returns to the bees and attempts to inscribe an "approximation" of their vastly different way of seeing. In the second stanza of "Coda"/"Song", he writes

> And something about¬//¬bees~~too and their recognition
> ||||| of colour. To see ultra~violet as a true colour ||||||||
> and to recognize the four distinct primal qualities
> of the inner reticulate world ... (*Humming*, 93)

In this instance, the comparison goes far beyond the first-person versus imperative-mode point of view discussed above. Noting the difference in perceptual range between the human and bee makes an obvious point, but the use of typographic symbols gives it a visceral effect, disrupting even our "human" reading experience. Of this passage, Scully himself has said, "In these lines I'm talking about how foraging bees see the world. The symbols cannot be given voice, cannot be read by the human eye, just as we cannot see the world through a bee's eyes. I'm trying to configure interference with the reading eye" ("An Interview", 19–20). In so doing, he provides another example of ways in which form in *Humming* converges with idea, acting in concert on the page rather than relying on explanation or exposition.

There are a number of other kinds of "interference" throughout the text. For example, Scully's particular handling of the poetic image destabilises our perception of the supposed reality of the material world.

He is a very imagistic poet at times, but his images don't stand still—they are often commented upon, exploded, turned inside out. They are a kinetic form of imagism rather than the pure imagism of early Ezra Pound, who asserted in "A Retrospect" (1918) that imagism should render a "Direct treatment of the 'thing'" (3). One example of Scully's kinetic imagism is the opening of another "Song," which reads:

> Brick glistens a little where a
> snail recently slid. Split. Sun
> through a dusty shed window
> under a tree: as yr pen-tip tou
> ches paper a long thin shadow
> shadows it to the right. Write
> that. Tell it. So. (*Humming*, 14)

There are actually two distinct images here — the glistening snail slime on brick, and the sun coming through the shed window — separated by a "split," as if pictured in tandem on a split-screen TV. For Pound in the 1910s, the static image would be enough. But Scully's kinetic image segues to his poet's pen in the act of writing, simultaneously within the scene and sketching it. Departing from Pound's modernist dictum, Scully implicitly argues that "direct treatment of the 'thing'" is simply not possible, or at least not for a poet cognisant of the "plane of immanence … upon which everything stirs, slows down or accelerates" (Deleuze and Guattari 255). There are numerous, wonderful images in *Humming*, but at just about every turn he undermines the notion that they are in any way capable of giving us the thing itself. Thus, the image is not the image, but a simulacrum of itself, broadcast ephemerally via light waves, unable to be disentangled from the writing of it, as if continually in motion, continually becoming in the play of light and shadow.

Accepting that human perception of the material world is limited, and that beyond it we are at an even greater loss, Scully nonetheless engages in the work of seeking a poetry that, as he set out decades ago, "records an apt humility in face of the complexity it sees but fails to transmit" ("As I", 10). Continuing with the same "Song" discussed above, he writes "(Art's lateral, even if / life's tiny – see?)" (*Humming*, 14). In other words, if nature refuses to work simply and linearly, his art similarly will move "laterally" – sideways, this way and that (or, as we have seen, might even loop back recursively). Life is "tiny," a brief moment of coming into and out of existence before dispersing once more into the ineffable. Here, Scully introduces a motif that occurs several times in *Humming*, that of "polishing" the lens or the glass: "You open yr glasses case, / … polish the lenses, put them on, begin" (14).[6] It is as if to say, it's all we can do to sharpen our apparatus of vision as best we can, to see the world for what it is, even if we ultimately "fail to transmit" it. As Eric Falci observes, Scully's work "[attempts] to apprehend the immediacies of the actual world while fronting its own mediations of this engagement …. Catching the immediacies of experience within the non-immediacies of the poetic page requires a commitment to detail[ing] acts of perceiving and modes of knowing, but also a relinquishment to the varieties of flux that aren't catchable" (149).

Later in this "Song," Scully stages the successive "burning" of deeper and deeper "layers" of perception:

> The First-Surface layer
> (op cit) carries the lies we're used to.
> Massed beds stitched with precision. Burn.
> The second-surface layer we get to know.
> Burn. A third-surface I infer. Burn!
> The fourth & so on down – dig, burn, dig –
> signals that buckle their receptors. (16)

Taking its terminology from the science of the "premelting" of solid substances ("First-Surface layer," where the abbreviation "op cit" prompts the reader to look it up), this passage also has wider resonance. If this first layer "carries the lies we're used to," then it can also be read as our everyday perception of reality which, being "lies" (as it is constructed via the unreliable human senses), any curious thinker would want to "burn" through. The next layer "we get to know," perhaps by studying physics or philosophy, but this too is an incomplete form of knowledge and must also be burned. The third layer, past the sensory and the scientific, can only be inferred. The process might well become never-ending, as there is always something further that is incomprehensible, until ultimately the "signals" become distorted, and the mind's "receptors" must "buckle." As Mills argues, "Rather than saying that nothing is

---

[6] The phrase "polishes / the / lens" also occurs in *Humming* on pages 19–20, "lens" on 93, "glasses" on 82, while "window" is found in various contexts passim.

unless it is held in the mind of a human observer, [sustainable poetry] asserts that many things are that have never been perceived, and that for most things that are perceived, the perception is imperfect" (np). In *Humming*, there is an interesting tension in that Scully seems at times to want to apprehend ("dig, burn, dig –") what lies beyond the bounds of human perception (beyond the mind, beyond the world, beyond life — immanent but unknowable), while at the same time understanding that to frame such categories as "self" and "beyond-self" only reifies the binary he has elsewhere called into question.

Being an elegy, *Humming* is also ineluctably about death, raising questions regarding how we should approach or conceive of it. For Scully, it too is ineffable, out of the reach of the senses (or, as Falci put it, a "[variety] of flux that [isn't] catchable" [149]). As Fryatt has contended, *Humming* is also a kind of "self-elegy" (7), and perhaps this is so of most elegies; Deleuze and Guattari maintain that "Whenever a musician writes *In Memoriam*, it is not so much a question of an inspirational motif or a memory, but on the contrary of a becoming that is only confronting its own danger…" (299). Perhaps the closest Scully in *Humming* comes to framing his own vision of death is at the end of "For Seven Auditions":

> settle bring your dust to settle
> your turbulence to settle your
>
> rigid amphitheatre of pain … hey.
> Hard work.
>
> Hard work.
>
> Close window
>
> Close window
> to return to
> main page
>
> Sing: close window to return to
> main page. (87)

The metaphor of settling dust and turbulence is frequently employed in Eastern philosophical frameworks such as Taoism[7] and Buddhism to signify the clarifying of perception, the clearing of the mind of delusion or distortion in order to see reality as clearly as possible, which as discussed above is one of the concerns of Scully's project. Settling turbidity reveals existence as a "rigid amphitheatre of pain" that takes "hard work" to confront and live in (despite the many moments of joy and ebullience, which we have also seen earlier). Similar to his statement that "life's tiny," here Scully likens it to a pop-up window that is but one facet of a much larger website. The suggestion is that existence is a small window in time and space, which when closed (by death) returns us to the "main page" – in other words, that we return to the ineffable fabric of being explored earlier, becoming "molecular," or are scattered to the void, the non-being that precedes being.[8]

Toward the end of *Humming*'s final "Song," Scully writes of "the fabric / through which twists *this* to *this*, fluid thread, un- / dancing thread, appearing/disappearing…" (93–94; italics in original), reiterating the major themes of the book: the immanent, cosmic hum that permeates all ("the fabric"); kinetic becoming ("twists *this* to *this*, fluid") rather than static being; and the ephemerality of existence itself ("appearing/disappearing"). In the final picture, the philosophical underpinning to this work and Scully's formal strategies for executing it complement each other, and ecopoetics provides a useful frame for discussing *Humming* and quite often even Scully's work as a whole. As Reilly writes, "ecopoetics reflects yet another in a series of human decenterings, as from an ecological perspective, the self dissolves into the gene pool and the species into the ecosystem" (257). There can, however, be nothing more "decentering" than death. In Maurice Scully's elegy, death is the transformation of the illusory self, the event that

---

[7] In *Several Dances* (2014), Scully twice has the word "dhow" (112, 136), which Romana Huk argues "is also, of course, a homonym of Tao, which views life as ungraspable via concepts but intuited in one's everyday being as it partakes of shared 'is-ness'; its interswimming yin and yang might be seen to augment the volume's orbiting images of interconnectedness… " (116).

[8] This ("the void," or emptiness) is the Eastern view, that of Taoism and Buddhism – that being inexpressibly springs from nothingness, though this can also be said to accord with the theory of the Big Bang. In any case, Scully ends one "Song" with the couplet, "post office notice on an envelope from Japan: / 'nothing may be contained in this letter'" (*Humming*, 70; italics in original).

hastens our reintegration with the (eco)system of nature from which all things spring, and into which they pass again.

Works Cited

Breatnach, Pádraig A. "The Poet's Graveside Vigil: A Theme of Irish Bardic Elegy in the Fifteenth Century". *Zeitschrift für Celtische Philologie* 49–50 (1997): 50–63.

Deleuze, Gilles, and Félix Guattari. *A Thousand Plateaus: Capitalism and Schizophrenia*. Trans. Brian Massumi. Minneapolis, MN: University of Minnesota Press, 1987.

Falci, Eric. "Joinery: Trevor Joyce's Lattice Poems". *Essays on the Poetry of Trevor Joyce*. Ed. Niamh O'Mahony. Bristol: Shearsman Books, 2015. 128–54.

Fryatt, Kit. "The Poetics of Elegy in Maurice Scully's *Humming*". *Irish University Review* 46.1 (2016): 89–104.

Goodby, John. "'Repeat the changes change the repeats': Alternative Irish Poetry". *The Oxford Handbook of Modern Irish Poetry*. Ed. Fran Brearton and Alan Gillis. Oxford: Oxford University Press, 2012. 607–28.

Huk, Romana. "'Out Past / Self-Dramatization': Maurice Scully's *Several Dances*". *Irish University Review* 46.1 (2016): 105–18.

Mc Elroy, James. "Ecocriticism & Irish Poetry: A Preliminary Outline". *Estudios Irlandeses* 6 (2011): 54–69.

Mills, Billy. "Sustainable Poetry". *Elliptical Movements*. 4th March 2013. <ellipticalmovements.wordpress.com/2013/03/04/sustainable-poetry/>. Accessed 25th May 2019. np.

Pound, Ezra. "A Retrospect". *Literary Essays of Ezra Pound*. New York, NY: New Directions, 1968. 3–14.

Quartermain, Meredith. "The Bees". Review of *Humming*, by Maurice Scully. *Golden Handcuffs Review* 1.14 (2011): 233–37.

Reilly, Evelyn. "Eco-Noise and the Flux of Lux". *)((eco(lang (uage(reader)): The Eco-Language Reader*. Ed. Brenda Iijima. New York, NY: Portable Press at Yo-Yo Labs / Nightboat Books, 2010. 255–74.

Satris, Marthine. "Selection as Rewriting: Maurice Scully's Re-Envisioning of *Things That Happen*". *Golden Handcuffs Review* 1.16 (2013): 195–200.

Scully, Maurice. "As I Like It". *the Beau* 3 (1983/1984): 10.

———. *Humming*. Exeter: Shearsman Books, 2009.

———. "An Interview with Maurice Scully." Conducted by Marthine Satris. *Contemporary Literature* 53.1 (2012): 1–30.

———. *Livelihood*. Bray, Co. Wicklow: Wild Honey Press, 2004.

———. *Several Dances*. Bristol: Shearsman Books, 2014.

———. *A Tour of the Lattice*. London: Veer Books, 2011.

Scully's *Several Dances* and the Play of Genre

Eric Falci

The line upon which contemporary poetry in Ireland has been divided is clear: between a mainstream fully invested in the value of the well-made lyric poem and an experimental wing that follows up on and extends the innovations of modernist and late-modernist writers. Because there are fewer poets in Ireland than in the United States or Britain, and because Irish poetry has long punched above its weight within the wider field of English-language literature, the larger split in the field of poetry is refracted and magnified within Irish poetry. The distinction between the mainstream and what Maurice Scully playfully calls "we Experimental Freakos" has been both wholly imaginable and all too easy to maintain (Satris 17). Because of the massive transatlantic success of, most notably, Heaney, Boland, and Muldoon, as well as the prominence of Northern Irish poets like McGuckian, Carson, and Longley, the presence of the "mainstream" is utterly palpable. And because, for the most part, the majority of Irish poets have remained committed to some version of the well-made lyric poem, even if that commitment has been – for many – entwined with varieties of invention, and because these poets have tended to be published by a small number of Irish presses – with the most prominent finding a home on the lists of major publishers in England and the United States – a "mainstream" in Irish poetry is remarkably easy to pinpoint. At the same time, the marginality and small size of the experimental wing has, perhaps counter-intuitively, allowed it to punch above *its* weight, or at least to use that marginality as a kind of propulsive force.

This isn't the place to reprise the full history of experimental formations within late twentieth-century Irish poetry – Michael Smith and Trevor Joyce's founding of New Writers' Press in the 1960s, the rediscovery of Irish modernists from the 1930s, the early careers of Maurice Scully, Billy Mills, and Randolph Healy and their small press projects and reading series in the late 1970s and 1980s, the emergence of Catherine Walsh in the mid-1980s, the cross-channel and transatlantic connections that catalysed and sustained Irish experimental writing, the return of Trevor Joyce to the fold in the 1990s, the fortuitous coming-together of many of the above figures at the Assembling Alternatives Conference at the University of New Hampshire in 1996, the importance of the SoundEye Festival in Cork, and the slow emergence of these figures as nationally and internationally recognized poets.[1] But it is worth reminding ourselves that the story of experimental poetry in Ireland has been told almost exclusively through the work of a very small handful of writers – Smith, Joyce, Scully, Mills, Walsh, Healy, David Lloyd, and Geoffrey Squires. To be sure, younger poets such as Fergal Gaynor and Sarah Hayden have become part of the story, but our accounts of Irish experimental poetry generally rest on the writers mentioned above, with Joyce, Scully, and Walsh the most prominent among them. Whatever the other effects of such a scenario, it has meant that – strangely enough – the experimental, innovative wing of Irish poetry has remained remarkably stable over the past several decades. This isn't to say that the work of any one of these writers resembles that of the others or that these writers produce work that's all of a piece. Rather, it is to suggest that, compared to experimental poetry formations in North America or in England, the Irish experimental scene is – if only because it has been so small – relatively easy to get one's head around.[2]

Of course, relying on a stark mainstream-experimental divide is ultimately limiting. It neither recognizes the inventions of "mainstream" figures such as Carson or McGuckian; nor provides a satisfying way to understand the particularities of a given poet's body of work; nor offers a way to value such work on its own terms without some blunt critical cudgel being brought down upon it; nor gives a means to account for the poetry of someone who seems to straddle the divide, such as Thomas Kinsella; nor suggests how we might read the experimental texts of Walsh, Scully, or Joyce as extensions or overturnings of "mainstream" lyric practices and form. And of course, neither term is adequate to describe all the work that we attempt to gather under it. Even when dealing with such a small field as Irish experimental poetry, using the term "experimental" to describe and categorize Walsh's radically splayed pages, Squires' phenomenological miniatures, Joyce's procedural poems, or Scully's serial projects is constricting, and perhaps only useful as an initial step into analysis, rather than an outcome of it.

And yet, even as we understand that the divide is overly simple, and even as we continually malign its existence and point out all of

---

[1] For accounts of this history, see Davis, O'Mahony, and Falci.

[2] For a clear-eyed take on just how difficult it is to get one's head around and keep up with contemporary poetry in a North American context, see Dworkin.

the ways in which it is inadequate, it remains – for nearly all critics and even some poets – remarkably handy. Within the world of Irish poetry, such a distinction certainly remains in force. In his introduction to a 2016 special issue of the *Irish University Review* devoted to "Irish Experimental Poetry", David Lloyd offers a concise and provocative sketch. Using Beckett's 1934 review essay, "Recent Irish Poetry" as a starting point, Lloyd distinguishes between "conventional", "well-made" poetry and the "experimental" poetry that is the topic of the special issue. Unsurprisingly, "conventional" poetry takes a beating in Lloyd's account, while experimental poetry is distinguished both from its "conventional" counterpart and from actual scientific experimentation:

> 'Conventional' poetry gives the impression that its materials have been processed to furnish a convenient metaphorical or anecdotal vehicle – a 'theme' – for the expression of a subject secure in its self-possession: one is all too familiar with the happy procedure of the poem that commences with a 'vividly realized' experience, draws from it some metaphoric thread, and winds up with a moral payload, validated by a nice turn of phrase, that brings metaphor and experience into graceful concord again. The procedure of the 'well-made poem' is handily available for recycling and the world yields ample material for exploitation in this mode. The experimental, on the other hand, is paradoxically quite the opposite of what a scientific analogy might imply: where the scientific experiment must be repeatable in order to be tested, the poetic experiment cannot in principle be repeated nor can its forms be adopted as conventions for future writing. (11–12)

Of course, Lloyd's gambit is meant to provoke, and were one so inclined one could spend time counter-punching, suggesting Lloyd paints with too broad a brush and that his depiction of "'conventional' poetry" might best be seen as a kind of catalytic overstatement, useful for the sake of launching a polemic, but perhaps not entirely adequate to describe the huge swath of work that presumably falls under the shadow of Lloyd's scythe-like phrase.

More intriguing than Lloyd's characterization of so-called "conventional" poetry is his description of experimental poetry. For Lloyd, "experimental poetry" pushes strenuously against both of its constitutive terms. It is opposed to all of the conventional writing that is too easily identifiable, and commodifiable, as poetry, and its modes of experimentation are contrary to the scientific process. Rather than the outcome of an experiment that is replicable, experimental poetry is always *sui generis*. Lloyd provides a more precise gloss on what he has in mind:

> The conception of the 'experimental' that informs the essays gathered here refers at once to the formal aspects of the poems discussed and to the relation to language and to the phenomenal world of perception or sensation that they manifest. That distinction, useful in some regards, remains suspect: the experimental in poetry is defined by the condition that the form does not precede the material, but is determined and continually transformed by the very process of the poem's engagement with the things of its world. (11)

The experimental quality of experimental poetry, in Lloyd's account, derives from a double condition: it is inherent in the poem's processual or open (rather than conventional or traditional) form as well as in its orientation toward the "things of its world". Its orientation would be apparent in its form, and each is a force within a dialectical process that ceaselessly routes the fluctuating "phenomenal world of perception and experience" through the system of language and an ever-transformative poetic structure. Here, Lloyd gives an elegant version of a familiar notion about modernist poetry, one that can be traced back to Pound's critical writings of the 1910s (and, to be sure, even earlier), and that has taken many different routes as it wended its way through artistic movements and poetic formations over the course of the twentieth century.

One of the most influential articulations of this notion, and one with which Lloyd's especially resonates, is Charles Olson's "Projective Verse" (1950). "Projective or OPEN verse", which Olson also calls "composition by field" (all capitalized in Olson's text), is based in kinetics, energy, and process (239). A poem is a "high-energy construct", a switch point between poet and reader: "A poem is energy transferred from where the poet got it (he will have some several causations), by way of the poem itself to, all the way over to, the reader" (240). Lloyd's sense of an experimental poem's singular, non-repeatable form is, for Olson, an entailment of "projective verse": "From the moment he ventures into FIELD COMPOSITION – puts himself in the open – he can go by no track other than the one the poem under hand declares, for itself" (240). And Lloyd's condition for experimental poetry – that "the form does not precede the material" – is a variation on Olson's crib from Creeley:

> FORM IS NEVER MORE THAN AN EXTENSION OF CONTENT. (Or so it got phrased by one, R. Creeley, and it makes absolute sense to me, with this possible corollary, that right form, in any given poem, is the only and exclusively possible extension of content under hand.) (CC)

"Projective verse" privileges both process and movement ("get on with it, keep moving") and positions the breath – the poet's breath as scored by the typewriter – as the engine and fulcrum of form (240). Lloyd's insistence that "the experimental in poetry... is determined and continually transformed by the very process of the poem's engagement with the things of its world" is a late reflex of Olson's sketch of "objectism" in the latter part of his essay:

> the kind of relation of man to experience which a poet might state as the necessity of a line or a work to be as wood is, to be as clean as wood is as it issues from the hand of nature, to be as shaped as wood can be when a man has had his hand to it. Objectism is the getting rid of the lyrical interference of the individual as ego, of the "subject" and his soul, that peculiar presumption by which western man has interposed himself between what he is as a creature of nature. (247)

Olson's call for a poetry that banished the "lyrical interference of the individual as ego" has remained a foundation stone upon which the mainstream-experimental divide has been produced and maintained, even as the actualities of Olson's practice and the genuine ambiguities of the phrase have obscured its polemical (and even critical) value.

Leaving aside all of the problematic aspects of Olson's theories, it is useful to note the ways in which Lloyd's description of experimental form accords with Olson's famous definition of "projective or OPEN verse".[3]

---

[3] "Projective verse" is a familiar term for most critics, but "open verse" is somewhat less so. While "projective verse" is, by now, reified as a critical phrase, the

For critics who favour what can be broadly construed as experimental or innovative, the terms in which it is favoured are relatively consistent: they either derive from notions of estrangement or defamiliarisation adapted from Viktor Shklovsky and Russian Formalism on the one hand and Stein on the other, or from conceptions of process and flux that emerge out of the work of Pound, Williams, Olson, Cage, and others. The major experimental nodes of the past half century – Language Poetry, Prynne's Cambridge School, the New York School, Conceptual Poetry – tend to work by braiding together, at varying ratios, these two inheritances from modernist aesthetics, often situating them within a framework of Marxian critique.

In the same passage from his introduction, Lloyd suggests another aspect of contemporary experimental poetry's modernist legacy: this kind of poetry "place[s] demands on readerly engagement and active alertness that do not make such work apt for classroom teaching or casual acquaintance" (12). Because such poems do not abide by conventions – whether those conventions are formal, metrical, generic, modal, grammatical, or thematic – and because each experimental poem generates its own form, they are difficult to read: unfamiliar as a matter of course, rebarbative of a reader's expectations, and recalcitrant to meaning. The argument over the value of literary difficulty both is venerable and remains undecided, but it is important to focus on the conjunction, within such discussions in the field of postwar poetry, of difficulty and open-ness. A poem's difficulty – its discursive impenetrability, its avoidance of normative grammar, its refusal of reference or its eschewal of sense – has also been understood to be concomitant with its process-based model of form. As Olson and so many others have suggested, an experimental poem experiments midflight. Its form, as Lloyd suggests, is "determined and continually transformed by the very process of the poem's engagement with the

---

strange and paradoxical force that binds "open" to "verse" still registers. The unstable coupling of open form and metered language – "open verse" – has attracted very little critical attention. For the most part, poetry in traditional meter has generally fallen on the "mainstream" side of the divide, while experimental poetry in the past half century has eschewed, at least explicitly, metricality. This characterization, as is often the case, certainly oversimplifies the matter, and one need only look toward poets from the Prynne-centred Cambridge School to find a variety of experimental practice deeply interested in the formal and critical possibilities of verse writing.

things of its world". If such a text partakes of conventional or traditional forms – as in Ted Berrigan's *Sonnets* or Keston Sutherland's *Odes to TL61P* – it is under the sign of parody or parasitism or Adornian negation and critique. Short and medium-sized poetic texts could rely on a chosen formal condition (a repeating stanza shape, a self-generated rhythm of lines, a resemblance to a familiar lyric duration, the simple space of a page, an iterative grammatical or syntactical structure) or could just go wherever they liked, confident in a reader's ability to find a way to yoke together (or try to) seemingly disparate bits. Long poetic texts either took on some kind of pre-fabricated scaffolding or simply unfolded serially, adding part to part as the work disclosed itself over a period of years or volumes, or simply became the overall form of the poet's corpus (Nathanial Mackey's intertwined series *The Song of the Andoumboulou* and *Mu* might be the signal contemporary example here). Unlike those poems that do make themselves "apt for classroom teaching or casual acquaintance", experimental poems are bound to be intractable if only because the terms of their unfolding are, under Lloyd's reading, necessarily unfamiliar. Lloyd's compound definition of experimental poetry, which, as I've suggested, can be said to be broadly representative of a widespread line of thinking within contemporary poetry scholarship and criticism, argues for two different modes of flux. On the side of composition, such an experimental text is always in process because it is "determined and continually transformed by the very process of the poem's engagement with the things of its world". On the side of reception, a reader is charged with following the course of an open and variable process, usually without the kinds of cues (generic, modal, and formal) that help to shape and organize one's reading.

In so many ways, Maurice Scully's poetry fits perfectly within Lloyd's terms, and so, at a larger level, within the central accounts of experimental and innovative poetry that have circulated for more than half a century. Like other contemporary long poems – such as Mackey's twinned sequences, Rachel Blau DuPlessis' *Drafts*, Ron Silliman's *Ketjak*, or Allen Fisher's *Place* and *Gravity as a consequence of shape* – Scully's major work, *Things That Happen* (1981–2006) is an open form text that appeared over many years and in a number of volumes. As is the case in a variety of open form poems, *Things That Happen* is premised upon a blurring of the distinction between the poem as process and the poem as linguistic artefact; it is "about" the various modes of perception and thought that constitute it. As Scully suggests in this passage from *5 Freedoms of Movement*, the earliest volume of the project, it simultaneously lays down and follows its own path:

> this music goes like this   hollows   twists
> pauses developing in places
> you follow   then
> wonder how it works (*Doing the Same in English*, 17)

John Goodby suggests that Scully's project is "kept alive by the alertness, fluidity, and subtlety with which consciousness is rendered in ejaculation, interrogation, commentary, parody, self-mockery, qualification, ventriloquism, and even lyric afflatus" (623). By shuttling between discursive registers, embedding multiple temporal and spatial frames, incorporating materials from a variety of sources, and jumping among units that make sense intrinsically but not necessarily together, *Things that Happen* makes a virtue of capaciousness and aims to splice together the act of the poem and the poem as object. David Wheatley puts the matter deftly: "the scaffolding is the façade" (100).

And yet, Scully's work diverges from other postwar open form projects in notable ways. Unlike long poems by Mackey or Blau DuPlessis (or, for that matter, by Pound, Olson, or Duncan), *Things that Happen* isn't primarily serial, and so one doesn't read it in quite the same way as one does a long, ongoing project that is organized as a series of successive parts. Rather, Scully's long poem is reticular or radial.[4] In a note to *Things that Happen*, Scully promotes a remarkably open approach to the text:

> *Things that Happen* in its entirety is written around motifs and sub-motifs. The motifs interlace in waves and eddies which echo and deepen as the reader progresses. The project is structured radially so that you can dip in almost anywhere and pick up the music of the interlacing motifs. (*Doing the Same in English*, 200)

The interlacing of the long poem's "motifs and submotifs" is decoupled from the forward progression of the project: it isn't simply that these "motifs and submotifs" accrue significance as *Things that Happen*

---

[4] I discuss the reticular aspects of Scully's work in "Joinery: Trevor Joyce's Lattice Poems," in O'Mahony.

advances. That is to say, *Things that Happen* affords a mode of readerly attention marked by reversals, splices, and jump-cuts, rather than by forward momentum or accretion. In an interview with Marthine Satris, Scully differentiates between two kinds of poetic form, the "architectural and the fibrous," and suggests that most of his work

> is fibrous – structure below ground. But *structured* for sure. The mycelium, the threaded web, connecting roots over long distances. Symbiotic, not parasitic. My poetry has that sort of fibrous connectedness. It's part of the way we all experience the world, I think. (13–14)

The analogy is both compelling and a bit of a feint. In Scully's formal imagination, texts are networks – nodal, radial, with hubs and spokes – rather than teleological progressions. And yet *Things that Happen* doesn't quite present itself to a reader as a "threaded web," but as a sequence of books that comprise a sequence of pages. As Scully suggests, a reader should be able to "dip in almost anywhere," but it is also incumbent upon a reader to pick up on the various interlacings of "motifs and submotifs," which would require a more thorough engagement with the text. And because a reader is likely to take the cue of the books' layout and begin the book at the beginning rather than repeatedly "dip in almost anywhere", the kind of improvisatory reading that Scully suggests is in dialectical tension with the kind of reading afforded – and enforced – by the technology of the book.

This tension is even greater because Scully's work is, from another angle, remarkably "architectural." Rather than unfolding serially (i.e., in numbered parts) or appearing as a simple amalgam of short forms, *Things that Happen* is a compound work that suggests a hierarchical structure to complement the "threaded web". While it does not have a narrative arc, it isn't simply a massive compendium. It is heavily demarcated, with numerous preludes, postludes, interludes, and codas strewn throughout. However, we aren't given the sense of inexorable forward progression implied by those relational terms, but rather something like the ghost of teleology or temporality – scaffolding without any building's façade. *Things that Happen* asks to be read relationally, even if one cannot ascertain how the contents of the texts – the things that happen – correspond to the titular terms that seem to correlate them. A reader is presented with two modes of approaching *Things that*

Happen – as a "threaded web" that can be dipped into anywhere, and as a sequence of parts that are ordered in some way – which are neither fully articulated nor totally incommensurable. Readerly expectations – which is to say, conventions – are both activated and deferred.

Such a double manoeuvre is also apparent in Scully's frequent invocation of traditional genres – most frequently the sonnet. However, the poems that are attached to conventional generic or formal tags generally eschew all of the features implied by the tag. At one level, this is a way to parody, rupture, or evacuate traditional forms, and it is a common tactic among writers of all stripes. At another level, it becomes for Scully a transpositional tactic: he takes a recognizable feature of a traditional form – such as the 14 lines of a sonnet – and uses it to shape a different aspect of the poem. As he says in his interview with Satris, many of the poems he calls "Sonnet" will have "fourteen elements," although it isn't always clear what constitutes an element (20). Rather than shun the conventions of genre and form, as we might expect for an experimental writer, Scully positively revels in them, even if the revelry is at times inscrutable.

Indeed, one of the unexpected ramifications of Scully's work is that it undertakes a rich investigation of the role of genre within experimental and innovative practice. This investigation is not limited to poetic genres but extends across the arts: the use of "prelude", "postlude", and "coda" in *Things that Happen* are, unlike Scully's cagey deployment of "sonnet", indications of his attempt to think across artistic media. And this, at long last, brings us around to *Several Dances*. If *Things that Happen* embedded an inquiry into genre within the larger sweep of its open, radial form, then *Several Dances* permits us to examine more directly Scully's insistence on the value of cross-genre and cross-arts experimentation, allowing us to ask not only about the ways in which experimental poetry inevitably mediates and repurposes conventional forms, but also about the value of such mediations and, more broadly, of the value of experimental poetry's general commitment to process and open form. If, to return to Lloyd one final time, the value of experimental poetry inheres both in its generation of linguistic forms that register the continually transformative "process of the poem's engagement with the things of its world" and in its making available a space of "readerly engagement and active alertness" that is neither predetermined nor repeatable, then how might we think these two conditions together? And what is the role of generic convention

– which entails repeatability – within such experiments, especially in cases in which poems adapt genres from other media?

If we approach the notion of genre capaciously – not merely as a titular tag or prefabricated structure, but as a dense configuration of formal features, projected settings, rhetorical tendencies, and tonal orientations – then *Several Dances* is steeped in generic context. Most of the poems in *Several Dances* are marked by double or triple generic entailments. They are all, of course, poems rather than songs or dances, but many are named for dances or musical compositions. In his interview with Satris, Scully glosses his thinking about the titles in the volume:

> In the book I'm currently working on, *Several Dances*, the titles themselves often have two elements, in tune with the idea of synchronized dancing – often a painting with a dance, or a painting with a painting or painting genre, separated, or *joined*, by a colon. I think of the colon as the hands, the hands of the dancers in contact. Joyce, I think, sometimes used colons as "eyes" – look at the opening page of the *Portrait*. And because several of the titles in *Several Dances* have these elements, they read laterally across the book, suggesting connections. The titles of my pieces are often not simply descriptive, or descriptive at all. With regard to the "poems" in various books, well, the books are not "collections" of disparate "poems", but pieces, tesserae, that make up a larger shifting picture, or thought-sound-world. (14)

As we've come to expect from Scully's motivic practice, *Several Dances* emerges as a lattice, a "threaded web," that is constituted by a proliferating cache of rhetorical, grammatical, and formal gestures. The poems in the volume frequently activate familiar generic energies even if the poem as a whole can't be generically categorized (such as the brief elegy that appears in the middle of "On a Dark Ground: Work Dance"; the paired poems of childhood recollection, "Tango" and "Sunlight"; and the ekphrastic moments in "Thorns Spindles Twigs", to name only a few examples). And as we've also come to expect, Scully incorporates visual motifs – both iconic drawings and abstract patterns – into his books, usually as part of the volume's paratext, and also supercharges diacritical marks, as in his sense of the scopic function of the colons. All of these features of his practice work to make Scully's poetry difficult to excerpt, as a number of critics have noted.

Some such difficulties remain when approaching *Several Dances*, but one of the major differences between *Several Dances* (and, for that matter, *Humming*) and the volumes that constitute *Things that Happen* is that *Several Dances* adjusts the relationship between tesserae and mosaic. Poems in *Several Dances*, despite their participation in the volume's "larger shifting picture", appear primarily as discrete texts even as they ramify with those that precede and follow them in the volume, a double condition of emergence that Scully articulates at the end of "Parallax: On Vellum":

> Yr glowing bristles in the dark,
> yr temporary arrangements in the
> larger Temporary Arrangement
> of interlaced overall design, pits &
> peaks, a piglet upside-down blowing
> on a chanter in the margin, its
> tune mute, moving over moving
> water, ripple & twirl, working,
> walking, working, walking off. (*Several Dances*, 70)

In Scully's hands, form and genre become "temporary arrangements in the / larger Temporary Arrangement". And, as I've suggested and will go on to describe in a bit more detail, generic categories and affordances become a means to modulate the ratio between the discrete poem and the volume's webby totality, or between the multifarious goings-on in the margins and the vellum's larger pattern. The overlapping of vision (the designs on the vellum), sound (the chanter's "tune mute"), and motion indicate the ways in which the volume both seeks and abjures an "interlaced overall design". Before turning to a more extended example, then, it will help to spend a bit of time on the implications of the volume's overall structure and on the ramifications of that structure on a reader's activity.

One could make the argument that certain strands of experimental poetry end up just as domineering as the "self-possessed" sorts of conventional poetry against which Lloyd and so many others have railed. It isn't that such poetry is simply too difficult, but rather that it has failed to honour the model of energy transfer that Olson preached, if not always practiced ("A poem is energy transferred from where the poet got it [he will have some several causations], by way of the poem itself to, all the way over to, the reader"). In such a poem, all of the energy is bound up in the initiating concept or in some aspect of composition, and there is no space for the reader within the poem's system. This is manifestly not the case in Scully's work and in *Several Dances* in particular. Unlike *Things that Happen* (both as a whole and within the individual volumes that constitute it), *Several Dances* has no superstructure: it contains 49 poems, followed by a "Coda" of three poems. Even this superstructural feature is negated because the three poems of the "Coda" are not the final poems. After the "Coda" and a page of notes, there is an additional poem titled "Backing Vocals" – a bonus track of sorts. After "Backing Vocals," there is a page that is blank apart from a very brief biographical note ("Maurice Scully was born in Dublin on 2nd June 1952. He has published close on a dozen books over the past 35 years", 133). Even now, however, the volume will not close: three pages of poetry appear after the biographical page, each one recalling an earlier poem in the volume and all three printed in lighter ink than the rest of the volume, almost as though they are meant to mimic the fading out of one of the song forms on which the volume spends so much time riffing.

Several Dances is in this sense paratactic rather than serial or sequential – what the volume's opening poem calls "meshes of energies made visible" (14) – which allows for a mode of readerly play that fulfils Scully's desire for *Things that Happen*, that one can "dip in almost anywhere". The particular kind of pressure that Scully places on generic conventions (whether in terms of poetry, music, or dance) is best seen in the condensed activity within each poem: the performative tension between a title and the poem that follows it, the toggling between tenses and moods (especially the abundance of imperative verbs in the volume), the enfolding of multiple artistic media as structural and discursive analogues, and the related vacillation between sensory modalities that most of the texts encourage. In this way, the volume undertakes an attempt to think together process and convention, to understand the inexorable intertwining of two approaches to writing and reading poetry that are often set in diametrical opposition: one that privileges an experimental process (whether a species of open form or a predetermined but newfangled set of constraints) and the other that adheres to (while inevitably adapting) some kind of familiar generic scaffolding. In the remainder of this essay, I will focus on one of the most intriguing texts in *Several Dances* in order to give a sharper sense of what Scully is up to and why it matters.

Along with a precise attention to local conditions and to what is "to-hand,"[5] the poems in *Several Dances* often pair description with instruction, a process of invitation and attunement that begins with "On a Light Ground: Eye Dance," the volume's opening poem:

> Dapple of mother-spider
> at the centre of its wet
> web between a hedge & a
> trellis. After work, the
>
> wait. Place your foot
> there. Then place it
> there. Pitch a rock
> in the pond: hear that
>
> difference over there.
> I-me-myself are moving
> forward
>   forward
>
> to that left behind, through
> air, to that placed shimmer
> ahead. Forward. Carry your
> spinning circle, a drop
>
> lands, little by/connects
> [pendent speck] reverberant.
> Hold still. I do. Move. Stare.
> Are you ready? What? ... (13)

This is *Several Dances'* initial gesture and in many ways it condenses its key manoeuvres. A focused description of the spider in its web is paired with a set of instructions that function both to call the reader into the poem and to thicken the space in which the poem unfolds. The tightly-drawn moment that begins the poem then dilates, enmeshed in a larger spatial frame and placed in time ("After work, the / wait"). After the opening visualization, the poem begins to activate additional sensory

---

[5] In an interview, Scully describes his aesthetic practice in such terms (see Fryatt 136).

channels, moving from the visual to the haptic to the ambulatory. It is as though the poem aims to construct the deictic and diegetic body of its reader, the "you" who is the implicit addressee of the cues ("Place your foot / there"). A further dilation occurs when the space is made to sound: after the figure/reader is asked to see and move, it is then required to interact with its environment and to hear the effects of that interaction. The rippling circles of water once the rock has been pitched in the pond double the spider web's concentricity, and the reader is asked finally to use hearing to conceptualize difference – the splash of the rock into the pond as compared to the echo of that splash. The poem's first major moment of arrival is itself a marking of such difference: "I-me-myself are moving".

This compound subject then begins to address the spider rather than the reader who has been called into the poem: "Carry your / spinning circle". After several stanzas in which the spider's movements are tracked, the poem's backdrop shifts: instead of a natural scene, we are presented with an artistic surface:

> To cross
>
> which pattern a/pattern a/
> [black] ripple of leaf-shadow
> over those books there
> restless surges & retreats
>
> smooth fluid undulations
> that move across a vase
> sketched in to burn care-
> fully across representations
>
> of small flowers on a curved
> ceramic edge complications.
> Pause. Meshes of energies
> made visible. (13–14)

Simultaneously presenting its visual field and accounting for its own compositional motion, the poem spins together figure and ground and continually rescales itself. The remainder of the poem unspools several further limnings of the scene – or, limnings of some series of incompatible scenes – before turning its gaze upon the artist and closing with a strange little declaration that could either come from artist or spider:

> (small paint-marks on my palm,
> wonder-swirl skin pattern, red
> giant, white dwarf)—yes I
>
> think I'll live here for a bit
> not across no but along. One.
>   Border. Forever. (14)

The artist's palm – another instauration of the spider web, rippling pond motif – is briefly turned galactic before the poem begins to settle itself. We might say that living "not across no but along" is what the entire poem is trying to do, and what *Several Dances* as a whole attempts. This moment of "being with" the world is, however, upended by the concluding tag. What seems like a repurposed political chant also serves to disclose the tension between stasis and motion – artefact and process – that underlies nearly all of Scully's work. "One. / Border. Forever" denotes unity while performing separation, and so the border at issue is both invoked and elided. Such a wavering is not only a function of Scully's commitment to presenting the vicissitudes of thought, sensation, and feeling as they intersect each other within the ambit of experience, but also – and perhaps more significantly – an effect of his continual, though quite subtle, inquiry into the means by which poems mediate any such content through their own representational and formal practices and via other artistic media.

The poem functions as an "eye dance," affording a reader a series of images in accordance with Pound's notion of *phanopoeia*. It also embeds its own music: the images are sonically charged (Pound's *melopoeia*) such that consonance and assonance serve to bind together and spur forward the quickly moving quatrains (*dapple/spider, hedge/trellis, pitch/rock/pond*). Scully networks the image clusters and sound chains by establishing a diegetic space in which they interact ("on a light ground") and sets the reader moving, seeing, and listening within that space. It is as though Scully extends *logopoeia* (which Pound famously describes as "the dance of the intellect among words") into a fully phenomenological register – not only establishing patterns of cognition and conceptualisation, but also those of perception and bodily activity. Romana Huk distinguishes

Scully's phenomenology from a more familiar Heideggerian version by describing it as a "'both/and', inclusive phenomenology", and one of the primary modes by which Scully's work encourages such inclusion is by foregrounding and setting out for display the primary channels through which readers come to and move along his poems (107). The play of perception and attention afforded a reader unfolds within a transformative generic space. It is not only a space of lyric diegesis that Scully means to construct, but also a space of generic and modal instability. A reader can't approach "On a Light Ground: Eye Dance" as she would a poem in a conventional genre or mode, but, nonetheless, the poem – like so many others in *Several Dances* – is saturated with generic information and suggestion. Many of the poems in the volume seem generically overdetermined even as they can't be conceived of adhering to a set of generic conventions. Rather, Scully's poetry asks a reader to consider generic formations as themselves "threaded webs", as fibrous configurations of linguistic and literary materials.

"On a Light Ground: Eye Dance" establishes some of the volume's major parameters and provides an initial instance upon which and against which readerly expectations will gather, but it does not designate a programmatic core. As in all of Scully's work, the incorporation of seemingly tangential materials, varieties of montage, haphazard turns, and experiential miscellany is central to both his compositional process and a reader's pleasure. While it does recycle a handful of phrases, intertexts, and topics, it precisely doesn't fit together into an "interlaced, overall design", nor do the volume's motifs fit together into a single overarching pattern. *Several Dances*, like his earlier work, allows a wide variety of things to happen within each poem and from poem to poem, and these happenings yield neither a cohesive arc nor an extended series of fragments. And this comes to the most beguiling aspect of Scully's work, one that my approach in this essay has so far skirted around, but which might ultimately prove useful in better understanding his poetry. What seems to me most difficult and beguiling about his poetry is its simultaneous limpidity and opacity. For all of its varieties of formal experimentation, Scully's poetry is often disarmingly straightforward, and can often be said to be "about" (either in part or in full) a particular topic: work and economic need, the writing of poetry, the Irish language, the politics of the Irish literary world, contemporary Irish society, the natural world. And while it would be too much to call his work autobiographical, much of it orbits around his own domestic space in Dublin. Indeed, the cover photograph of *Several Dances* features Scully's writing shed, taken by the poet's son, which is the clear setting of many of the poems in the volume. While Scully's poems in no way resemble the slickly-packaged conventional lyrics that, to return to Lloyd for the *final* final time, offer a "'vividly realized' experience" which then becomes the vehicle to deliver "a moral payload", Scully's poems often resemble such poems by beginning in bare "experience". To offer just a few opening lines from *Several Dances*: "Cleaning my glasses with a cloth / she made for me as a child years ago"; "It is 6:40 a.m."; "Sun shines on a quiet Friday morning"; "Squeeze some ink on to the palette"; "When the church bell rings hold on / a sec I mean"; "The kids leave for / school now in a haze of / colour at the door" (44, 45, 71, 88, 110, 129). One can imagine any number of poems that could be painted with Lloyd's brush following from any of these lines. While Scully does have, as he has suggested, a "to-hand aesthetic," in which "wherever I am whatever books (or sounds or people and so on) I'm surrounded with can become part of the elements I'll use to make the work," his poems never remain comfortably ensconced in those surroundings (Fryatt 136). Or, they do remain in those surroundings, because they don't seek to leverage those surroundings into epiphany or transcendence. Scully has managed to find a way to both draw from that well of experience, memory, intellection, and perception that has long (for better and worse) underwritten lyric poetry, and to orient his poetry along quite different lines than any other contemporary Irish poet.

In her reading of *Several Dances*, Huk suggests a different aspect of this larger concern: "this volume engages 'art' (broadly defined) as an inescapable part, *already*, of any 'material circumstances' that give rise to perception or poetry – indeed made *in order to* experience materiality" (107). What has interested me here are the particular ways that genre and ideas about genre inflect this capacious engagement. It isn't that one is meant to determine the particular kind of poem an "Eye Dance" is, or that one is meant to find a precise way to transpose one of the volume's many cross-arts titles ("Mountain Railway: Gavotte", "Tap Dance", "Sonnet: Print", "Bluebells in a Wood: Waltz", "Blackbird: Jig", to name a few) into a satisfactory literary analogue. Nor is it that the titles are empty gestures. Rather, it is that Scully is keen to fissure the generalized notion of "process" that underwrites a good deal of experimental poetry in order to understand it both as a mode of composition and reception. In *Several Dances*, this fissuring occurs as an extended exploration of just how composition and reception are enmeshed within that network of shapes, forms, habits, and orientations that we too quickly gloss as *genre*. Scully raises the stakes of this investigation by thinking across the arts and asking readers to approach his poems from impossible, inexorable angles – to read a text as poem, dance, and song all at once.

Works Cited

Davis, Alex. *A Broken Line: Denis Devlin and Irish Poetic Modernism*. Dublin: University College, Dublin Press, 2000.
Dworkin, Craig. "Seja Marginal." *The Consequences of Innovation*. Ed. Craig Dworkin. New York, NY: Roof Books, 2008. 7–24.
Falci, Eric. *Continuity and Change in Irish Poetry, 1966–2010*. Cambridge: Cambridge University Press, 2012.
Fryatt, Kit. "Interview with Maurice Scully." *Metre* 17 (2005): 134–143.
Goodby, John. "'Repeat the Changes, Change the Repeats': Alternative Irish Poetry." *The Oxford Handbook of Modern Irish Poetry*. Ed. Fran Brearton and Alan Gillis. Oxford: Oxford University Press, 2012. 607–628.
Huk, Romana. "'Out Past/Self-Dramatization': Maurice Scully's *Several Dances*." *Irish University Review* 46.1 (2016): 105–118.
Lloyd, David. "Introduction: On Irish Experimental Poetry." *Irish University Review* 46.1 (2016): 10–19.
Olson, Charles. "Projective Verse." *Collected Prose*. Ed. Donald Allen and Benjamin Friedlander. Berkeley and Los Angeles, CA. University of California Press, 1997. 239–249.
O'Mahony, Niamh, Ed. *Essays on the Poetry of Trevor Joyce*. Bristol: Shearsman Books, 2015.
Satris, Marthine. "An Interview with Maurice Scully." *Contemporary Literature* 53.1 (2012): 1–30.
Scully, Maurice. *Doing the Same in English: A Sampler of Work 1987–2008*. Dublin: Dedalus Press, 2009.
———. *Several Dances*. Bristol: Shearsman Books, 2014.
Wheatley, David. "Using the Space" [review of *Livelihood*]. *Poetry Ireland Review* 84 (2005): 98–100.

The Shed of Poetry

Mairéad Byrne

I

> *a triangle of sun*
> *light on a*
> *wall of a*
> *shed.*
> "Fire," *i.m.: Paul Klee*

In a note to *5 Freedoms of Movement*, Tony Baker writes of Maurice Scully's poetry:

> If we don't hear the voice speaking to us, we can exploit the privilege of silent reading and dwell on the bright detail at the cost of the idea in time. An idea in Scully's work is something that's made to happen; a reading that ignores the voice and suspends time, stands outside events and is bound to be a misreading to some degree. (95)

There's no doubt that the sound of the human voice is one of the most luscious attributes of Maurice Scully's poetry (with delight in diction coming a close second). This is colloquial soliloquy, neither stagey nor convivial, a sort of conceptual DMZ, a no-man's or Scullyland, between public and private, starred with its own clematis, fugitive species, spiders, birds, hieroglyphs.

Scully's tone is awash with other tones, borrowed colloquialisms, echoes of Herbert, Dickinson, Whitman, Stevens, Williams, Eliot, Pound, Kavanagh, Hartnett, most of all Beckett, and distilled Joyce. Witty, elliptical, minimalist, he's a kind of Erik Satie, touching the clear notes of Irish, Sesotho, Swahili, Kikuyu, Italian, Tzuba ("which exists only in the author's imagination"), in passing, between other things. This is very cleanly stitched collage.

And though the tone is avuncular, and the reader/listener implied, there is always a sense of talking to the self, tolerantly, humorously, playfully, at the edge of despair.

It is not just a matter of voice. There is great attention to sound in the imagery too:

>   That sound of traffic on wet streets
> some streets away sending a delicate intertexture
> of intermittent sound intact this far. And
> a baby's babbling. Intermittence. Tiddle-dum-dee. And
> a leaking roof. This too. Tap. And pattern : sitting down,
> taking notes, time, notice, drip, play, counter it –
> though graceful bits fit over "the truth"
> awkwardly, don't they? (15)

The methodology is that of the motif – "Bright berry in a blackbird's beak" ("And Through", *Doing the Same in English*, 40–41). And the motif is intensely visual:

> **sonnet/**There is a grey sky.
>   there is a white gull
>   on a black aerial
>   on a black roof
>   opening its yellow beak
>   wide & silently
>   calling calls. (*Livelihood*, 21)

What looks good sounds good in poetry and vice versa—"calling calls" works for both ear and eye. In setting out to hail the aural primacies of Scully's work, we arrive at the visual.

'the privilege of silent reading'

There is an inner ear as well as an inner eye. A silent reading is not silent to the one who reads but charged with the pressure of blood. In the inner world, both sound and vision vibrate. They are alike as much as they are different.

In lyric poetry (an interregnum between public and private), the line break serves both eye and ear, a capacity Scully exploits:

> typewriter
> blunt on
> its desk
> in front
>
> of me em
>
> phatically
> plastic steel
> rubber maybe
> a copper fil
>
> ament or two
> becoming ob
> solete at speed
> yes is not
>
> cannot
> be my Brother.
> *(Sonata*, 95)

The performance of the words is in appearance as much as in sound, on the page as much as in speech. Yes, Scully is a remarkable reader, fluid, jocular, quizzical, low-toned. But that Brother needs its capital B, invisible in speech. And how the lines break relates more "em/phatically" to their mechanical means of production than to the conversational voice. Scully dares more visually, often, than aurally.

The punctuation marks which pepper the text, inventive, extravagant in their minimalism, are the visual yields of decisions about sound. The poem is scored and not wholly playable. Its bullet points, batteries of marks, separations, decorations, glyphs, italics, diacritics, formulae, language traces and smears, neologisms, underlinings, parentheses, are breaks in the voice, miniscule pitfalls, moments of silence in text set in the greater silence of the page.

'the bright detail'

Scully's gulls and blackbirds seem iconic, like the motifs in Michael Hartnett's *Inchicore Haiku*. The haiku itself is iconic, for Hartnett a somewhat alien form, in a somewhat alien language, in a somewhat alien city. It is part of Hartnett's genius that he can make Inchicore as familiar as home ground:

> On a brick chimney
> I can see all West Limerick
> in a jackdaw's eye. (10)

Both Scully and Hartnett hold allegiance with their Gaelic masters. Hartnett's form in *Inchicore Haiku* is miniaturist, while the images appear gigantic. Scully's form, by contrast, is molten, carrying myriad motifs, literary/typographic, referential/self-referential, graphic/photographic, in its drift.

The monk in Maurice loves colour, or more precisely illumination. Shine is a colour. "[G]old-gold" (*Sonata*, 67), "mica-/glint-" (*Sonata*, 67) "ink-pool glisten" (*Several Dances*, 90), and "screen-glow" (*Several Dances*, 20) are colours, as much as "gold-black" (*Tig*, 73), "reddish-brown/black" (*Sonata*, 56), "pink bluepink" ("The Dun Copy", 120), and the colours of the notebooks in *Zulu Dynamite*.

Scully flirts with Concretism, including drawings, emblems, embroideries, as necessary and desultory as the flourish of Uncle Toby's cane. The poems are shaped, picking their way through the pages as if words were flagstones, the white space of the page as much gleaming sand as water. It's almost as if words are curios, and tone a kind of tide to hurry them along:

> a
> song
> is
> a
>
> sh
> ap
> e (*Tig*, 65)

All is organized lightly, like the breeze making a third party to the partnership of word and page, a bird gathering materials for the nest of the poem. The *weave/mesh/lattice/trellis/reticle/web/filigree* is Scully's metaphor for how the little bits are held in the magnetic field of the poem.

As Tony Baker also writes: "Scully's writing is so thoroughly meshed that lines that appear in one place are likely to reappear in entirely different contexts in different pieces so that a reader's sense of what the lines are, what they do, depends on the entire weave ... " (*5 Freedoms of Movement*, 95).

Repetition, variants, variegation, become ways to gain ground and make things happen, correcting iconicity, hand-in-hand with this mesh-gathering of "tiny bright word*k*s of / discorded invention" (*Livelihood*, 29).

'at the cost of the idea in time'

Yes, the image can stop time:

> A sodium lamp glows in a laneway outside,
> rose ... orange ... dandelion.

But voice is not the only way to get it flowing again. And flow is not the only metaphor for time. A cognitive, or mechanical, switch can be flicked, as here:

> A sodium lamp glows in a laneway outside,
> rose ... orange ... dandelion. Pause. Detach.
> The house is quiet. My children sleep, my wife
> sleeping. We plan to leave this place soon, the
> outrageous rent, the stinking toilet, the born-
> again Xtian landlord. No sound. 1 a.m. ... (*Livelihood*, 93)

The line is not solely dependent on voice. It is geometric and doubles back, makes shapes, defines spaces which are themselves occupied by lines. Or silence. And silence in poetry is a generative substance, which makes things happen.

"Frost at Midnight" may be our poster poem:

> The inmates of my cottage, all at rest,
> Have left me to that solitude, which suits
> Abstruser musings: save that at my side
> My cradled infant slumbers peacefully.
> 'Tis calm indeed! so calm that it disturbs
> And vexes meditation with its strange
> And extreme silentness. (Coleridge 231)

For both poets, quietness disrupts. And gets things moving.

"Frost at Midnight" is almost without sound but hardly without time. The poem is replete and heavy with it. Time hangs most thickly in the low-ceilinged room where Coleridge stares into the smaller chamber of the hearth and travels in time, backwards, then forwards.

The owlet cries, twice, to set the poem in motion. The breathing of the sleeping child carries the lines, as close to, and distant from, stillness as possible. Otherwise all sound in the poem is mediated, through memory, or anticipation. Even the poet's voice, clothed in blank verse, is imagined by himself, and us.

The image can be still, like the icicle with which Coleridge attempts to freeze the poem, to nail it shut. But the banter begins at the instant of the icicle's formation, moving it from stillness into dialectic, from silence into dialog, "Quietly shining to the quiet Moon". Just before we have the icicle, we have "eave-drops", and just after, in the erased stanza, we know the "sharp keen points" will yield "pendulous drops". The image can be still, but not for long. The most unpromising image in the poem, the "stranger", or film of ash on the grate, is the most lambent, in equal parts material, evocative, presageful.

The still image has a job to do – to end the poem, just as the owlet's cry has a job to do – to open it. But in "Frost at Midnight", sound and image are arrayed on a spectrum, not only in relation to the active properties of the former and the static properties of the latter but also in relation to one another. Frost is silent, yet it performs its ministry. Bells peal – in daydream or memory; they stir and haunt, announcing what is to come. They lull, inhabiting a temporal interregnum rather than signifying any actual event striking the tympanum. The image of the redbreast on the bough doesn't turn toward a special providence or fall but pans sideways to the steaming thatch, then the eave-drops between lulls in the wind, the secret ministry of frost, returning to where the poem begins, looping the drops back into icicles, shining respondents to the shining moon.

Nesting, echoing, mirroring, doubling score the poem. The child's breathing can be heard only when there is a break in the poet's thought, the eave-drop only when the blast lulls. The poet has a self, with its own dimensions of time, within the poem, and that self in the poem has a younger self, also with his own dimensions of time. The poet has a child too, Hartley, with his own short past, slumbering present, and expansive future.

There is a sense that ideally apprehension is unified. In the future, Hartley may "see and hear / The lovely shapes and sounds intelligible / Of that eternal language" which God utters. God is the only unpaired One. But language doubles Him, refracting and cusping images through the clouds and mountains, to get to us.

At midnight, everything outside the cottage is shrouded in silence and darkness. Inside, the poet's eye is fixed on the *stranger* fluttering on the grate. But Coleridge doesn't see it as much as see through it, just as the child Coleridge at Christ's Hospital sees through the "swimming book". What is seen in the poem is absent in the room: the hoped-for visitor.

"Frost at Midnight", a structure in blank verse, functions as a kind of capsule through which, when it is held in the hands and tilted, time shifts. Writing is a way of standing outside time, or seeming to, by the simple act of building smaller structures which we can, to some extent, control within the larger structures which contain us.

In this poem, Coleridge, like Whitman in "Crossing Brooklyn Ferry", recognizes the reader. Whitman claims the right to look straight at the reader, through time, as the reader looks at him. Coleridge is shyer, fixing on the *stranger* on the grate. The *stranger* is the reader, perceived across time, just as in Whitman. Coleridge had both God and confidence in a reader. Whitman had, at the least, certainty in a reader. What of the poet today, who has neither?

'something that's made to happen'

When I asked Tony Baker what he meant by his concatenation of idea/happening/time/voice in his note to *5 Freedoms of Movement*, his answer – and answering – gave me grounds for continuing, just as his note had provoked me to begin:

Maurice's work strikes me as utterly vocal, a voice talking, a voice making sense out of patterns of sound and thought. Even if you read and take it apart to 'analyse' it … I really don't see how it makes sense unless you can grasp it as a whole — a progress in time — in the same way that we do mostly unquestioningly with music. … Some poets can be very metaphysical obviously, but I hear Maurice as the reverse: physical, a talker, a builder with mouth-sounds. His narrative to my ears works rhythmically in ways similar to conversation, with surges and hesitations and curiosities in parenthesis and threads getting lost and found. And to get that rhythm — which is integral to sense — I need to go with the sound in time. (email 11/27/17)

In Maurice Scully's poetry, I see patterns too – in terms of space as well as voice. I see architecture and design. I see rooms with antechambers and back halls telescoping away. I see the book laid out like the floor plan of a Roman villa. I see something like Heinrich Böll's graphic work plans for his novels.

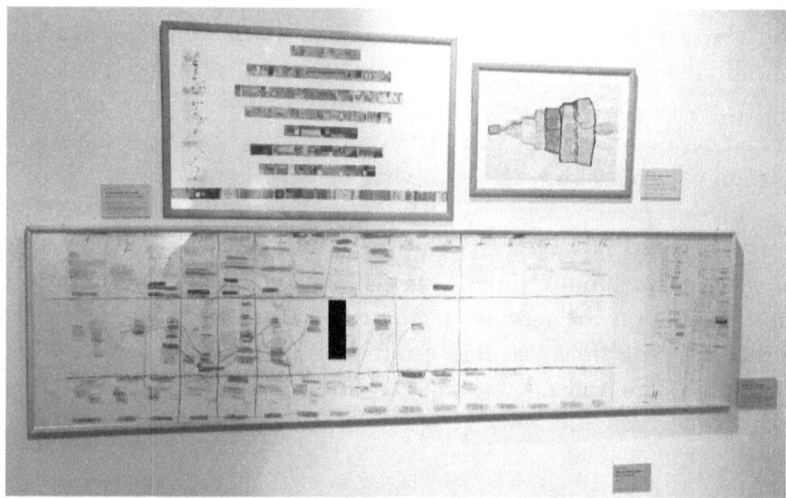

Mairéad Byrne, *Photo from the exhibition* Different Points of View: Böll and Grass, *Gunther Grass House, Lübeck, 2017*

I see blank pages, and shovelfuls of creamy space. I see the diacritics' pepper and spice. I hear the voice, of course, but sometimes I think it's talking to itself, as I wander through the rooms. I take permission for my own perspective from Tony's ownership of his:

> I imagine that working as a musician gives me a very particular slant on all this; and it's a sensibility as well – sound appeals to me. It can make sense of itself. This might not seem so to someone else more attracted to other aspects of language in writing. But I'm not sure you can escape it with Maurice because his ideas are embedded in the talk; talk is their lungs and without hearing it (in time) I don't know how they can seem to breathe. (email 11/27/17)

I hadn't quite thought to refuse the voice but now Tony's words dare me to show that Maurice is a builder of rooms too, and his ideas are embedded there too, and we can walk and breathe there. Although our perspectives are different, Tony allows our comradeship-in-arms:

> Looks to me as if you're describing probably the visual counterpart to what I was approaching from the aural/oral angle – the two overlapping as score I suppose. At any rate, it looks a good way to go to me as they seem aspects of one another. (email 11/28/17)

When I brought Tony's note in *5 Freedoms of Movement* back to him, he said "It's rather satisfying to so lose touch with something you've written that you'd forgotten you'd ever done it. It returns as a stranger and as a surprise".

In Tony's warm response to my inquiry, I found my own *stranger* – not just another perspective but the pleasure of entertaining perspectives, with partial concordances.

II

'a reading that ignores the voice'

I like Tony Baker's idea of Maurice Scully as a builder. I see him as a builder of architectural as well as vocal spaces. This is a bold 20th century move on Scully's part because the inheritance under colonization tends to be intangible culture. The privileging of voice over artefact is a given in that context. The ornamentation and variation of Scully's work – the "little bits", and the reticle, mesh, lattice, trellis, weave, web, filigree that lightly binds them – speak to this heritage. But Scully makes a keen bid for materiality too, in the inclusion of marks which cannot be sounded, lavish use of blank space, and most of all the planned build of the book, and set of books. This constructivism comes as a relief, a kind of solid structure, or the promise of one. Unlike the work of Imran Qureshi, Scully's miniaturism is not subversive. He's subversive when he goes – or tries to go – big. That's where he rocks the tradition.

The dismal heritage remains – in the prevalence of hint over statement, repetition over change, hesitation over experience. But hesitation becomes a design tool. I don't associate the recursiveness and indirection of Scully's multiple beginnings and endings with any sort of tantalization but with anxieties about how to enter and leave a space. The negative legacy of colonization may lend a hopelessness to the work, a sense of poetry as organized despair. Perhaps the only house that *can* be built is the house of the book in the shed. Nevertheless, the building of the book is a bracing move. We know this local habitation is drawn from airy nothing. It is still grounding. It can't quite be occupied but it occupies:

> They are building a house, note
> and accrete, tat-tat. On the map.
> That. I. But. Building a place
> on a place so that/is yr cell
> in yr hive quite adequate? Patches
> of leaf. Conduit, shadow. Walling
> and windowing, dooring and flooring,
> a wandering idiot, humming and
> hawing, hello-ing and no-ing, oh
> yes. Shimmer of advancing futures,
> oily consecutive links, building
> a dream on a fact. (*Livelihood*, 193)

Scully is preoccupied with domestic space, and the relation of the writing space to the house. The house is longed for, coveted, necessary, but never owned. Houses are occupied but transient. The same struggle with money, the same solace of writing, the same peripheral evidence of family – "My children's feet in their shoes on the floor" ("In Praise of Painting

Doors"), and forays outside the walls, happens with every house:

> I wish I had a house, wheedle and whine, I wish
> I had a bit of money, closing the door,
> opening the window. Soul's ability
> to ripple through crisp watermarks – vertical
> layers – mud and wattle cabins and a tidy
> compound. Only a house. In. The.
> Breathing. For instance. I wish I had a
> roof, my two kids, my one wife. Less
> nomadics, but then a whole haversack
> of heartstopping examples: wash-basins,
> wainscot, rain-pearls on a clothesline,
> a clean spread of glasspane deep in its framebed,
> whatever you've got, a folded view through
> gold and developing veins underground,
> small traditional poems – or even less
> traditional poems even – or even less. (*Livelihood*, 155)

The house is bound up with poetry, and poetry is bound up with poverty:

> This is the house I live in now. It is to be poor.
> It is to be decided on without grounds. It is to
> spend one's life thinking, and be thought an idiot;
> to live by dint of intensive works, and be thought
> lazy; to cherish one's wife and children and
> be thought ga-ga. Dance! (*Livelihood*, 158)

Inside the house is the study, the place where the work of poetry is done:

> Writing, deleting, writing again, patient, persistent,
> dogged to the point of /(?)/ is what was reflected on
> that surface leering up, magnetic & stupid, up from
> whose hopelessness you could eat through to the next
> depth barely. (*Sonata*, 100)

The study is shored up against the pressure of the house, one love against another – "A brick or two against that broken door to keep my little daughter out" (*5 Freedoms of Movement*, 15).

Houses, in Scully's poetry, are transitional spaces, and studies are borrowed too, like books from a library:

> Table facing a square window
> inset in a deep white wall
> of a quiet room
> on loan to me (*Livelihood*, 117)

The more material the one, the less material the other.

Whether rented, borrowed, or visited, they make as much or as little impact:

> I always liked being there
> that dark & haunting house
>
> off the South Circular
> at the canal end where
>
> colossal mirrors
> spread out their
>
> cloth ducks in flight
> across a wall (*Tig*, 36)

Ultimately, there will be a move – what poetry at least is well equipped for.

Scully's house is chimerical, transient, desired even lusted after, at the same time apparently occupied and unattainable. It is not like Auden's house in *About the House* (1959):

> Territory, status,
>
> and love, sing all the birds, are what matter:
>   what I dared not hope or fight for
> is, in my fifties, mine, a toft-and-croft
>   where I needn't, ever, be at home *to*

> those I am not at home *with,* not a cradle,
>   a magic Eden without clocks,
> and not a windowless grave, but a place
>   I may go both in and out of. ("Thanksgiving for a Habitat", 7)

Scully's house is cluttered with lustrous children, the very beings who, if anyone or anything does, bring him outside. Relative to Auden, who takes Psalm XVI, 6 for his epigraph, or even MacNeice whom Auden invokes in "The Cave of Making," Scully's inheritance is shaky, whether in terms of language, tradition, recognition, or recompense. Neither Auden's nor MacNeice's dads were "porphyry-born" but they're doing alright, while Scully's patrimony (Ó Scolaí) is simply the name of *student* which, despite his mastery, accompanies him for life.

The homes Auden warms to, "though seldom wealthy, always convey a feeling / of bills being promptly settled // with checks that don't bounce" ("The Common Life"). Scully's homes, wherever they are, seem moored in anxiety:

> my wife & I worry about our debts & our spirited
> baby daughter. & the difficulty of getting out of
> this mess & learning the language & dodging main
> streets at rush-hour so as not to run into anybody
> we might owe money to. (*Livelihood*, 97)

Scully's house is not like Auden's house, nor like Richard McGuire's house in *Here*, a small space through which vast time flows. It is not a palimpsest. It is without history or geography. It doesn't seem to matter whether it is in Lesotho or Ireland.

Scully doesn't have it in him to be urbane, as Auden is – "After all, it's rather a privilege / amid the affluent traffic / to serve this unpopular art ("The Cave of Making"). Everything costs too much. And for all that Auden appreciates that "a cellar never takes umbrage" ("Down There"), he probably wouldn't write "In Praise for a Habitat" in an abject space. Scully, on the other hand, goes into the shed joyfully:

> And then I woke up. It was early. I was
> in a shed in a garden in spring, snow
> melting from roof and branches, a cock
> robin foraging under a hedge and I knew

> ... I knew it was time to open my notebooks
> again with a clear mind and a long memory
> and make a start. (*Livelihood*, 291)

The shed, even more than the study, seems a place of relief for Scully:

> Do you like it?
> Yes, I do.
> Your shed
> your books
> your notebooks
> your time. (*Several Dances*, 87)

It is outside the house, an abject place, a place of relief and admission, consonant with Kavanagh's rueful "I am King / of banks and stones and every blooming thing" in "Inniskeen Road". There's a sense that you can't go any lower and there's a comfort in that: "Maybe a year since suddenly I began / sipping hot tea in a cold shed" (*Several Dances*, 110).

It's a familiar space, from the days of the watchman's hut:

> *And then I woke up. I was at a table in a*
> *small shed on a building site in Dublin. It*
> *was 1983 and I'd just written the words: "Site*
> *normal. Nothing to report" in the logbook.* (*Livelihood*, 65)

The shed is a workroom, a place of making: "intent at desk in shed. relaxed / at table. reading in bed. working" (*Several Dances*, 16). It does scald that this work is not productive of cash:

> give me some money. give me some
> money to live. I'm willing to work.
> I'm willing to work well. I'm willing
> to work well and apply what talents
>
> I have to the job. you will not get all
> of me no but then I'll not get all of yr
> money. give me some money. give
>   me some money now.   (*Several Dances*, 17)

Where the house is indistinct, and barely defined, the shed is the bottom-line. It is very real and understood: "that's a roof / over my head not a leprachaun's inkcap" (*Sonata*, 22).

More than a poet of interior spaces, Scully is a poet of the liminal. In this sense, the shed is perfect. The skin of the shed barely separates inside from outside. You can see light through the walls even if there are no windows. The rain almost falls on you but is stopped by the thin roof.

The shed is also monk's cell, "yr hut-in-hiding" (*Several Dances*, 53), a parenthesis, nonetheless material for being spiritual. You can smell the shed, while you just glimpse the clutter of the house. In the shed, unlike the house, there is a sense of palimpsest. The shed, definitively transient, is a kind of constant. You can be as bitter as you like in the shed, it has nothing to do with the shed:

>   in this
> particular out-building to the Forgotten
> Gaelic Tradition I find that Blackbird of
> Anywhere-At-All quite likely to be in two
>
> minds on one branch. leaf-swish. between
> your dictionary & its air-shapes, an inter-
> mission. try harder. bigger vistas, less
> credulity. *cementery* is good. yes?
>
> sing Amor. (*Tig*, 29–30)

The shed is a redolent fact. There's more than a grim satisfaction in this being the marginalised space for a marginalised art in a marginalised tradition, not just poetry or Irish poetry in English – but experimental Irish poetry in English. You win the trophy and stigma of "Art Made in a Shed" (*Several Dances*, 90). There is no rent to pay. No-one wants to work here. It is absolutely ideal for the purposes of invention:

> here you are
> in a shed in a garden
> in the cold wondering what's
> the next
> move
>
> (in a trap) (*Several Dances*, 35)

The shed is a place of work but also a child's hut, a place of solitude and making-up. The shed, a temporary structure by definition, may not travel in time exactly but time travels through it, modulating Scully's modernism with postcolonial Ireland's tenant legacy. As with De Certeau's renters, Scully knows "how to insinuate [his] countless differences into the dominant text" (De Certeau xxii).

Auden, having a house, writes a book *About the House*. Scully, craving a house, writes a book about the house too, not in the sense of *regarding, concerning, respecting* but *around, throughout, over, through, on every side of*. Scully plots, plans, lays out, installs, constructs, and decorates his house within the book. And then invites us to visit: "a book if you can afford it / is a fat paper object / & it can open anywhere" (*Livelihood*, 43).

There is a sense in which nothing quite rivals the success of the blank page:

> The paper is open. ▢   (*Humming*, 67)

Scully's books offer a luxuriance of space. There are pages with nothing but space; diamond-shaped stanzas remind us that space is the setting; the space between words can be opened and shut like a fan. We know this house is built in the air. If it were a real house, it would be made of glass and full of light:

> parquet
>
> white   wall
>
> parquet
>
> white wall   blue window
>
> parquet
>
> blue window   square picture
>
> parquet
>
> picture parquet

                    square wall

    picture picture picture picture picture

                DOOR (*Humming*, 62)

He is greedy for space, to the extent that he can't resist compartmentalizing, delaying his approach, and demonstrating equal reluctance to leave, repeatedly repurposing titles, and lines.

As an architect, Scully is a minimalist, a wit, making follies of his glass boxes, generous with blank pages, extravagant with tiny detail. The drive to ornament, to hint, to pun, to derive joy from the story of Johnny McGory, ensures that things will never be quite "picture parquet". There will always be some sedition nudging into life, keeping the minimalism fertile, tumbling into the lattice, sphagnum, host of golden raffle-tickets, mesh of possibility.

The table of contents of *Tig* (2006) is both building and poem (see overleaf).

These books have many entrances and exits, foyers and back halls, structural performances of a recursivity and indirection imbued in Irish culture – the downplaying of arrival, obligatory sheathing of any request, and near-impossibility of dislodging a departing visitor from the step.

And of course *Tig* closes with an encapsulation of the three book project, *Things That Happen* which of course has a coda (*Tig*) which of course contains everything else, head and body and limbs, as well as its inclusive self. *The Basic Colours, Zulu Dynamite, Priority, Steps*, and *Adherence* precede *Livelihood*, which contains them. *Things That Happen* becomes *A Tour of the Lattice* and *Doing the Same in English* as the city limits are re-drawn. The old structures hum and dance and work alongside the new books.

Actually, Scully's book project is a conurbation, with neighbourhoods organized in retrospect. His houses are a library, disordered after work.

The books are meticulously planned, considerately sectioned, divided, subdivided, and numbered, the poems obligingly titled ("Sonnet" or "Song" or "Rain") but can you genuinely find your way around? It's Borgesian, OuLiPoean, both planned and haywire, with parallelism, doubling back, intersections and loops, signposts bearing the same names pointing to different things. The naming project is intense

Contents

Stepping	7
I.	
[Blessing the Animals]	11
II.	
[Backyard]	17
[Waterway]	20
[Backyard]	25
III.	
[A Falling Leaf]	33
[Picking Persimmon]	35
Coda	
[A Place to Stay]	43
Sonnet	46
Coda Coda	
Sonnet Ode: Blessing the Animals	51
Bread	59
I.	61
II.	67
III.	75
Coda	81
Coda Coda	93
[A Place. To Stay]	95
Notes	101

but to what end? Citations become their own poetic form, nested like a url. The outcome is paradoxical: on the one hand, apprehension of the collective rather than the particular (which is paradoxical in itself given the emphasis on particularity); and on the other, the simultaneous Apollonian and Dionysian character of the work.

In *Humming* (2009), the first new book after *Things That Happen*, the table of contents is a poem, slipped in before the title page, a miracle of function and form:

CONTENTS

Song	9
Song	23
Ballad	29
Sonnet	41
Ballad	59
Song	65
Song	71
Jam	79
Coda	91

How is this gleaming orb drawn from this nest?

"Nest", Louis Scully, Several Dances *cover image (2013)*

It's tempting to see English as the house and Irish as the shed – "The clutter of yr shed is different / from yr English language, no? Yes" (*Sonata*, 100). But it's not so much the language, or the cultural and political divide. It's more the difficulty of any art, emerging from confusion and myriad possibilities:

> Years of grinding technique roll back
> to be imploded through one or two pages
> of pure fire. (100)

'stands outside events'

The shed is a place and space of practice, in De Certeau's terms. It is not proper enough to be simply a place. So it is a space:

> A space exists when one takes into consideration vectors of direction, velocities, and time variables. Thus space is composed of intersections of mobile elements. It is in a sense actuated by the ensemble of movements deployed within it. Space occurs as the effect produced by the operations that orient it, situate

> it, temporalise it, and make it function in a polyvalent unity of conflictual programs or contractual proximities. (117)

You can see De Certeau inch crablike sideways claiming space in the act of describing it. He goes on to relate space to the spoken word:

> On this view, in relation to place, space is like the word when it is spoken, that is, when it is caught in the ambiguity of an actualization, transformed into a term dependent upon many different conventions, situated as the act of a present (or of a time), and modified by the transformation caused by successive contexts. In contradistinction to the place, it has none of the univocality or stability of a "proper". (117)

Sound and vision are sensibilities, ways to see or sound or snare the thing. They are not the thing. They are all verb, compatible as the many processes of a living body are compatible, active in the act of reading:

> In short, space is a practiced space. Thus the street geometrically defined by urban planning is transformed into a space by walkers. In the same way, an act of reading is the space produced by the practice of a particular place: a written text, i.e., a place constituted by a system of signs. (117)

III

As important as the shed is the path between the house and shed. There is a joy in taking the shining line, in the early morning, in solitude:

> You'd slept well and rose immediately,
> kettle on, bundle of papers out to your shed
> at the end of the garden through the dewy grass.
> In detail and proliferation (hoverfly's
> pulsing abdomen, secret nectary opened out)
> a ladybird beetle ambling past through
> the proliferate grass. Is that the word for it?
> A woodlouse dropped off a door-jamb, so quiet you
> could hear it drop. (*Livelihood*, 196)

And you get to do it again:

> You rise of a morning, early, shirt,
> underpants, pants, sandals, in the half-light,
> quiet. Toilet. Downstairs through hall,
> kitchen on tip-toe, through the garden
> to the shed at the back of the house
> with your bundle of papers. Beginning
> is a change of sound and that changes things,
> and things tell each other where you are and
> how to be and—how do you feel about that?
> Blackbird on a wall. (*Doing the Same in English*, 34)

And again:

>   If you
> wake in the morning overjoyed before a tide of worries in the
>   dark.   If the smell of rain in the air brings rain. (*Sonata*, 13)

The path to the shed is as much the real thing as the shed, and as magical. It is worn by practice, and cuts both ways. The shed is a lot of things. It is ignominious. It is a relief. It is a soft rock bottom. It is a hut, an outhouse, a work place, a cell. But Scully is not a monk. There is a house, rented, borrowed, mortgaged, coveted, crowded. And there is a path over the grass between the two, inside the garden walls, with the city on the other side. Whether the enclave is in Africa or Rathmines, the dilemma is the same: the space of poetry *vs* the space of family. Scully's achievement is not so much the raising of the shining poem from the nest as the faithful creation of the line between house and shed. As much as any work done in the shed, the making of the path between shed and house is his daily practice.

This is the main difference between Scully's shed and the hut as represented by J.H. Prynne in his extended riff (2008) on William Collins' *Odes* (1746): Scully is intensely uxorious. For Prynne, "the hut is a marginally safe haven which connects very closely to the threatened invasion of cold and wet from the wild outside, and this is the vantage that the poet must summon courage to occupy, the distance from a settled and socialised habitation" (615). For Scully, the vantage for the occupation of which courage must be summoned is a space in tense proximity to, not at a distance from, the house.

There are other distinctions. The shed is urban, a customary appendix to the house, while the hut is bucolic, primitive, strategic. For Prynne the hut is an escape – a place of seasonal practice. For Scully the shed is aligned with the house – a place of daily practice. There's a sense too that the "settled and socialized habitation," to which Prynne's hut provides a makeshift alternative, is the owned house – Auden's house – while for Scully both house and shed are makeshift, transitional. If the hut is a meeting place of opposing forces, i.e., the lyric and the primal, the shed relinquishes such opposition. Everything is made of molecules, even letters, to quote David Jhave Johnston, with their "kinetic skins" (194).

Outside the shed is the garden, garden walls, "my friends, the sounds in the street" (*Livelihood*, 109), vague cityscape beyond, indistinct as "all the numberless goings-on of life" in Coleridge's "populous village", or the "dim-discover'd Spires" of William Collins' "Ode to Evening". The shops, the post box, the places where bills are paid, the city, the country, the encounter in the street have a vagueness in no way to be compared to the vivid light and dust of the shed, and the rain on its roof.

The main thing that's outside the shed is the rain. And it's just barely outside. If the roof is tin the sound of the rain is amplified. Only a thin sheath separates inside from outside. Rain is a web, a drizzle, a reticle, a *calligramme*, a mesh. It is another kind of path. Learning may not be wholly real for Scully (despite his name), or memory, and questions may not "*really* exist" (*Sonata*, 74). But rain is real, and Scully knows exactly what it is:

> water falling from the sky
> is one of the most
> important of all
> of all phenomena that make life
> life possible on land
> possible (*Livelihood*, 95)

Rain is the very embodiment of small drops that make things happen. Rain, shimmering, has certainty, and uncertainty in equal part – a definition of evanescence, particularity, pattern, surprise, velocity, fertility:

> Tentative rain, contending
> rain, unbending rain, amending rain, attentive rain,
> a tent. Of rain. Question-mark, dart and date. Point,
> hack. Circles and arrows. Flint instruments. Needled,
> need I say, a stolen music. Not poetry. The point is:
> *hand over those beautiful garbles.* City washed and
> scintillant after it, a gully opening up. (*Livelihood*, 157)

Hesitation and repetition of attempt are what save Scully's minimalism from sterility. It becomes lavish, fanning into variation, fertilizing itself. "Patterns of scratches on the / surface of my desk" (*Sonata*, 58); "paring a pencil / carefully, its / frill, its dark // dust"; "sharp-pointed // curves" of the nail clippings "cut with / pleasure thinking / together into a / little heap" – "all these little pieces" can be watched, tilted, "shifting sideways" slightly (*Sonata*, 59–61), to make.

And it is the maker's privilege to see tiny differences. In poetry, we are sensitive to the weight of a comma. Likewise, an image-maker registers dimensionality accorded by practice. Still photos are not still to the photographer who sees photography, no less than cinematography, as a time-based art, every image staged both in production and perception. Robert Rauschenberg referred to his flat white paintings as clocks which could be read – "If one were sensitive enough ... you would know how many people were in the room, what time it was, and what the weather was like outside".

'a misreading to some degree'

In poetry, there's no shame in misreading. As a way to get somewhere, misreading has a part to play. In Linda Bierds' delicious "Lawrence and Edison in New Jersey: 1923", Edison, deaf, hears everything in terms of "motion and sound", while Lawrence sees everything, past and present, in terms of the image. Together, mishearing every word the other says, they produce the finale of the poem, each with his own set of lines, his own thrilling denouement, as they sit close to one another, ear to confounded ear. Maurice Scully's poetry is ruffled by its own misreadings. Small, incremental adjustments serrate what is seen and what is heard. Slippage is a lubricant, integral to the dynamics of the poetics:

> Having shed clutter, to the next house go, with a light
> pocket, a light heart, a light touch, a fire in the mind,
> and a plan, lightly carried, as lightly let go.
> *(Doing the Same in English*, 49)

Works Cited

Auden, W. H. *About the House*. New York, NY: Random House, (1959) 1965.
Bachelard, Gaston. *The Poetics of Space*. Trans. Maria Jolas. New York, NY: Penguin Books, 2014.
Baker, Tony. Email. 11/27/17.
———. Email. 11/28/17.
———. Note to *5 Freedoms of Movement*. Buckfastleigh: etruscan books, 2001.
Bierds, Linda. "Lawrence and Edison in New Jersey: 1923". *The Profile Makers*. New York, NY: Henry Holt & Company, 1997. 47–48.
Coleridge, Samuel Taylor. "Frost at Midnight". *Complete Poems*. London: Penguin, 1997. 231.
de Certeau, Michel. *The Practice of Everyday Life*. Trans. Steven Randall. Berkeley, Los Angeles, CA & London: University of California Press, 1988.
Hartnett, Michael. *Inchicore Haiku*. Dublin: Raven Arts Press, 1985.
Johnston, David Jhave. *Aesthetic Animism: Digital Poetry's Ontological Implications*. Cambridge, MA: The MIT Press, 2016.
Kavanagh, Patrick. "Inniskeen Road". *Collected Poems*. New York, NY & London: W.W. Norton, 1973.
McGuire, Richard. *Here*. New York: Pantheon Books & Random House, 2014.
Prynne, J. H. "Huts". *Textual Practice* 22:4 (2008): 613–633.
Rauschenberg, Robert. Quoted in Jiehao Su, Rhode Island School of Design MFA in Photography thesis draft, March 2018. <https://www.sfmoma.org/artwork/98.308.A-C/research-materials/document/WHIT_98.308_005/#transcript>.
Scully, Maurice. *5 Freedoms of Movement*. Buckfastleigh: etruscan books, (1987) 2001.
———. *Doing the Same in English*. Dublin: Dedalus Press, 2008.
———. *Humming*. Exeter: Shearsman Books, 2009.
———. *Livelihood*. Bray, Co. Wicklow: Wild Honey Press, 2004.
———. *Several Dances*. Bristol: Shearsman Books, 2014.

——. *Sonata*. Hastings: Reality Street Editions, 2006.
——. *Tig*. Exeter: Shearsman Books, 2006.
——. *A Tour of the Lattice*. London: Veer Books, 2011.
Whitman, Walt. "Crossing Brooklyn Ferry". *Poetry Foundation*. <https://www.poetryfoundation.org/poems/45470/crossing-brooklyn-ferry>. Accessed 28th May 2019.

Between the "Canon" and "Oblivion": Looking in the Books of Maurice Scully

Philip Coleman

> *When you open your notebook to begin again*
> *and a shadow-image of a pen descending in a*
> *dream to dream-paper entering a dream-place,*
> *shadow over shadow, shivering, to that space in*
> *silence that cradles a deeper silence out of time,*
> *again, opens, you open a notebook, flat, and again,*
> *begin.*
>
> Maurice Scully, "PROPS" from *Play Book*

1. Beginning with *Marvell*?

Looking in Maurice Scully's first book, *Love Poems & Others*, published by Raven Arts Press in 1981, the first thing one sees – after Leo Duffy's striking cover photographs[1] – is an epigraph, placed before the first section of the book begins, taken from Andrew Marvell's poem "The Garden":

> *Mean while the Mind, from pleasure less,*
> *Withdraws into its happiness:*
> *The Mind, that Ocean where each kind*
> *Does streight its own resemblance find;*
> *Yet it creates, transcending these,*
> *Far other Worlds, and other Seas;*
> *Annihilating all that s made*
> *To a green Thought in a green Shade.* (*Love Poems & Others*, 4)

---

[1] Leo Duffy is credited with both the cover design and the photography used in *Love Poems & Others*. The front cover image – a black-and-white photograph of sunlight flooding a room containing what looks like an old-fashioned perambulator and a single bed standing against a wall – provides an interesting visual backdrop of urban dereliction for the poems in the book itself. The back cover image of Scully reading a poem (presumably) is also striking.

The gesture – represented here exactly as it appears in the book, in italics and retaining some of the original spelling – is perhaps an unexpected one when considered in the light of the poet's later work, though it is important to note that *Things That Happen*, which would not be completed until 2006, was started around the same time that *Love Poems & Others* appeared. What did happen between the publication of *Love Poems & Others* in 1981 and *5 Freedoms of Movement*, the first instalment of *Things That Happen*, in 1987? To look at and into the two books is to encounter two very different approaches to the art of poetry – so much so that readers rarely consider the earlier volume as anything more than juvenilia. While the poems gathered in *Love Poems & Others* are strikingly unlike his later works, however, not least because it is a "collection of poems" in a way that no other book by him is, the book nonetheless establishes a number of important contexts within which the development of the poet's later work may be positioned. Beginning *Love Poems & Others* with Marvell, Scully flags a project of close and complex engagement with the history of Anglophone poetry – and literature in general – that has expanded in unexpected and radical ways in the course of his career. Looking in the books of this poet, in short, is to find oneself continually directed towards other books – books by the poet himself, at times, as one finds when reading through the "books" that comprise *Things That Happen* – but also the books of other writers (and not just the books of other poets).

This makes sense for a poet who has claimed that his unit of composition is the book: "books" matter to the way we read Scully's work in the same way that the breath mattered for Charles Olson, say, or the image occupied a central position in the poetics of Ezra Pound.[2] *Love Poems & Others*, then, inaugurates a career committed to the idea that the book in and of itself may constitute a fundamental unit of measure in poetry, and it achieves this partly by establishing the self of the poet "Between Towers of Books", as Scully writes in "Piece for viola", from Part II of his first collection (*Love Poems & Others*, 23). Divided into four parts – the final comprised of a single, revealing poem entitled "En Route", in which the speaker imagines himself and another "Tinkering with the time and the space of the future and wishing they'd burst / And send us careering backwards into ourselves in reverse" (*Love Poems & Others*, 40) – the volume displays a degree of

---

[2] Scully says that his "unit of composition is the book rather than the poem" in his reading at Unnameable Books in Brooklyn on March 10, 2018.

bookish self-reflexivity that is most obviously conveyed, and reinforced, by its opening sonnet, "Lake Garda". Unlike the sonnets Scully would go on to write in his later volumes – the exploded sonnets in *Steps* (1994) or *Sonata* (2006), for example, or pieces such as "Sonnet: Print" and "Sonnet: On Tiptoe" in *Several Dances* (2014) – "Lake Garda" appears to appropriate a more traditional formal template of fourteen lines and a regular rhyme scheme. It begins *in medias res* – relating things as they are in the process of happening – and it quickly becomes clear that the poem represents the final section of a letter:

> Then crossing the mountains we got stranded one night
> In a deserted wooden chapel where I lit
> Squat candles and looked at the *Ex Voto* pictures.
> We slept at last in a hay hut and woke at dawn
> In, as it seemed, an Alpine pot with a high, green
> Meadow for a bottom. Language a damn stricture
> Though we finally got this tranquil spot on Lake
> Garda. Peach, bamboo and Catullus. While I make
> Friends with his fine wife, Frieda chats old Pietro
> The landlord. Do come. Or send somebody you know
> Would like a holiday. Am hugely pleased about
> *Love Poems & Others*. Only F. thinks they are
> Trivial. Naturally she wants the ones about
> Herself to blossom forth. Yours, of course, as ever…
> (*Love Poems & Others*, 6)

But who is speaking here, and who are these characters, Frieda and Pietro? Could it be that this poem relates in some way to D.H. Lawrence, who spent a period of time living at Lake Garda in Italy in the second decade of the twentieth century with his wife (Frieda) and who, indeed, published a book entitled *Love Poems and Others* – "and" not "&" – in 1913? A little bibliographical sleuthing leads one to the first volume of Lawrence's correspondence, in which one finds a letter, written to Edward Garnett in September 1912, containing many of the details (the peach and the bamboo are there, but not Catullus) and whole phrases used in Scully's poem. Here is the letter's conclusion: "I am hugely pleased about *Love Poems and Others* – and I shall correct the proofs in Gargnano. What bliss. Only F. thinks they are trivial poems. She wants those concerning herself to blossom forth" (Lawrence 454).

Scully's *Love Poems & Others*, then, replaces Lawrence's *Love Poems and Others* in his (Scully's) transposition and poetic reorganisation of the Lawrentian text, but the introduction of the English Edwardian writer into the frame of reference, following Marvell, signals the young Irish poet's desire to begin his poetic project outside of a local or national cultural frame of reference. This is a writer having fun with the canon, as it were, but where is he going with it? Scully responds to certain themes introduced by Marvell's "The Garden" in the poems of his first volume. In "Bachelor's Walk", for example, the desire to retreat from the cares of the world into a space of creative meditation is dramatized in a manner that recalls the withdrawal of the mind from the inferior pleasures of physical experience in Marvell's poem. Spurning those "otherwise stupendous individuals, these boring / couples embracing along the quays [...] all talc and *noli me tangere*", Scully's vision is directed towards the abstract, towards a position of "delicious solitude," to use Marvell's term, where art – here represented in the musical form of a "Pavane" (replete with Poundian associations[3]) – is singled out as "an end" in itself that surpasses the expectations of the "pillars of society":

> Beauty is difficult:
> A climax – sea-hammerings at Killiney,
> Ribboning neon in the river in the night,
> And an end – Rimbaud in agony at Marseille,
> Pavane. (*Love Poems & Others*, 22)

This poem, "Bachelor's Walk", is a kind of *anti*-epithalamium that participates in Lawrence's dismantling of conventional views about love and romance – "The parasites, the guests panting for the telegrams and speeches and applause and public maternal tears" (*Love Poems & Others*, 22) – but on other occasions, too, it has to be said that Scully's first collection is reminiscent of the "pre-raphaelitish slush" that Pound rebuked in Lawrence's debut volume (Pound 149). This, in a way, is part of the fun of it, notwithstanding the mild embarrassment lines such as these, from a poem called "1968," might cause Scully today:

> Margaret Dunne.
> I name you for the magic of it,

---

[3] New Directions Press published a volume of Pound's "lighter" verse under the title *Pavanes & Divagations* in 1975.

> Your marvellous school uniform
> Still on. (*Love Poems & Others*, 30)[4]

These poems, in other words, are attuned to the emotional and aesthetic registers and interests of the volume's named precursors – Marvell, Lawrence, Rimbaud – but it is not simply that Scully is struggling here to find a way out from under the influence of these and other figures in some kind of Oedipal quarrel, as a Bloomian reading of these engagements might have it.[5] What he terms the "pleasurable passageway to discovery" in "Spring song of hope", moreover, is not just the journey into sexual consciousness anticipated by the young male poet in "1968" (*Love Poems & Others*, 33). It is also the realisation that books by other writers may form an important and positive part of his creative emergence over and above the vicissitudes of his own private, intimate experience.

This may seem like an obvious discovery. Poets read and sometimes the things they read make it into their poems. In *Love Poems & Others*, however, the traces of Scully's early reading in non-Irish literature, in particular, flag the development of an intertextual technique that will evolve into a profoundly complex and engaging method over the next few decades. Beginning with Marvell, and directing the reader in playful, allusive ways towards other writers along the way – Catullus, Rimbaud, Lawrence, and many more – *Love Poems & Others* is a book in which Scully demands that the reader work with the books of other writers if they are to fully understand what is going on in his poetry. For readers familiar with T.S. Eliot's insistence that "poets in our civilization, as it exists at present, must be *difficult*", this will not come as a surprise, but for all of their ostensible surface simplicity Scully is decidedly a poet writing with a modernist conception of poetic complexity (Eliot 65; emphasis in original). As Eliot puts it: "The poet must become

---

[4] Dermot Bolger, who published Scully's *Love Poems & Others*, quoted from this poem in his review of Pat Boran and Gerard Smyth's anthology *If Ever You Go: A Map of Dublin in Poetry and Song* (Dublin: Dedalus, 2014), in Dublin's *Evening Herald* in March 2014. The review can be found online at: https://www.herald.ie/lifestyle/if-you-ever-go-to-dublin-town-youre-likely-to-meet-a-poet-30079037.html.

[5] The key text in which Harold Bloom outlines his theory of poetic misreading, in which Nietzsche and Freud are "the prime influences," is of course *The Anxiety of Influence: A Theory of Poetry* (2nd ed. Oxford: Oxford University Press, 1997).

more and more comprehensive, more allusive, more indirect, in order to force, to dislocate if necessary, language into his meaning" (65). As one moves from *Love Poems & Others* to Scully's later books, it becomes clear that he has absorbed the full force of Eliot's injunction.

It is for this reason, then, that the "lyrics" of *Love Poems & Others* are already moving away from the traditional lyrical domain of their inception at the very moment of their arrival – in the same year, importantly, that Scully was starting to work on *Things That Happen*. Refusing, ultimately, the sentimental, and resisting an inclination towards straightforward lyric autobiography, Scully's first book anticipates an escape that is brilliantly confirmed by the poet's subsequent output, but this is a far cry from the poet sitting in a "dingy room in Parnell's Square teaching English equivalents of idiocy to the adolescent offspring of the Spanish upper-bourgeoisie," as he puts it in "Piece for viola" (*Love Poems & Others*, 23). In a related poem, "Private tuition," he writes:

> Wings of jet-planes tip and fold over the crystalline outlines of
>   the Alps,
> Ice sunshine of the extremities of speed and comprehension where
>   clocks compute between our problems.
> In twenty years you'll barely be my age, sonny.
> No, no.... sit down in this bar and fly, said Soul to Body.
>   (*Love Poems & Others*, 37)

The "Alps" here could be compared to the "glaciers" and "crags" of Pound's *Cantos*, as Basil Bunting thought of that long work (Bunting 110). Scully, in other words, is not anticipating the beginning of a life to be spent among the jet-set in "Private tuition". Rather, the poem – which is about self-instruction as much as it concerns the business of teaching other people – describes the poet's realisation that he must embark on a difficult course of discovery that will lead him towards his own unique form of "comprehension" (the term echoes Eliot's formulation). Scully learns this lesson, in the early stages of his career, less through the activity of actual travel – although he is a well-travelled poet who has lived for periods of time in countries such as Italy, Spain and Lesotho – than he does through the process of engaging in deep ways with other writers and their books. Part of the pleasure of reading him, in turn, is due to the ways in which he engages creatively, and often radically, with the works of others.

2. "between the paper and the trees": From Crane to Samperi

Scully's use of D.H. Lawrence's letter to Edward Garnett at the start of *Love Poems & Others* signals an interest in writers' letters that is picked up in another of the book's key poems, "But I'll rest up on the boat" which, a footnote explains, takes its title from *"Hart Crane's last letter before his (presumed) suicide by drowning"* (*Love Poems & Others*, 36; italics in original). Crane's luxuriant language and excessive style is echoed throughout the poems of Scully's first volume, and in some ways the early twentieth-century US American poet is a dangerous role model for a young poet – just as dangerous, perhaps, as Lawrence. *5 Freedoms of Movement* represents a decisive break with these figures in many ways, however, and the notion of "movement" in itself is useful as a way of marking the formal distance between the lyrics of *Love Poems & Others* and the more expansive texts within the later work. The photographs included in *5 Freedoms of Movement* place a particular emphasis on the activity of jumping. Yves Klein's remarkable image of a man leaping from a building onto a suburban street, before the book's opening section ("unauthorised credits") finds an interesting parallel in Eadweard Muybridge's front- and side-profile photographs of an athletic figure preparing to do the long jump just before the concluding section ("one wallflower") (*5 Freedoms*, 5, 75). The movement represented by these figures vacillates between death and energetic well-being: Klein's figure is, presumably, about to commit suicide, while Muybridge's man is the very picture, as it were, of masculine health and vigour.

As one turns from Scully's first book to his second, then, one is struck very forcefully by the poet's decisive movements in form and style, and the title of *5 Freedoms of Movement* announces this at the same time that it numbers the five parts ("A" to "E") of its "Contents" (*5 Freedoms*, 89). While the book is formally very different from the one that precedes it, however, it still records the poet's concern with the business of writing – including the difficulty of surviving as a writer while trying to bring up a young family – and it also directs the reader towards certain books that informed its production. The following piece from Section E of *5 Freedoms* (the section is called "two caterpillars") is interesting because it explicitly records the poet's emergence into a new kind of critical awareness regarding the formal and thematic possibilities for his work:

> between the paper & the trees where the sun
> gets through between the branches to the grass
> under a leaf on a curving stem – the pseudo-fairytale
> before the 'lyrics'/two actors play beforehand too –
> how's this? a girl goes by from elsewhere
> to set street music its cryptic rhythm against another
> how you can live to a different beat an old radio
> in a hut on a deserted building site paid little to
> live & as to writing/well! but between stations
> to pick up the possible & go on with that from there
> (*5 Freedoms*, 64)

There is so much going on here, but the text brings together a number of concerns that recur throughout Scully's work, including the relationship between the natural world and the world of art – "between the paper & the trees" – and the disconnection the artist feels between the desire to make art, on the one hand, and the pressure to make ends meet, on the other.

The piece may be said, also, to question the status and value of Scully's earlier "lyrics" and to provide a "cryptic" account of the poetic re-tuning of his poetic voice and approach as these were being reconfigured by him in the making of *5 Freedoms of Movement*. Marking an even more radical departure from the canonical poets flagged in *Love Poems & Others*, this piece dramatises the poet caught up in a process of fundamental re-invention, tuning into "stations" of suggestion that include, for example, R.J. Harrison's *Textbook for Medicine with Relevant Physiology and Anatomy* (1977) and Michael Tweedie's *Insect Life* (1977), as well as poems by Lee Harwood, Gianni Rodari and William Bronk. These sources are revealed in the "Notes" section of *5 Freedoms of Movement*, but they prompt the reader to move beyond the confines of the given text, to seek out these and other texts in order to perceive the bigger picture of Scully's project. Looking into *5 Freedoms of Movement* – especially in the first Galloping Dog Press edition – is to experience poetry as visual art as much as it is to encounter a printed, verbal text. The poet's interest in and commitment to the visual is marked everywhere in the text, most importantly in the drawings by him that are given on the covers and endpapers, based on North African cave paintings, and in the reproduction of images by Klein, Muybridge and others, as mentioned above. The textual material, however, is also explicitly concerned with the activities of looking, seeing, and *reading* – with the business of relating one's textual experience of certain books, drawn from a wide range of interests, to the observed world as it appears "where the sun / gets through between the branches to the grass / under a leaf on a curving stem" (*5 Freedoms*, 64). The word "leaf" here, of course, suggests both a blade of grass and the page of a book.

It is one thing for a poet to reveal their sources, however, and quite another to say precisely how a cited text relates to a larger poetic artwork. In relation to Scully's earlier poems, the problem is not quite so vexed: the connections with Lawrence in "Lake Garda", for example, or Crane in "But I'll rest up on the boat," are fairly easy to untangle. The problem becomes more difficult in *5 Freedoms of Movement* because the domain of reference becomes larger, encompassing not only literary figures but also visual artists, entomologists and anatomists. In a sense, then, Scully's range of influence expands beyond the literary sphere, or to put it the other way around, the literary sphere is expanded to accommodate others, so that his poetic method is increasingly born out of a sense of the connection between the process of observing the world, on the one hand, and recognising the ways in which various textual reproductions of those observations function in our consciousness, on the other. For Scully, if "living" is "writing" then *reading* is also synonymous with the experience of existence. Reading Scully, then, is not merely a matter of appreciating the poet's representations of nature, domesticity, and so on. While it is true that many of his works do provide interesting and illuminating insights into various aspects of experience, they are more fundamentally concerned with the problem and process of representing the world in itself – with the activity, which is constant, of reading what one finds as one opens one's eyes on the world of immediate sensory perception:

> A quality when the sky opens
> cloudless in early morning
> November and your breath stays
> around and the laketop's flat
> and receptive to light that comes
> clear through otherwise
> hills melting into cloud
> is that a heron?
> stripped from the sky

leafless treetops in pools
in the road in the sky

silver grey brown green (*5 Freedoms*, 25)

Sight and the delineation of details in a landscape reduce here to colours, but the process performed by this text affirms the importance of seeing the world as a matter of paying readerly attention to it, while not necessarily being sure what all of its separate details mean. When Scully's speaker asks "is that a heron?" he continues to read the world before him, even if he is unsure how to identify or understand its constituent parts and inhabitants exactly.

Leaves and sunlight recur throughout *5 Freedoms of Movement* as signal motifs – culminating in "[a]n erotic dream of green / where each leaf is different" in the work's closing section ("E": "one wallflower," *5 Freedoms*, 77) – but Scully is no botanist. Rather, as Billy Mills has put it, "this is a poetry of learning to live with and in the world, not of explaining and improving on it" (Mills, "Sustainable Poetry"). The poet reveals some of the texts that informed the making of *5 Freedoms of Movement* in the "Notes" section of that work, then, because he wants the reader to be aware of the materials that have helped him in his own encounters with the strangeness of the world around him. This is a very different way of thinking about the poet's engagements with sources to what one encounters in his first volume, and it also points to the development of an intertextual method that is central to his later artistic practice. As Marthine Satris has observed, this poetry represents "the interaction of the writer's reflecting mind with [...] daily life": since the writer's reading is a central part of his "reflecting mind", consequently, it is no surprise that the poet's work should point us, in direct but also in oblique ways, towards the books that he has himself looked into in the process of making his poetry (Satris 1).

This process is present to Scully's early work in the gestures his poems make to the books of others, but it is extended in important ways later on. Is this a matter of chance? In a piece called "Sunlight" from *Several Dances* (2014) – a book that echoes *5 Freedoms of Movement* in its reproduction of several details, textual and visual, from the earlier work – he writes:

> ... Stand back, invent. Back-to-back. Meant. Stand.
> *I dteanga an ghasúir—rince.*
> In the child's folding land-ridge—long ago & far away—echoes
> echo everywhere. Everywhere. So.
> Solid. Blend. Sink. Breathe. Chance. (*Several Dances*, 23)

Invention is one part of the process of making art, the poet suggests, but the work of art, once made, may also echo and have folded within its structures experiences, memories, and ideas that took place "long ago & far away". On one level, then, "Sunlight" in *Several Dances* concerns what the poem calls "the circle of the mind", but it also echoes the sunlight "between the branches" in *5 Freedoms of Movement* and, further back, the light flooding into the room on the cover of *Love Poems & Others*. As the American poet Frank Samperi puts it, in a text used as an epigraph to *Several Dances*: "Sunlight is / on things" (Samperi 2; Scully 9). Who owns the sunlight, though, and where does it originate? Is the Irish poet's "Sunlight" the same as Samperi's? As with his earlier transposition of a private text written by D.H. Lawrence in "Lake Garda", Scully's sense of the world in his later work is formed in profound ways by his reading of other poets and, indeed, by his incorporation of their texts into the composition of his own texts.

Scully's engagement with Samperi in *Several Dances* is related to the Irish poet's broader dialogue with US American poetic culture, and one of the pleasures of reading him is precisely this interest in figures who do not always make it into the anthologies of the mainstream. The Samperi epigraph opens up a network of textual and cultural possibility and exchange – Williams, Zukofsky, Reznikoff, Oppen – but specifically Samperi's own *The Prefiguration* (1971), itself part of a project that "reconciles the interior vision of Dante and the objectivist [sic] fact of American poetry in light of Zukofsky and Williams", as John Martone has argued (Samperi ix). In an important sense, then, Scully is not only in dialogue with Samperi in *Several Dances*, but the quotation from Samperi's work invites the reader to read Samperi and Scully *both* in relation to a broader network of artists that extends back at least as far as Dante. Scully's work invites us to engage with other writers and their ideas through this bibliographic prompting, but it is also one of the ways in which his art accrues meaning, through a process of dialogue with others, of being-in-the-world as reader. Indeed, Scully is a "knowing reader" in the way that Martone has described those who read and admired Samperi – Robert Creeley, Robert Kelly, Will Petersen and others (Samperi vii). Like them, Scully is a poet for whom the process of making poetry involves deep knowledge of other writers and poets. His art is not that of the observing ego operating in splendid isolation but, rather, it is born out of a sense of the creative self as a student engaged in the process of continuous, often scholarly, reading of others. As Robert Kelly has said of Samperi:

> He used the word study to identify this night labor of his. While the rest of us were experimenting among the nocturnals with passions and potions, he was studying the masters. Aristotle, Aquinas, Shankara the acharya he spoke of as his masters, and Dante, closest of all. He wrote from among their company, not as a modern going back for insight and system, but as one of their contemporaries…. (Samperi xi)

As we look into his books from *Love Poems & Others* through to *Several Dances*, and beyond, it is clear that Scully is a poet less concerned with describing his experiments "among the nocturnals" than he is with using poetry to map his journey in knowledge, through his engagements with figures ranging, for example, from Hart Crane to Frank Samperi. Scully assumes his place among these poets, and many other kinds of writers, as a student but also as a peer. Only by looking into his work as students, however, can we begin to appreciate the depth and range of his labours.

3. "Between Towers of Books" (2018): Bibliographical Interlude

On the first day of March 2018, as Ireland prepared to shut down because of the arrival of Hurricane Emma and the so-called "Beast from the East", the writer and his wife Mary took one of the last flights out of Dublin bound for the United States, where the poet gave a reading at the aptly named "Unnameable Books" bookstore on Vanderbilt Avenue, Brooklyn, the following week.[6] Before he left Dublin, Scully started to clear out his writing shed – his desk and some of the surrounding shelves can be seen on the cover of *Several Dances* in a photograph

---

[6] A full recording of the reading is available on Pennsound, as listed above.

entitled "Nest", taken by his son Louis in 2013 – and he donated a few bags of books to a local charity shop.

Before two of these bags of books were brought to the shop, I had a chance to look through their contents, which are described in brief bibliographical outline here. Together they constitute a remarkable insight into the range of Scully's reading and interests going back many years. Whether he read all of these books or not – though some of the books were clearly read by him given the evidence they present in the form of annotations and other markings – they bear out the idea, explored in the preceding sections, of Scully as a scholar-poet, working out of a process of close engagement with a wide and eclectic range of other writers and thinkers.

The image of Scully writing "Between Towers of Books" occurs, as mentioned above, in his early poem "Piece for viola" (*Love Poems & Others*, 23). These, then, are just some of the books among which he has worked over the last number of decades. Many of them are works of poetry by friends and colleagues in Ireland, the United Kingdom and the United States – Harry Gilonis, Gael Turnbull, Rosmarie Waldrop, for example – while others reflect Scully's particular interest in the visual arts, music, science, and the environment. Some of the books will come as a surprise and one may well wonder what they are doing here – Peter Fallon's *Winter Work* is a case in point (prompt for an abandoned parody, perhaps?) – but the diversity of the selection as a whole is more significant than the presence of any specific text in itself. Taken together, the books complicate the idea that Scully's work can be explained in relation to any single source or influence, no matter how prominent they may be in the story of his overall development.

Alféri, Pierre. *Night and Day*. Trans. Kate Lermitte Campbell. Iowa City, IA and Paris: La Press, 2012.
Anderson, Beth. *Overboard*. Providence, RI.: Burning Deck, 2004.
Anderson, Elliott and Mary Kinzie, eds. *The Little Magazine in America: A Modern Documentary History*. Yonkers, NY: Pushcart Press, 1978.
Anon. *Go Ask Alice*. London: Prentice-Hall, 1971.
Auden, W.H. *Thank You, Fog*. London: Faber and Faber, 1974.
Behrle, Jim. *She's My Best Friend*. Boston: Pressed Wafer, 2006.
Beirne, Eric. *A Layman's Guide to Psychiatry and Psychoanalysis*. Harmondsworth, Penguin Books, 1986.
Beltrametti, Franco. *Three Poems*. [np]: Kater Murr's Press, 2005.
Bittleston, Adam and Jonathan Westphal, eds. *The Golden Blade*. London: Rudolph Steiner Press, 1982.

Blaser, Robin and Meredith Quartermain. *Wanders*. Vancouver, BC: Nomados, 2002. *Bongos of the Lord* 5 (May 1998).
Bosquet, Oscarine. *Present Participle*. Trans. Sarah Riggs and Ellen LeBlond-Schrader. Iowa City, IA and Paris: La Press, 2013.
Bradshaw, Robert. *The Fugitive Years: The True Story of a Compulsive Gambler*. Harmondsworth: Penguin Books, 1986.
Cain, Séamas. *Marannan*. Edinburgh: Forest Arts Centre, 2005.
———. *Tríd an gcoill*. Dublin: The Red Jasper, 2008.
Carpenter, Erica. *Perspective Would Have Us*. Providence, RI: Burning Deck, 2006.
Chinese Literature: Fiction, Poetry, Art (Autumn 1985).
Cobbing, Jennifer Pike. *Scrunch*. 2nd ed. London: Veer Books, 2010.
Corso, Gregory. *Mind Field*. Madras and New York: Hanuman Books, 1989.
Cross, Del Ray. *Lub Luffly*. Boston: Pressed Wafer, 2006.
Czurda, Elfriede. *Almost 1 Book. Almost 1 Life*. Trans. Rosmarie Waldrop. Providence, RI: Burning Deck, 2012.
de Buitléar, Éamon. *Wild Ireland*. Dublin: Amach Faoin Aer Publishing, 1984.
Doppelt, Suzanne. *Ring Rang Wrong*. Trans. Cole Swenson. Providence, RI: Burning Deck, 2004.
Fallon, Peter. *Winter Work*. Dublin: The Gallery Press, 1983.
Gallace, Maureen. [untitled]. Dublin: Douglas Hyde Gallery, 2004.
Gilonis, Harry. *eye-blink*. Rpt. London: Veer Books, 2011.
Grosjean, Jean. *An Earth of Time*. Trans. Keith Waldrop. Providence, RI: Burning Deck, 2006.
Harding, Gunnar. *They Killed Sitting Bull and Other Poems*. Trans. Robin Fulton. London: London Magazine Editions, 1973.
Harris, Dylan. *europe*. Portarlington: Wurm Press, [2008].
John, Laurie, ed. *Cosmology Now*. London: British Broadcasting Corporation, 1973.
Kain, Richard M. and James H. O'Brien. *George Russell (A.E.)*. Lewisburg, PA: Bucknell University Press, 1976.
Keery, Neville. *Temple Hill: A Suite of Poems*. Dublin: [privately printed], 2009.
Kenneally, Michael, ed. *Poetry in Contemporary Irish Literature*. Gerrards Cross: Colin Smythe, 1995.
Lennon, Seán. *Irish Gothic Writers: Bram Stoker and the Irish Supernatural Tradition*. Dublin: Dublin Corporation Public Libraries, [nd].
Lucas, E.V. *"The More I See Of Men...": Stray Essays on Dogs*. London: Methuen & Co., Ltd., 1930.
Lyons, J.B. *Oliver St. John Gogarty*. Lewisburg, PA: Bucknell University Press, 1976.
McCardle, Aodán, Piers Hugill and Stephen Mooney. *Shuddered*. 2nd ed. London: Veer Books, 2010.

Marriott, D.S. *Schadenfreude*. Hebden Bridge: Open Township, 1989.
Martenson, Jennifer. *Unsound*. Providence, RI: Burning Deck, 2010.
Maxwell, Gavin. *A Reed Shaken by the Wind*. London: Four Square Books, [nd].
Meadows, Deborah. *Itinerant Men*. San Francisco, CA: Krupskaya, 2004.
Muckle, John. *The Cresta Run*. Newcastle upon Tyne: Galloping Dog Press, 1987.
Ní Lamhna, Éanna. *Wild Dublin: Exploring Nature in the City*. Dublin: The O'Brien Press, 2008.
Picabia, Francis. *Who Knows: Poems and Aphorisms*. Trans. Remy Hall. Madras and New York, NY: Hanuman Books, 1986.
Prunty, Randy. *Van Gogh Talks*. Atlanta, GA: 3rdness, [nd].
Quartermain, Meredith. *Abstract Relations*. Vancouver, BC: Keefer Street Press, 1998.
Ravelle, Lou. *Fit in Three Months: An Infallible Guide to Physical Fitness for Men*. London: Four Square Books, 1965.
Rivera, Eléna. *Two Poems*. [np]: Kater Murr's Press, 2005.
Robinson, Elizabeth. *Under That Silky Sky*. Providence, RI: Burning Deck. 2006.
Roth, Gerhard. *The Will to Sickness*. Trans. Tristram Wolff. Providence, RI.: Burning Deck, 2006.
Royet-Journoud, Claude. *i.e.* Trans. Keith Waldrop. Providence, RI.: Burning Deck, 1995.
Russell, Raymond. *Early Keyboard Instruments*. London: Her Majesty's Stationery Office, 1967.
Sanders, Edward. *Thirsting for Peace in a Raging Century: Selected Poems 1961–1985*. Minneapolis, MN: Coffee House Press, 1987.
Selby, Spencer. *Barricade*. Providence, RI: Paradigm Press, 1990.
Simpson, Eileen. *Poets in the their Youth*. London: Picador, 1984.
Strong, Eithne. *Songs of Living*. Dublin: The Runa Press, 1961.
Swenson, Cole. *Numen*. Providence, RI: Burning Deck, 1995.
Tait, Neal. [untitled]. Dublin: Douglas Hyde Gallery, 2002.
Tardi, Mark. *Airport Music*. Providence, RI: Burning Deck, 2013.
The Royal Art Lodge. *Serpentine Musings*. Dublin: Douglas Hyde Gallery, 2005.
Tóibín, Colm. *The Sign of the Cross: Travels in Catholic Europe*. London: Picador, 2010.
Turnbull, Gael. *The Small Change*. Ulverston: Migrant Press, 1980.
———. *Amorous Greetings In Terms Of…*. Staines: Vennel Press, 1998.
Tyson, Nicola. *Where Laughter Comes In*. Dublin: Douglas Hyde Gallery, 2005.
Waldrop, Rosmarie. *Psyche & Eros*. Peterborough: Spectacular Diseases, 1980.

Waterhouse, Peter. *Language Death Night Outside: Poem Novel*. Trans.
  Rosmarie Waldrop. Providence, RI: Burning Deck, 2009.
Wilkinson, John. *Proud Flesh*. Łodz: Equofinality and Liverpool: Délires, 1986.
Williamson, Aaron. *A Holythroat Symposium*. London: Creation Press, 1992.
Zambaras, Vassilis. *Triptych*. [np]: Kater Murr's Press, 2005.

4. Between the "Canon" and "Oblivion"

In a section from *Play Book* read in Unnameable Books in Brooklyn in March 2018, the poet ends "a piece of prose called 'Poetry'" with the image of "two arrows" pointing in "opposite directions": "To: The Canon" and "To: Oblivion". "Now," he says at the end of the piece, "plant your acorn there" (*Pennsound* 16:47–17:05).

Acorns – "the fruit of the oak" – have long been associated with "fecundity and immortality", as Farrin Chwalkowski explains in a consideration of the oak as a "sacred tree" in a wide-ranging study of ancient cultures and traditions (169). Scully's invitation to the reader to "plant" their "acorn" at the intersection of the "Canon" and "Oblivion", then, is an interesting way of signposting the source of creative production. For Scully, as the "Towers of Books" reproduced in the preceding section suggests, the poet's art is a product not just of their engagement with materials drawn from a wide and diverse lifetime of reading. Looking into these and other books has been one of the ways in which Scully's own books have came into being. Books by and/or about Marvell, Lawrence, and Crane, for example, provided crucial stimuli in the making of *Love Poems & Others*, while other books, by figures ranging from R.J. Harrison to William Bronk, were essential resources for the poet as *5 Freedoms of Movement* was being written. This is not to suggest that the poet does not have his own intellectual, imaginative, and experiential resources, of course, but it means that the activity of reading him demands a process of active looking – of looking into his books to see which other books, in turn, have informed the making of his highly original and radical poetic formations.

The process of looking into the books of Maurice Scully – or any poet worth their salt, for that matter – in the manner described here is, of course, an endless one. It is endless, rather, if the writer or artist under consideration is worth the effort, in which case the reader (critical or otherwise) may return to the work again and again to find new things there. This is the case with the work of Maurice Scully, for whom the process of locating the origins of language, memory and the shared space between them has been a central theme in his published work to date. Consider "PIP," for example, which was first published in *Golden Handcuffs Review* in 2018. The piece is concerned, in an important sense, with the idea of linguistic origins:

> what was that
> word that
> first word that
>
> [.................]
>
> that first
> word a fabric
> in the past
> absorbed by
>
> passing time may
> be makes orb or
> its coherence
> yr memory my
>
> chance our lives
> together over
> there hold still
> now in the dark
>
> what was it? ("Pip", 98–9)

The poet is less troubled by the idea of actually locating the origins of "that word", however, than he is with affirming the fundamental significance of the search in itself, of being willing to approach the world through a process of:

> listening
> saying
> noticing
> something

a change
a beginning
a to each
retrodicting

differently
both each
noticing both
passing

the over-
lapping
regions of
preparation

& hoping to
shift an inch
or two
on –

plinth – clock
time – a long way
back – &
so ... ("Pip", 99–100)

As "Pip" proceeds, the reader is taken, surprisingly, towards "the Congolese / pygmy word / for love" (101). Proceeding through the text, however, one cannot know, before getting there, that we are being brought towards this particular linguistic destination. Moreover, the final point of arrival does not ("retrodictively") undo the initial search posited by the speaker in the opening lines, towards which, in a way, the reader is repeatedly drawn back, even if it seems "a long way / back". The poem posits the idea of the text as a kind of "fabric" in which the "first / word" has been "absorbed by / passing time", but where should the reader seek for this "word" if not, at least in the first instance, in the works (and words) of the poet himself and then, widening the net, in the works (and words) of those he has read? "Like any poet who takes the art seriously", as Billy Mills has written, Scully "has read widely and learned deeply and then turned what he has learned to his own ends" (Review of *Several Dances*).

The process outlined here can be theorised in many ways – most obviously, perhaps, with regard to the idea of intertextuality (or "transposition"), as Julia Kristeva, and others, have defined that term. Nerys Williams, responding specifically to Scully's most recent work, has also suggested that certain kinds of Game Theory may provide useful tools for understanding the formal and thematic complexities of the work. What I have called "the books of Maurice Scully" in this essay includes not only his own published works but, also, the poet's own working library, a snapshot of which has been included here with the poet's permission. That "library" can be extended to include the other authors and works mentioned in the first two sections of this essay, and the process of reading through its contents is, to use Andrew Marvell's phrase – in the poem with which we (and, in a sense, Scully) began – one that involves "uncessant labours":

> How vainly men themselves amaze
> To win the palm, the oak, or bays,
> And their uncessant labours see
> Crown'd from some single herb or tree,
> Whose short and narrow verged shade
> Does prudently their toils upbraid;
> While all flow'rs and all trees do close
> To weave the garlands of repose. (Marvell)

Maurice Scully is a poet who has proceeded with his work over several decades without "win[ning]" very much recognition compared to some of his contemporaries in Ireland. This situation is changing, and as it does so readers will apply various kinds of critical and theoretical models to the work of this highly complex and engaging poet. In this essay, I have attempted to show why it is important to pay attention to what may be found simply by looking into the writer's books in themselves – by looking carefully at what may be found there, in terms of their processes and strategies of direct quotation, cross-reference, and allusion. It is a process that takes us to a space somewhere, as Scully puts it himself, between "the Canon" and "Oblivion". As he writes in *Livelihood*:

> you were saying? that was
> precisely. a clue. dis-
> carded invention. our problem

was how the question was the
more I thought I knew the more I
"knew" I sank into those relative
shadows that seem to cover the a-
symmertrical skin that one begins
to suspect anyway covers everything.
full of. everything differently
precisely in each different net.
full of tiny bright word*k*s of
discorded invention. our lives,
glittering, reticulated. & from in
here that edge where what you've
been taught to imagine you know
meets more: quote cut quote & in
this dream of learning (a fish, a
frond, a ball, a calabash) the panel
twists, splintering: "I think I
let me see I *think* I wait I mean I ..." (*Livelihood*, 29)

Works Cited

Bunting, Basil. *Collected Poems*. Oxford: Oxford University Press, 1978.

Chwalkowski, Farrin. *Symbols in Arts, Religion and Culture: The Soul of Nature*. Newcastle upon Tyne: Cambridge Scholars Publishing, 2016.

Eliot, T.S. *Selected Prose of T.S. Eliot*. Ed. Frank Kermode. London: Faber and Faber, 1975.

Lawrence, D.H. *The Letters of D. H. Lawrence, Volume I, September 1901– May 1913*. Ed. James T. Boulton. Cambridge: Cambridge University Press, 1979.

Marvell, Andrew. "The Garden." *Poetry Foundation*. <https://www.poetryfoundation.org/poems/44682/the-garden-56d223dec2ced>. Accessed 28th May 2019.

Mills, Billy. "Sustainable Poetry." *Elliptical Movements* (March 2013): <https://ellipticalmovements.wordpress.com/2013/03/04/sustainable-poetry/>. Accessed 28th May 2019.

———. Rev. of Maurice Scully, *Several Dances*. *Elliptical Movements* (12 April 2015): <https://ellipticalmovements.wordpress.com/category/maurice-scully/>. Accessed 28th May 2019.

Pound, Ezra. Rev. of D.H. Lawrence, *Love Poems and Others*. *Poetry* 2.4 (July 1913): 149–51.

Samperi, Frank. *Spiritual Necessity: Selected Poems*. Ed. John Martone. Barrytown, NY: Station Hill Press, 2004.

Satris, Marthine. "An Interview with Maurice Scully." *Contemporary Literature* 53.1 (2012): 1–30.

Scully, Maurice. *Love Poems & Others*. Dublin: Raven Arts Press, 1981.

——. *5 Freedoms of Movement*. Newcastle upon Tyne: Galloping Dog Press, 1987.

——. *Livelihood*. Bray: Wild Honey Press, 2004.

——. *Several Dances*. Bristol: Shearsman Books, 2014.

——. "PIP." *Golden Handcuffs Review* II.24 (2018): 98–101.

——. "Reading at Unnamable [sic] Books, New York [sic], March 10, 2018." *Pennsound*. <https://media.sas.upenn.edu/pennsound/authors/Scully/Scully-Maurice_Unnamable-Bks-NY_3-10-18.mp3 >. Accessed 28th May 2019.

Williams, Nerys. "Listening and Commemoration: Maurice Scully." *Golden Handcuffs Review* II.24 (2018): 223–32.

Bibliography

Poetry: Books and Pamphlets

Love Poems & Others. Dublin: Raven Arts Press, 1981. 40pp.
5 Freedoms of Movement. Newcastle upon Tyne: Galloping Dog Press, 1987. 86pp.
1, 2, 3 Procedures. Dublin: Coelacanth Press, 1986. 6pp.
Unauthorised Credits. Dublin: Coelacanth Press, 1986. 9 leaves.
The Tree Beside the Water. Dublin: Coelacanth Press, 1987. 6pp.
History. Dublin: Coelacanth Press, 1987. 6pp.
English-Greek Dialogues. Dublin: Coelacanth Press, 1987. 6pp.
Paper Token. Dublin: Coelacanth Press, 1987. 2pp.
Prior. Durham: Staple Diet, 1991. 10pp.
Over and Through. Cambridge: Peter Riley, 1992. 12pp.
Certain Pages. London: Form Books, 1992. 10pp.
Priority. London: Writers Forum, 1994. 60pp.
The Basic Colours: A Watchman's Log. Durham: Pig Press, 1994. 60pp.
Prelude. Bray, Co. Wicklow: Wild Honey Press, 1997. 14pp.
Interlude. Bray, Co. Wicklow: Wild Honey Press, 1997. 14pp.
Postlude. Bray, Co. Wicklow: Wild Honey Press, 1997. 28pp.
from Zulu Dynamite. Brattleboro, VT: Longhouse, 1997. 8pp.
Steps. London: Reality Street Editions, 1998. 70pp.
Five Freedoms of Movement, revised ed. Buckfastleigh: etruscan books, 2001. 91pp.
Livelihood. Bray, Co. Wicklow: Wild Honey Press, 2004. 336pp.
from Tree with Eggs. Dublin: hardPressed Poetry, 2004. 16pp.
Tig. Exeter: Shearsman Books, 2006. 102pp.
Sonata. Hastings, East Sussex: Reality Street Editions, 2006. 103pp.
Doing the Same in English: A Sampler of Work, 1987–2008. Dublin: Dedalus Press; Syracuse, NY: Syracuse University Press, 2008. 202 pp.
Work. Old Hunstanton, Norfolk: Oystercatcher Press, 2008. 36pp.
Five Dances: Poems. Tokyo, Japan and Burlington, Ontario: Ahadada Books (online), 2009. 13pp.
Humming. Exeter: Shearsman Books, 2009. 97pp.
A Tour of the Lattice: from Things That Happen (1981–2006). London: Veer Books, 2011. 155pp.
Rain. Smithereens Press (online), 2013. http://smithereenspress.com/publications/sp2.html. 14pp.
Several Dances. Bristol: Shearsman Books, 2014. 137pp.
Plays. Smithereens Press (online), 2016. http://smithereenspress.com/publications/sp18.html. 20pp.
hardPressed Dual Poets Reader: Three, with Jordi Valls Pozo. Limerick: hardPressed Poetry, 2019. 64pp.
Play Book. Tipperary: Coracle, 2019. 188pp.

Poetry: Periodicals and Anthologies

'News' and 'On the Wall'. In *Aisling* (1973): 4–5.
'True Troy at O'Donoghue's', 'Loving/Damning', and 'Getting Places'. In *TCD Miscellany* (25th October 1974): np.
'For Fergus: 1973', 'Evolution', and 'Watch'. In *Aisling* (1974): 2–3.
'Function' and 'Being One'. In *TCD Miscellany* (15th November 1974): np.
'Gabrielle in a White House'. In *Aisling* (1974/75): 8.
'But I'll Rest Up on the Boat'. In *Icarus* 68 (1975): np.
'Ebb'. In *TCD Miscellany* (14th February 1975): np.
'Spring Poem of Hope' and 'Loving/Damning'. In *Icarus* 70 (1976): np.
'Waves (from a Train of Events)'. In *Funge Arts Centre Broadsheet* (1976): np.
'But I'll Rest Upon the Boat'. In *Words & Images*. Lurgan: Ronan Press, 1976. np.
'The Great Irish Novel', 'Ars Poetica, Perhaps', 'O Schopenhauer where are you now?', and 'Hang it all Paddy Kavanagh'. In *Icarus* 72 (1977): 4–8.
'The Paddy's Lament Shuffle' and 'The Money Shuffle'. In *Icarus* 73 (1977/78): 60, 66.
'Sonnet' ('One should be in love…') and 'Sonnet' ('The Character to the Author'). In *Icarus* 76 (1979): 71–72.
'Note'. In *Iron* 29 (1980): 21.
'Viola D'Amore' and 'The Poem without a Word'. In *The Poetry Ireland Review* 3 (1981): 26–27.
'Lake Garda'. In *Anna Livia* 1.1 (1981): 24.
'Time to Talk'. In *Oak* 1.1 (1981): 6.
'Out on a Limb', 'You could lie by th'Indian Ganges Side', 'Orchid', 'Kiss', 'Quarries', 'Flow', 'Ebb', and 'Sexton Lund's Daughter'. In *Feathers & Bones: Ten Poets of the Irish Earth*. Edited by Sevrin Housen. Sacramento CA: Halcyon Press, 1981. 72–79.
'Exhibition Piece', 'Communion', and 'Watch'. In *Iron* 32 (1981): 36–37.
'Rue Chardon Lagache', 'Old Friends & Anniversaries' and 'Poiema'. In *The Poetry Ireland Review* 5–6 (1982): 17–19.
'Periphera'. In *Ulster Tatler* 16.6 (1982): 4.
'An Lár'. In *Wealth Indeed*. Edited by Thomas Nelson. Maynooth: Cardinal Press, 1982. 15.
'On Looking Out a Shed Door' and 'Two Shots, in the Dark'. In *The Poetry Ireland Review* 7 (1983): 23–24.
'Distances'. In *Speak to the Hills: An Anthology of Twentieth Century British and Irish Mountain Poetry*. Edited by Hamish Brown and Martyn Berry. Aberdeen: Aberdeen University Press, 1985. 157.
'3 Sections from 'Four Freedoms of Movement''. In *Poesie Europe* (1985): 8.
'The Geometry of Soap Bubbles'. In *Poesie Europe* (1986): 44–45.

Bibliography

'crowded eggpouches in a crevice by the corner...'. In *Voicefree Broadsheet* 7 (1987): np.
'The Wave'. In *The Poetry Ireland Review* 22–23 (1988): 56.
'Steps (from *The Basic Colours*)'. In *The Salmon* 21 (1989): 59–60.
'from *5 Freedoms of Movement*' and 'Touring the Lattice'. In *New American Writing* 8&9 (1991): 152–155.
'from Sonnets on Site'. In *Stet* 7 (1991): 5.
'Sonnet' and 'Maturity'. In *Critical Quarterly* 34.4 (1992): 72–73.
'Prior'. In *Tel-let Pamphlet Series* 18 (1992): np.
'Steps' ('It rises with the strange crisis...'), 'Sound', 'Maturity', 'Steps' ('To go in one machine on the road...'), 'Reticle', and 'A Personal Note'. In *Active in Airtime* 2 (1993): 7–13.
'In Praise of Painting Doors'. In *World Letter* 5 (1994): 28–29.
'Marching Song'. In *Angel Exhaust* 10 (1994): 6–9.
'from the book *Adherence*'. In *West Coast Line* 17 (1995): 80–84.
'Interlude'. In *Etruscan Reader IV*, with Bob Cobbing and Carlyle Reedy. Edited by Nicholas Johnson. Buckfastleigh: etruscan books, 1996. 27–37.
'In the Music'. In *Books Ireland* 196 (1996): 182.
'Lullaby', 'Steady', and 'Steps: Work Day'. In *Talisman: A Journal of Contemporary Poetry and Poetics* 16 (1996): 156–159.
'Permission', 'Rain' ('then cut the wood'), 'Steps' ('driving in a red...'), 'Aisling', 'Reticle' ('Years ago one winter...'), 'Steps' ('wake dreaming...'). In *Shearsman* 28 (1996): 2–11.
'Fire' ('Moving through the shadows...'), 'In the Music' ('The route turns sharply...'), 'Fire' ('low sky...'), 'Maturity' ('The smell of cypress...'), and 'Four Corners'. In *Shearsman* 29 (1996): 2–8.
'Forgetting Everything III'. In *Books Ireland* 201 (1997): 29.
'Fire' ('Moving through the shadows...'), 'Sound' ('What cruder machine...'), 'Aisling', 'Fire' ('low sky...'), and 'Responsibility'. In *Fire* 4 (1997): 139–148.
'In The Music' ('The route turns sharply under the railway track ...'). In *Shearsman* 31 (1997): 8.
'Two Poems from *Zulu Dynamite*'. In *Shearsman* 32 (1997): 10–11.
'Prior'. In *Metre* 5 (1998): 49–55.
'Work Day'. In *At the Year's Turning or Volge L'Anno: Responding to Leopardi*. Edited by Marco Sonzogni. Dublin: Dedalus Press: 1998. 225.
'from *Prelude*, The Pillar and the Vine'. In *Talisman* 8 (1998): 114–121.
'Steps' ('driving in a red dustcloud...'). In *Human Rights Have No Borders: Voices of Irish Poets*. Edited by Kenneth Morgan and Almut Schlepper. Dublin: Marino Books, 1998. 153–154.
'The Red Notebook' and 'The Dun Copy'. In *the Journal* 1 (1998): 3–15.
'The thing about understanding...'. In *For the Birds: Proceedings of the First Cork Conference on New and Experimental Irish Poetry*. Edited by Harry

Gilonis. Suton and Dublin: Mainstream Poetry and hardPressed Poetry, 1998. 13.

'Two Caterpillars' and 'Cohering'. In *Etruscan Reader IV*, with Bob Cobbing and Carlyle Reedy. Edited by Nicholas Johnson. Buckfastleigh: etruscan books, 1999. np.

'Variations'. In *Other: British and Irish Poetry since 1970*. Edited by Richard Caddel and Peter Quartermain. Hanover, NH: Wesleyan University Press, 1999. 223–230.

'Seven Variations'. In *News for the Ear: A Homage to Roy Fisher*. Edited by Robert Sheppard and Peter Robinson. Exeter: Stride, 2000. 76.

'A Walk-On Part'. In *The Hip Flask: Short Poems from Ireland*. Edited by Frank Ormsby. Belfast: Blackstaff Press, 2000. 98.

'An Aside'. In *April Eye: Poems for Peter Riley*. Edited by Peter Hughes. Cambridge: infernal methods, 2000. 38–39.

'Trial / Peace'. In *Angelaki* 5.1 (2000): 159–164.

'Fire'. In *Twentieth Century British and Irish Poetry*. Edited by Keith Tuma. Oxford: Oxford University Press, 2001. 830–834.

'Ballad'. In *Metre* 11 (2001/02): 91–95.

'from Tig'. In *The Gig* 8 (2001): 6–11.

Three Pages from 'Broken Ceremony'. In *The Poetry Ireland Review* 73 (2002): 103–105.

'Coda'. In *The Burning Bush* 8 (2002): 5–7.

'from *Tig*'. In *Cyphers* 53 (2002): 20–23.

'Rain', 'Responsibility', 'In the Music', 'Fire', and 'Point'. In *Metre* 13 (2002/03): 62–66.

'TIG, Part II'. In *Poetry Salzburg Review* 5 (2003): 167–173.

'from Adherence (Book V of Livelihood)'. In *Cyphers* 56 (2003): 42–43.

'Sonnet' ('at the Rhapsody & Squash…') and 'Sonnet' ('From your previous life…'). In *The Burning Bush* 11 (2004): 20–23.

'RSVP', 'Steady', and 'Testing'. In *The Poetry Ireland Review* 79 (2004): 67–71.

'Sonnet' ('when I follow the patterns of scratches…'). In *Metre* 15 (2004): 157.

'from *Sonata*'. In *Cyphers* 57 (2004): 12–13.

'Sear Search'. In *The Poetry Ireland Review* 84 (2005): 36–37.

'Song' ('On the field of beginning…'). In *Further Evidence of Nerves: Cambridge Poetry Summit 2005*. Edited by Sara Crangle and Sam Ladkin. Cambridge, UK: Cambridge Series Poetry, 2005. 61–62.

'this three-&-a-half inch long'. In *Kore Broadsheet Series* 2 (2005): np.

'from *Sonata*'. In *Metre* 17 (2005): 126–133.

'Sonnet' ('did you / get that…'). In *Shearsman* 65/66 (2005–2006): 65–72.

'A Song (& a Dance)'. In *The Poetry Ireland Review* 87 (2006): 66–71.

'Snow'. In *On Literature and Science: Essays, Reflections, Provocations*. Edited by Philip Coleman. Dublin: Four Courts Press, 2007. 251.

'Country Dance / With Some Applause' and 'Mountain Railway: Gavotte'. In *The Poetry Ireland Review* 92 (2007): 32–34.

'Two-Step: Still Life with Skull'. In *Veer Away*. Edited by Stephen Mooney. London: Veer Books, 2007. 36–39. [Note: Author's name erroneously spelled 'Morris'].

'Artist & Model: Polka' and 'Locket'. In *Great Works* (online): 2007. Edited by Peter Philpott. http://www.greatworks.org.uk/poems/scully/ms1.html

'Fallaí Luimní: Tree with Eggs', 'Thorns Spindles Twigs', '[Hungarian] Folk Dance: Artist's Studio', and 'Butoh: Coup de Soleil'. In *Golden Handcuffs Review* 1.9 (2007–08): 154–172.

'Geometric (for gamelan)'. In *Veer Off*. Edited by Stephen Mooney. London: Veer Books, 2008. 26–30. [Note: Author's name erroneously spelled 'Morris'].

'Sonnet' ('when I follow the patterns of scratches…'), 'Sonnet' ('From your previous life…'), and 'Sonnet' ('from the nine facts the typist is…'). In *The Reality Street Book of Sonnets*. Edited by Jeff Hilson. London: Reality Street Editions, 2008. 205–208.

'3 Songs from *XXI Songs*'. In *Poetry Salzburg Review* 15 (2009): 85–89.

'In the Music' ('the flower of the banana tree…'), 'In the Music' ('Suddenly I could hear…'), 'Point', 'In Praise of Painting Doors', and 'Permission'. Translated by Guido Leotta and Monica Pavani. In *Immagini d'Irlanda in Umbria*. Edited by Fernando Trilli. 2009. np.

'Baint an Fhéir / Baint an Fhéir' and 'Parallax on Vellum / Saobhdhiallas: ar Pár'. Translated by Gabriel Rosenstock. In *Wurmfest Programm*. Dublin: wurm im apfel, 2009. np.

'Foxtrot' and 'Motet'. In *Past Simple* 6 (2009): online. http://www.pastsimple.org/ps6mscully.html.

'This is to Say: Sonnet' and 'Pavane'. In *Succour* 10 (2009/10): 20–23.

'Miniature' and 'from Fire'. In *MATERIALpoetry*, a catalogue of American Irish Historical Society exhibition; 'Contemporary Objects from Ireland', Causey Contemporary, New York. Edited by Simon Cutts and J.C.C. Mays. Clonmel, Co. Tipperary: Coracle, 2010. np.

'In the Music' ('The flower of the banana tree…'), 'Point', 'In Praise of Painting Doors', and 'Permission'. Translated by Monica Pavani and Guido Leotta. In *Tratti* 83 (2010): 56–64.

'Sound', 'Liking the Big Wheelbarrow', and 'Lullaby'. In *The Penguin Book of Irish Poetry*. Edited by Patrick Crotty. London: Penguin, 2010. 843–845.

'Parallax: On Vellum', 'Heart', and 'Minuet'. In *Golden Handcuffs Review* 1.14 (2011): 57–63.

'Four Extracts from *Livelihood*'. Translated into Hungarian by Olga Pekova. In *PSI VINO* 58 (2011): 28–29. [Note: Erroneously attributed to 'Marice Scully']

'from Work: Self-Portrait as Oddity'. In *Sea Pie: A Shearsman Anthology of Oystercatcher Poetry*. Edited by Peter Hughes. Bristol: Shearsman Books, 2012. 29–30.

'To make a table…'. In *Menu of Poems*. Edited by Alice Lyons. Arts and Health Coordinators Project. http://www.artsandhealth.ie/wp-content/uploads/2013/08/menu_of_poems_20131.pdf. np.

'Song: Dance [knots in the grain]', 'Sonnet: On Tiptoe', and 'Backing Vocals'. In *Golden Handcuffs Review* 1.16 (2013): 10–17.

'Tap Dance', '[Hungarian] Folk Dance: Artist's Studio', 'To Balance', 'This to Say: Sonnet', and 'Poetry'. In *Poetry International* (online), 2014.

'Kiss' and '1968'. In *If Ever You Go: A Map of Dublin in Poetry & Song*. Edited by Pat Boran and Gerard Smyth. Dublin: Dedalus Press, 2014. 110, 113.

'When your horse…'. In *Regarding Susan Howe*. Edited by Jonathan C. Creasy. Dublin: New Dublin Press, 2015. 12–14.

'Tap Dance' and 'Mugapu'. In *Golden Handcuffs Review* 2.20, Special Issue: *Great Writers Occupy: Anthology of the New* (2015): 121–126.

'Key Dance'. In *Irish University Review* 46.1 (2016): 183–188.

'Placed', 'Pattern' and 'Particles'. In *Icarus* 67.1 (2016): 6–13.

'Print'. In *A Screw in the Shoe: Anthology of Challenges*. Edited by Lou Rowan. Seattle, WA: Golden Handcuffs Review Publications, 2016. 25–28

'Rain [signed piece]'. In *Trumpet* 6 (2017): 19–20.

'Particulars'. In *Tears in the Fence* 66 (2017): 31.

'Pass'. In *Gorse* 8 (2017): 152–154.

'Print'. In *Golden Handcuffs Review* 2.22 (2017): 25.

'PIP'. In *Golden Handcuffs Review* II.24 (2018): 98–101.

'Punnett'. In *Smithereens Literary Magazine* 1 (2018): 5.

Prose

'John Behan'. In *Icarus* 69 (1976): 24–28.

'As I Like It'. In *The Beau* 3 (1983/4): 10.

'Minority Publishing' (Letter to the Editor). In *Books Ireland* 109 (1986): 246.

'Space'. In *Colonies of Belief: Ireland's Modernists*. Edited by John Goodby and Maurice Scully. Special Issue of *Súitéar na n-Aingeal/Angel Exhaust* 17 (1999): 2–3.

'The Thing About'. In *News for the Ear: A Homage to Roy Fisher*. Edited by Robert Sheppard and Peter Robinson. Exeter: Stride, 2000. 65.

'A Personal Note'. In *On Leave: A Book of Anecdotes*. Edited by Keith Tuma. Norfolk, UK: Salt Publishing, 2011. 73.

'Rainfall'. In *Trumpet* 6 (2017): 18.

Art

Untitled piece (portrait of Michael Hartnett). Woodblock graphic. In *TCD Miscellany* (1974): np.
Untitled pieces. Two woodblock graphics (unacknowledged). *TCD Miscellany* (1974): np.
Untitled piece. Woodblock graphic, with poems by Des O'Grady, Hayden Murphy, and André Kozimor. *TCD Miscellany* (1974): np.
'Ebb' and two woodblock illustrations (unacknowledged). *TCD Miscellany* (1975): np.
Numbers. Clonmel, Co. Tipperary: Coracle, 2006. Limited edition [50 copies].

Children's

Was Sieht die Katze Bloss? / What is the Cat Looking at?, with Bianca Grünwald-Game. Leipzig: Faber and Faber, 1995. 30pp.

Editorial Work

Icarus 69 (1976). np.
Icarus 70 (1976). np.
'Interview with Anthony Cronin, by Maurice Scully'. In *Icarus* 70 (1976): np.
'Seeing the Horizon Tilt Up Gravely', Bilingual roundtable featuring Maurice Scully, Gabriel Rosenstock, Liam Ó Muirthile, Dáithí Ó Coileáin, and Seán Ó Corrain. In *Icarus* 70 (1976): np.
The Beau: An Annual Publication of & about Literature, no. 1. Edited by Maurice Scully. Dublin: Beau Press, 1981. 80pp.
The Beau: An Annual Publication of & about Literature, no. 2. Edited by Maurice Scully. Dublin: Beau Press, 1982. 88pp.
The Beau: An Annual Publication of & about Literature, no. 3. Edited by Maurice Scully. Dublin: Beau Press, 1983. 104pp.
Healy, Randolph. *25 Poems*. Edited by Maurice Scully. Dublin: Beau Press, 1983. 31pp.
Colonies of Belief: Ireland's Modernists, with John Goodby. Special Issue of *Súitéar na n-Aingeall/Angel Exhaust* 17 (1999): 137pp.
Annwn, David. *Arcs Through: The Poetry of Randolph Healy, Billy Mills & Maurice Scully*. Dublin: Coelacanth Press, 2002. 38pp.
Mays, J.C.C. *N11 A Musing*. Dublin: Coelacanth Press, 2003. 52pp.
Taking Figaries: Poems and Stories from North Tipperary. Tipperary: Tipperary County Council, 2004. 56pp.

Reviews

Review of *Site of Ambush*, by Eiléain Ní Chuilleanáin. In *Icarus* 69 (1976): 43–45.

Interviews

Interview by Kit Fryatt. In *Metre* 17 (2005): 134–143.
Interview by Marthine Satris. In *Contemporary Literature* 53.1 (2012): 1–30.
Interview by Jonathan Creasy. In *The Writers' Room* (Ep. #10): https://www.writersroomradio.com/?fbclid=IwAR24VQh-jDKegU6s3s2mDcnAWHxES_gICN5la6kYT9nMo_CM_lB2KxePoBw

Video/Sound Recordings

Philomena's Restaurant. Dublin: Grapevine Arts Centre and Raven Arts Press, 1981. Audio cassette.
Mouthpuller, with Randolph Healy. Dublin: Coelacanth; Bray, Co. Wicklow: Wild Honey Press, 2000. Compact disc.
'I am / that condition in the city…'. In *Soundeye*. Directed by Adam Wyeth. Edited by Kevin Walsh. Cork: A Wyeth & Walsh Film. 2005. Film. YouTube.com (online). https://www.youtube.com/watch?v=NPj_24Vbpn8.
Maurice Scully Reads at SoundEye, 1/5. Cork: Meshworks, 7th July 2007. YouTube.com (online). https://www.youtube.com/watch?v=l7Vsf96aX6g.
Maurice Scully Reads at SoundEye, 2/5. Cork: Meshworks, 7th July 2007. YouTube.com (online). https://www.youtube.com/watch?v=jhVOkX-Jj3A.
Maurice Scully Reads at SoundEye, 3/5. Cork: Meshworks, 7th July 2007. YouTube.com (online). https://www.youtube.com/watch?v=kTg0PnG87E4.
Maurice Scully Reads at SoundEye, 4/5. Cork: Meshworks, 7th July 2007. YouTube.com (online). https://www.youtube.com/watch?v=sWhkGQ2t3Q0.
Maurice Scully Reads at SoundEye, 5/5. Cork: Meshworks, 7th July 2007. YouTube.com (online). https://www.youtube.com/watch?v=UYtpfCBT87M.
The Holloway Series in Poetry, with Anne Tardos. University of California, Berkeley, 23rd September 2009. YouTube.com (online). https://www.youtube.com/watch?v=CDdqpIHQDH8.

Bibliography

'In Praise of Painting Doors'. Limerick: White House Poets, 5th November 2009. YouTube.com (online). https://www.youtube.com/watch?v=lY3QLJ_L3ew.

Maurice Scully - Wurm Im Apfel & Veer Books: Launch & Reading in Dublin, Ireland. Dublin: Hello Operator, 8th September 2011. Vimeo.com (online). https://vimeo.com/29483350.

'Exposure: Tuesday'. *Poetry Readings @ UCD.* James Joyce Library, University College Dublin, 9th September 2015. YouTube.com (online). https://www.youtube.com/watch?v=Q6g1ngHWeFo.

'For Treated Piano'. *Poetry Readings @ UCD.* James Joyce Library, University College Dublin, 9th September 2015. YouTube.com (online). https://www.youtube.com/watch?v=RfPbsOhsYNU.

'On a Dark Ground: Work Dance'. *Poetry Readings @ UCD.* James Joyce Library, University College Dublin, 9th September 2015. YouTube.com (online). https://www.youtube.com/watch?v=IY-LL_RgSvE.

'On a Light Ground: Eye Dance'. *Poetry Readings @ UCD.* James Joyce Library, University College Dublin, 9th September 2015. YouTube.com (online). https://www.youtube.com/watch?v=_K8xIc3vFAU.

'Sunlight'. *Poetry Readings @ UCD.* James Joyce Library, University College Dublin, 9th September 2015. YouTube.com (online). https://www.youtube.com/watch?v=HgVmSA3wwF8.

'Tap Dance'. *Poetry Readings @ UCD.* James Joyce Library, University College Dublin, 14th September 2015. YouTube.com (online). https://www.youtube.com/watch?v=Lghcfd9GuoY.

'Poetry'. *Poetry Readings @ UCD.* James Joyce Library, University College Dublin, 14th September 2015. YouTube.com (online). https://www.youtube.com/watch?v=kGCBlBezNQg.

'To Balance'. *Poetry Readings @ UCD.* James Joyce Library, University College Dublin, 14th September 2015. YouTube.com (online). https://www.youtube.com/watch?v=oqo50HhHZGI.

'Tap Dance'. *3rd Ó Bhéal Winter Warmer Poetry Festival Closed Mic.* Sample Studios, Cork, 20th November 2015. YouTube.com (online). https://www.youtube.com/watch?v=MbjMlSXYVZg.

Maurice Scully @ Phonica: One. 20th January 2016. YouTube.com (online). https://www.youtube.com/watch?v=VqaACzSKcjU.

'Platform/Going Forward'. In *Verbal Sun: Poems.* Edited by Philip Coleman and Diane Sadler. Dublin: NCBI Studios, 2016. Compact Disc.

'Reading at Unnamable Books, New York. March 10, 2018.' *Pennsound* (online). https://media.sas.upenn.edu/pennsound/authors/Scully/Scully-Maurice_Unnamable-Bks-NY_3-10-18.mp3.

Secondary Criticism

Annwn, David. *Arcs Through: The Poetry of Randolph Healy, Billy Mills & Maurice Scully*. Dublin: Coelacanth Press, 2002. 38pp.

Fryatt, Kit. "AW.DAH.' An allegorical reading of Maurice Scully's *Things That Happen*'. In POST 1 (2008): 59–87.

———. "Must not attempt escape / from here and now': Maurice Scully Reading Brian Coffey'. In *Other Edens: The Life and Work of Brian Coffey*. Edited by Benjamin Keatinge and Aengus Woods. Dublin: Irish Academic Press, 2010. 226–240.

———. 'The Poetics of Elegy in Maurice Scully's *Humming*. In *Irish University Review* 46.1 (2016): 89–104.

Gilonis, Harry. 'The Spider, the Fly and Philosophy: Following a Clew through Maurice Scully's *Livelihood*. In *The Fly on the Page* 3 (2004): 29–43.

Goodby, John. "Repeat the Changes Change the Repeats': Alternative Irish Poetry'. In *The Oxford Handbook of Modern Irish Poetry*. Oxford: Oxford University Press, 2012. 607–628.

Hadfield, Charles. 'No End to the Wriggle of the Mind'. In *Tears in The Fence* 21 (1998): np.

Huk, Romana. "Out Past / Self-Dramatization': Maurice Scully's *Several Dances*'. In *Irish University Review* 46.1 (2016): 105–118.

O' Donnell, Mary. 'Irish Cultural Connections in Poetry, Fiction and on the Street: The Writing of Jean O'Brien, Maurice Scully, Emer Martin and Other Irish Writers', in *Authority and Wisdom in the New Ireland: Studies in Literature and Culture*. Edited by Carmen Zamorano Llena and Billy Gray. Frankfurt am Main: Peter Lang Edition, 2016. 41–56.

Perry, Paul. 'Maurice Scully and the Avant Garde'. In *The Portable Poetry Workshop*. Edited by Nigel McLoughlin. London: Palgrave, 2017. 218–223.

Quinn, Justin. 'Chapter 6: The ends of Modernism: Kinsella and Irish experiment'. In *The Cambridge Introduction to Modern Irish Poetry: 1800–2000*. Cambridge: Cambridge University Press, 2008. 97–112.

Satris, Marthine Desiree. *Making it new, again: Innovative poetry and the reinvention of Ireland at the turn of the Twenty-First Century*. University of California, Santa Barbara, 2013. Ph. D. Thesis.

———. 'Selection as Rewriting: Maurice Scully's Re-Envisioning of *Things That Happen*'. In *Golden Handcuffs Review* 1.16 (2013): 195–200.

Williams, Nerys. 'Listening and Commemoration: Maurice Scully'. In *Golden Handcuffs Review* 2.24 (2018): 196–205.

Reviews: Periodicals and Newspapers

Begnal, Michael S. 'Beyond Tradition: The Wild Honey Poets'. Review of *Prelude*, by Maurice Scully. In *Burning Bush* 5 (2001): 14–17.

——. Review of *5 Freedoms of Movement*, by Maurice Scully; *Arcs Through*, by David Annwn. In *Burning Bush* 8 (2002): 52–53.

——. 'A Sustained Burst of Energy'. Review of *Sonata* and *Tig*, by Maurice Scully. In *Fortnight* 453 (2007): 28.

——. Review of *Tig*, by Maurice Scully. In *B'Fhiú an Braon Fola: Poetry, Literature, Whatever* (online), 2007. http://mikebegnal.blogspot.ie/2007/01/maurice-scully-tig.html.

——. Review of *Doing the Same in English: A Sampler of Work 1987–2008*, by Maurice Scully. In *An Sionnach: A Journal of Literature, Culture and the Arts* 5.1&2 (2009): 314–317.

——. Review of *Humming*, by Maurice Scully. In *B'Fhiú an Braon Fola: Poetry, Literature, Whatever* (online), 2010. http://mikebegnal.blogspot.ie/2010/02/maurice-scully-humming.html.

——. Review of *A Tour of the Lattice*, by Maurice Scully. In *B'Fhiú an Braon Fola: Poetry, Literature, Whatever* (online), 2011. http://mikebegnal.blogspot.ie/2011/11/maurice-scully-tour-of-lattice.html.

——. Review of *Rain*, by Maurice Scully; *from Pensato*, by Billy Mills. In *B'Fhiú an Braon Fola: Poetry, Literature, Whatever* (online), 2013. http://mikebegnal.blogspot.ie/2013/12/scully-mills-smithereens-chapbooks.html.

——. Review of *Several Dances*, by Maurice Scully. In *B'Fhiú an Braon Fola: Poetry, Literature, Whatever* (online), 2015. http://mikebegnal.blogspot.ie/2015/07/review-of-maurice-scully-several-dances.html.

——. Review of *Plays*, by Maurice Scully. In *B'Fhiú an Braon Fola: Poetry, Literature, Whatever* (online), 2016. http://mikebegnal.blogspot.ie/2016/11/maurice-scullys-plays.html.

Brennan, Rory. 'Making the Words Light Up'. Review of *Collected Poems 1962–1993*, by Richard Kell; *The Tamarit Poems*, by Federico García Lorca and Michael Smith; *Postlude*, by Maurice Scully; *Touching the Bones*, by Tom French; *The Ogham Stone: An Anthology of Contemporary Ireland*, by Gerald Dawe and Michael Mulreany; *The Reed Bed*, by Dermot Healy; *Slow Time: 100 Poems to Take You There*, by Niall MacMonagle. In *Books Ireland* 250 (2002): 157–159.

Bushe, Paddy. Review of *Dyckman-200th Street*, by Eamonn Wall; *Tim Drum Country*, by Sabine Wichert; *The Basic Colours*, by Maurice Scully. In *The Poetry Ireland Review* 47 (1995): 100–103.

Dunne, Sean. 'Landmarks'. Review of *Going Home to Russia* by Paul Durcan; *Pillars of the House: An Anthology of Verse by Irish Women from 1690 to the Present*; *I Bailed out at Ardee* by Tom MacIntyre; *5 Freedoms of Movement* by Maurice Scully; *Voices of Our Kind: Scottish Poetry from*

1920 to the Present by Alexander Scott; *Welsh Verse* by Tony Conran. In *The Poetry Ireland Review* 22–23 (1988): 39–43.

Ellis, Conleth. 'The Thing Contained'. Review of *The Strange Museum*, by Tom Paulin; *Rún Na gCaisleán*, by Gabriel Rosenstock; *The Shifting of Stones*, by Tony Curtis; *Brought up in Dublin*, by Derry Jeffares; *Paper Token*, by Maurice Scully. In *Books Ireland* 113 (1987): 100.

Fryatt, Kit. "Which is really where we are': Irish neo-Modernism and the Practical Critic'. Review of *Livelihood*, by Maurice Scully. In *Cyphers* 58 (2004): 49–53.

Goodby, John. 'Who's Afraid of Experimental Poetry?' Review of *Penguin Modern Poets 10*, by Douglas Oliver, Denise Riley, and Iain Sinclair; *Conductors of Chaos*, edited by Iain Sinclair; *Prelude, Interlude*, and *Postlude*, by Maurice Scully; *Rana Rana!*, *Flame*, and *Arbor Vitae*, by Randolph Healy. In *Metre* 5 (1998): 41–48.

Greacen, Robert. 'The Partial View'. Review of *Love Poems and Others*, by Maurice Scully; *Sensualities*, by Sydney Bernard Smith; *Cinema of the Blind*, by Anthony Weir; *Come When You Can*, by Rupert Strong. In *Books Ireland* 57 (1981): 180.

Horgan, Joe. 'Poetry'. Review of *Several Dances*, by Maurice Scully. In *Books Ireland* 362 (2015): 40–41.

Johnston, Fred. 'Us Abroad, and Others Here'. Review of *Steps*, by Maurice Scully; *After the Ball*, by Breda Sullivan; *Letter to America: Poems on the Thirty Year War in N. Ireland*, by Brendan Hamill, *Domestic Flight*, by James Ellis, *Libretto*, by Edoardo Sanguineti and Pádraig J. Daly; *Greetings to Our Friends in Brazil: One Hundred Poems*, by Paul Durcan. In *Books Ireland* 225 (1999): 273–275.

———. 'The engine laid bare — an Irish poet's commitment to modernism'. Review of *Play Book*, by Maurice Scully. In *Books Ireland*. February 2020. https://booksirelandmagazine.com/review-playbook/.

Jordan, John. Review of *Love Poems & Others*, by Maurice Scully; *Dánta Grádha*, by Augustus Young; *Dall Orlo Marino Del Mondo*, by Pádraig J. Daly and Margherita Guidacci. In *The Poetry Ireland Review* 3 (1981): 46–47.

Keatinge, Benjamin. 'Things That Happen'. Review of *Sonata* and *Tig*, by Maurice Scully. In *The Poetry Ireland Review* 91 (2007): 95–98.

Kiely, Kevin. 'Youthfulness'. Review of *An Paróiste Míoruilteach / The Miraculous Parish*, by Máire Mhac an tSaoi; *Speech Lessons*, by John Montague, *New and Selected Poems*, by Michael D. Higgins; *The Smile and the Tear: Poems and Songs of Ireland*, by Sean McMahon; *Tour of the Lattice*, by Maurice Scully. In *Books Ireland* 336 (2012): 10–12.

Makris, Christodoulos. 'A Tour of the Lattice, by Maurice Scully (and Kevin Keily's review)'. Review of *A Tour of the Lattice*. In *yes, but is it*

poetry (online), 12th March 2012. https://yesbutisitpoetry.blogspot.com/2012/03/tour-of-lattice-by-maurice-scully-and.html.
Mills, Billy. '*Several Dances*, by Maurice Scully: A Review'. In *Elliptical Movements* (online), 2015. https://ellipticalmovements.wordpress.com/2015/04/12/several-dances-by-maurice-scully-a-review/.
Perry, Paul. Review of *Humming*, by Maurice Scully. In *The Stinging Fly* 17.2 (2010–11): 111–114.
———. 'a gun filled with rhetoric'. Review of *A Tour of the Lattice*. In *Golden Handcuffs Review* 1.16 (2013): 201–205.
Riley, Peter. 'Books Noted and Worthy'. Review of *Play Book*, by Maurice Scully. In F*ortnightly Review*. March 2020. https://fortnightlyreview.co.uk/2020/03/spring-storms-2020/.
Wheatley, David. 'Using the Space'. Review of *Livelihood*. In *The Poetry Ireland Review* 84 (2005): 98–100.
———. 'Irish Poetry, Paul Klee of'. Review of *Livelihood*. In *georgiasam* (online), 9th December 2008. https://georgiasam.blogspot.com/2008/12/irish-poetry-paul-klee-of.html.
———. Review of *Doing the Same in English: A Sampler of Work 1987–2008*, by Maurice Scully. In *Times Literary Supplement*, 16th October 2009.

Dictionary Entries

Casey, Philip. 'Maurice Scully'. In *Irish Writers Online* (online), nd. http://www.irishwriters-online.com/scully-maurice/.
Fryatt, Kit. 'Maurice Scully'. In *Poetry International* (online), 2014. http://www.poetryinternationalweb.net/pi/site/poet/item/24372.

Contributors

Michael S. Begnal is author of the collections *Future Blues* (Salmon Poetry, 2012) and *Ancestor Worship* (Salmon Poetry, 2007), as well as the chapbook *The Muddy Banks* (Ghost City Press, 2016). He currently teaches writing at Ball State University in the U.S.

Mairéad Byrne's poetry collections include *Nelson & The Huruburu Bird* (Wild Honey Press 2003), *Talk Poetry* (Miami University Press 2007), *SOS Poetry* (/ubu Editions 2007), *The Best of (What's Left of)* Heaven (Publishing Genius 2010), and *Famosa na sua cabeça* (Dobra Editorial 2015). Current publications include two chapbooks, *In & Out* (Smithereens Press 2019), and *har sawlya* (above/ground press 2019); an essay, "Light in July," in a 13th volume (of essays by nine contemporary writers) accompanying David Jhave Johnston's 12-volume A.I./human poetry project, *ReRites* (Anteism 2019); and a poem plus commentary in *The Cast-Iron Airplane That Can Actually Fly: Contemporary Poets Comment on Their Prose Poems*, edited by Peter Johnson (MadHat Press, 2019). She emigrated from Ireland in 1994, earned a PhD in Theory & Cultural Studies from Purdue University, and works as a Professor of Poetry & Poetics at Rhode Island School of Design, teaching multi-media courses in Visual Poetry, Sound Poetry, Digital Poetics, Material Poetics, Contemporary Poetry, and poetry workshops. She is a co-curator of *Policromia*, an annual international festival of poetry and translation across the arts in Siena.

Philip Coleman is an Associate Professor in the School of English, Trinity College Dublin, where he is also a Fellow. He is the author of *John Berryman's Public Vision* (2014) and he has edited or co-edited several collections of essays including *George Saunders: Critical Essays* (2017) and *Robert Lowell and Irish Poetry* (with Eve Cobain, forthcoming). With Calista McRae he is currently editing a volume of John Berryman's letters for Harvard University Press.

Lucy Collins is Associate Professor of English at University College Dublin. Books include *Poetry by Women in Ireland: A Critical Anthology 1870–1970* (2012) and a monograph, *Contemporary Irish Women Poets: Memory and Estrangement* (2015), both from Liverpool University Press. She has published widely on contemporary poets from Ireland, Britain and America, and is co-founder of the Irish Poetry Reading Archive, a national digital repository.

Eric Falci is Professor of English at the University of California, Berkeley. He is the author of *Continuity and Change in Irish Poetry, 1966–2010* (2012) and the *Cambridge Introduction to British Poetry, 1945–2010* (2015), as well as a number of essays on twentieth- and twenty-first-century Irish and British poetry. Along with Paige Reynolds, he is the co-editor of *Irish Literature in Transition, 1980–2020*, to be published by Cambridge University Press.

Contributors

Kit Fryatt lectures in the School of English, Dublin City University. He has published four books of poems, most recently *Bodyservant* (Shearsman Books 2018).

Kenneth Keating is a Government of Ireland Postdoctoral Research Fellow in University College Cork. He is the author of *Contemporary Irish Poetry and the Canon* (Palgrave Macmillan 2017) and publishes widely on contemporary poetry. He is the cofounder of MEAS (Measuring Equality in the Arts Sector) and founder and editor of Smithereens Press.

David Lloyd, Distinguished Professor of English at the University of California, Riverside, works on Irish culture, settler colonialism, postcolonial and cultural theory, and visual art. His most recent books are: *Irish Culture and Colonial Modernity: The Transformation of Oral Space* (2011); *Beckett's Thing: Painting and Theatre* (2016); and *Under Representation: The Racial Regime of Aesthetics* (Fordham University Press 2019). *Arc & Sill: Poems 1979–2009* (Shearsman Books 2012) collected his new and selected poetry. Poetry collection *Bar Null* appeared from SoundEye Books and *Furrow Archive* from Magra Books, both in 2019. A bilingual French/English edition of his play, *The Press/Le Placard* was published by the Nouvelles Scènes series, Presses Universitaires du Midi, in 2018.

J.C.C. Mays retired from University College Dublin fifteen years ago and lives in Wicklow. His most recent books concern ways to read Coleridge's poetry, the latest being *Coleridge's Dejection Ode* (Palgrave Macmillan 2019).

Aodán McCardle's current practice is improvised performance/writing/drawing. His PhD is on 'Action as Articulation of the Contemporary Poem' though physicality and doubt are the site of meaning and the stance respectively where the action operates. He opened the Performance Month at Beton7, Athens 2015, and the Performance Philosophy Centre University of Surrey Sep 2016. He was a member of the anti-performance group LUC, London Under Construction and the Collaborative/Improvisational Performance group Cuislí. Two books, *Shuddered* and *ISing* from VEER, online chapbook *LllOoVvee*, Smithereens Press. Recent publications in *Wretched Strangers*, *Lumin Journal* and *Smithereens Literary Magazine*, and "Control – Information – Resistance – Game: Knowledge Systems in the poetry of Stephen Mooney", with Francis Gene-Rowe, in *Systems and Knowledge: Scholarship, Ecology and Mind in Science Fiction* Palgrave Macmillan), edited by Chris Pak and William Slocombe.

www.ingramcontent.com/pod-product-compliance
Lightning Source LLC
Chambersburg PA
CBHW032128160426
43197CB00008B/560